THE SARVA-DARŚANA-SAṂGRAHA

THE SARVA-DARŚANA-SAṂGRAHA

OR REVIEW OF THE DIFFERENT SYSTEMS OF HINDU PHILOSOPHY

MÁDHAVA ÁCHÁRYA

TRANSLATED BY
E. B. COWELL, M.A.
PROFESSOR OF SANSKRIT AND FELLOW OF CORPUS CHRISTI COLLEGE IN THE UNIVERSITY OF CAMBRIDGE, AND HONORARY LL.D. OF THE UNIVERSITY OF EDINBURGH.

and

A. E. GOUGH, M.A.
PROFESSOR OF PHILOSOPHY IN THE PRESIDENCY COLLEGE, AND PRINCIPAL OF THE MADRASA, CALCUTTA.

WILDSIDE PRESS

Note: The Diacritical marks in this book are not consistent throughout the book. The original Diacritical marks have been retained.

Published by Wildside Press LLC.
www.wildsidebooks.com

PREFACE.

I well remember the interest excited among the learned Hindus of Calcutta by the publication of the Sarva-darśana-saṃgraha of Mádhava Áchárya in the Bibliotheca Indica in 1858. It was originally edited by Paṇḍit Íśvarachandra Vidyáságara, but a subsequent edition, with no important alterations, was published in 1872 by Paṇḍit Táránátha Tarkaváchaspati. The work had been used by Wilson in his "Sketch of the Religious Sects of the Hindus" (first published in the Asiatic Researches, vol. xvi., Calcutta, 1828); but it does not appear to have been ever much known in India. MS. copies of it are very scarce; and those found in the North of India, as far as I have had an opportunity of examining them, seem to be all derived from one copy, brought originally from the South, and therefore written in the Telugu character. Certain mistakes are found in all alike, and probably arose from some illegible readings in the old Telugu original. I have noticed the same thing in the Nágarí copies of Mádhava's Commentary on the Black Yajur Veda, which are current in the North of India.

As I was at that time the Oriental Secretary of the Bengal Asiatic Society, I was naturally attracted to the book; and I subsequently read it with my friend Paṇḍit Maheśachandra Nyáyaratna, the present Principal of the Sanskrit College at Calcutta. I always hoped to translate it into English; but I was continually prevented by other engagements while I remained in India. Soon after my return to England, I tried to carry out my intention; but I found that several chapters, to which I had not paid the same attention as to the rest, were too difficult to be translated in England, where I could no longer enjoy the advantage of reference to my old friends the Paṇḍits of the Sanskrit College. In despair I laid my translation aside for years, until I happened to learn that my friend, Mr. A. E. Gough, at that time a Professor in the Sanskrit College at Benares, was thinking of translating the book. I at once proposed to him that we should do it together, and he kindly consented to my proposal; and we accordingly each undertook certain chapters of the work. He had the advantage of the help of some of the Paṇḍits of Benares, especially of Paṇḍit Ráma Miśra, the assistant Professor of Sáṅkhya, who was himself a Rámánuja; and I trust that, though we have doubtless left some things unexplained or explained wrongly, we may have been able to throw light on many of the dark sayings with which the original abounds. Our translations were originally published at intervals in the Benares Paṇḍit between 1874 and 1878; but they have been carefully revised for their present republication.

The work itself is an interesting specimen of Hindu critical ability. The author successively passes in review the sixteen philosophical systems current in the fourteenth century in the South of India, and gives what appeared to him to be their most important tenets, and the principal arguments by which their followers endeavoured to maintain them; and he often displays some quaint humour as he throws himself for the time into the position of their advocate, and holds, as it were, a temporary brief in behalf of opinions entirely at variance with his own.[1] We may sometimes differ from him in his judgment of the relative importance of their doctrines, but it is always interesting to see the point of view of an acute native critic. In the course of his sketches he frequently explains at some length obscure details in the different systems; and I can hardly imagine a better guide for the European reader who wishes to study any one of these Darśanas in its native authorities. In one or two cases (as notably in the Bauddha, and perhaps in the Jaina system) he could only draw his materials second-hand from the discussions in the works of Brahmanical controversialists; but in the great majority he quotes directly from the works of their founders or leading exponents, and he is continually following in their track even where he does not quote their exact words.[2]

The systems are arranged from the Vedánta point of view,—our author having been elected, in A.D. 1331, the head of the Smárta order in the Maṭh of Śṛingeri in the Mysore territory, founded by Śaṃkara Áchárya, the great Vedántist teacher of the eighth century, through whose efforts the Vedánta became what it is at present—the acknowledged view of Hindu orthodoxy. The systems form a gradually ascending scale,—the first, the Chárváka and Bauddha, being the lowest as the furthest removed from the Vedánta, and the last, the Sáṅkhya and Yoga, being the highest as approaching most nearly to it.

The sixteen systems here discussed attracted to their study the noblest minds in India throughout the mediæval period of its history. Hiouen Thsang says of the schools in his day: "Les écoles philosophiques sont constamment en lutte, et le bruit de leurs discussions passionnées s'élève comme les flots de la mer. Les hérétiques des diverses sectes s'attachent à des maîtres particuliers, et, par des voies différentes, marchent tous au même but." We can still catch some faint echo of the din as we read the mediæval literature. Thus, for instance, when King Harsha wanders among the Vindhya forests, he finds "seated on the rocks and reclining under the trees Árhata begging monks, Śvetapadas, Mahápáśupatas, Páṇḍarabhikshus, Bhágavatas, Varṇins, Keśaluñchanas, Lokáyatikas, Kápilas, Káṇádas, Aupanishadas, Ísvarakárins, Dharmaśástrins, Pauráṇikas, Sáptatantavas, Śábdas, Páñcharátrikas, &c., all listening to their own accepted tenets and zealously defending them."[3] Many of these sects will occupy us in the ensuing pages; many of them also are found in Mádhava's poem on the controversial triumphs of Śaṃkara Áchárya, and in the spurious prose work on the same subject, ascribed to Anantánandagiri. Well may some old poet have put into the mouth of Yudhishṭhira the lines which one so often hears from the lips of modern paṇḍits—

> Vedá vibhinnáḥ smṛitayo vibhinná,
> Násau munir yasya matam na bhinnam,
> Dharmasya tattvaṃ nihitaṃ guháyáṃ,
> Mahájano yena gataḥ sa pantháḥ.[4]

And may we not also say with Clement of Alexandria,

> μιᾶς τοίνυν οὔσης τῆς ἀληθείας, τὸ γὰρ ψεῦδος μυρίας
> ἐκτροπὰς ἔχει, καθάπερ αἱ βάκχαι τὰ τοῦ Πενθέως διαφορήσασαι
> μέλη αἱ τῆς φιλοσοφίας τῆς τε βαρβάρου τῆς τε
> Ἑλληνικῆς αἱρέσεις, ἑκάστη ὅπερ ἔλαχεν, ὡς πᾶσαν αὐχεῖ
> τὴν ἀλήθειαν, φωτὸς δ', οἶμαι, ἀνατολῇ πάντα φωτίζεται.

THE PROLOGUE.

1. I worship Śiva, the abode of eternal knowledge, the storehouse of supreme felicity; by whom the earth and the rest were produced, in *him* only has this all a maker.

2. Daily I follow my Guru Sarvajña-Vishṇu, who knows all the Ágamas, the son of Śárṅgapáṇi, who has gone to the further shore of the seas of all the systems, and has contented the hearts of all mankind by the proper meaning of the term Soul.

3. The synopsis of all the systems is made by the venerable Mádhava mighty in power, the Kaustubha-jewel of the milk-ocean of the fortunate Sáyaṇa.

4. Having thoroughly searched the Śástras of former teachers, very hard to be crossed, the fortunate Sáyaṇa-Mádhava[5] the lord has expounded them for the delight of the good. Let the virtuous listen with a mind from which all envy has been far banished; who finds not delight in a garland strung of various flowers?

CHAPTER I.

THE CHÁRVÁKA SYSTEM.

[We have said in our preliminary invocation "salutation to Śiva, the abode of eternal knowledge, the storehouse of supreme felicity,"] but how can we attribute to the Divine Being the giving of supreme felicity, when such a notion has been utterly abolished by Chárváka, the crest-gem of the atheistical school, the follower of the doctrine of Bṛihaspati? The efforts of Chárváka are indeed hard to be eradicated, for the majority of living beings hold by the current refrain—

While life is yours, live joyously;
None can escape Death's searching eye:
When once this frame of ours they burn,
How shall it e'er again return?

The mass of men, in accordance with the Śástras of policy and enjoyment, considering wealth and desire the only ends of man, and denying the existence of any object belonging to a future world, are found to follow only the doctrine of Chárváka. Hence another name for that school is Lokáyata,—a name well accordant with the thing signified.[6]

In this school the four elements, earth, &c., are the original principles; from these alone, when transformed into the body, intelligence is produced, just as the inebriating power is developed from the mixing of certain ingredients;[7] and when these are destroyed, intelligence at once perishes also. They quote the Śruti for this [Bṛihad Áraṇy. Up. ii. 4, 12], "Springing forth from these elements, itself solid knowledge, it is destroyed when they are destroyed,—after death no intelligence remains."[8] Therefore the soul is only the body distinguished by the attribute of intelligence, since there is no evidence for any soul distinct from the body, as such cannot be proved, since this school holds that perception is the only source of knowledge and does not allow inference, &c.

The only end of man is enjoyment produced by sensual pleasures. Nor may you say that such cannot be called the end of man as they are always mixed with some kind of pain, because it is our wisdom to enjoy the pure pleasure as far as we can, and to avoid the pain which inevitably accompanies it; just as the man who desires fish takes the fish with their scales and bones, and having taken as many as he wants, desists; or just as the man who desires rice, takes the rice, straw and all, and having taken as much as he wants, desists. It is not therefore for us, through a fear of pain, to reject the pleasure which our nature instinctively recognises as congenial. Men do not refrain from sowing rice, because forsooth there are wild animals to devour it; nor do they refuse to set the cooking-pots on the fire, because forsooth there are beggars to pester us for a share of the contents. If any one were so timid as to forsake a visible pleasure, he would indeed be foolish like a beast, as has been said by the poet—

> The pleasure which arises to men from contact with sensible objects,
> Is to be relinquished as accompanied by pain,—such is the reasoning of fools;
> The berries of paddy, rich with the finest white grains,
> What man, seeking his true interest, would fling
> away because covered with husk and dust?[9]

If you object that, if there be no such thing as happiness in a future world, then how should men of experienced wisdom engage in the agnihotra and other sacrifices, which can only be performed with great expenditure of money and bodily fatigue, your objection cannot be accepted as any proof to the contrary, since the agnihotra, &c., are only useful as means of livelihood, for the Veda is tainted by the three faults of untruth, self-contradiction, and tautology;[10] then again the impostors who call themselves Vaidic pundits are mutually destructive, as the authority of the jñána-káṇḍa is overthrown by those who maintain that of the karma-káṇḍa, while those who maintain the authority of the jñána-káṇḍa reject that of the karma-káṇḍa; and lastly, the three Vedas themselves are only the incoherent rhapsodies of knaves, and to this effect runs the popular saying—

The Agnihotra, the three Vedas, the ascetic's three staves, and smearing oneself with ashes,—

Bṛihaspati says, these are but means of livelihood for those who have no manliness nor sense.

Hence it follows that there is no other hell than mundane pain produced by purely mundane causes, as thorns, &c.; the only Supreme is the earthly monarch whose existence is proved by all the world's eyesight; and the only Liberation is the dissolution of the body. By holding the doctrine that the soul is identical with the body, such phrases as "I am thin," "I am black," &c., are at once intelligible, as the attributes of thinness, &c., and self-consciousness will reside in the same subject [the body]; like and the use of the phrase "my body" is metaphorical "the head of Ráhu" [Ráhu being really *all head*].

All this has been thus summed up—

> In this school there are four elements, earth, water, fire, and air;
> And from these four elements alone is intelligence produced,—
> Just like the intoxicating power from kiṇwa, &c., mixed together;

Since in "I am fat," "I am lean," these attributes[11] abide in the same subject,
And since fatness, &c., reside only in the body,[12] it alone is the soul and no other,
And such phrases as "my body" are only significant metaphorically.

"Be it so," says the opponent; "your wish would be gained if inference, &c., had no force of proof; but then they have this force; else, if they had not, then how, on perceiving smoke, should the thoughts of the intelligent immediately proceed to fire; or why, on hearing another say, 'There are fruits on the bank of the river,' do those who desire fruit proceed at once to the shore?"

All this, however, is only the inflation of the world of fancy.

Those who maintain the authority of inference accept the *sign* or middle term as the causer of knowledge, which middle term must be found in the minor and be itself invariably connected with the major.[13] Now this invariable connection must be a relation destitute of any condition accepted or disputed;[14] and this connection does not possess its power of causing inference by virtue of its *existence*, as the eye, &c., are the cause of perception, but by virtue of its being *known*. What then is the means of this connection's being known?

We will first show that it is not *perception*. Now perception is held to be of two kinds, external and internal [*i.e.*, as produced by the external senses, or by the inner sense, mind]. The former is not the required means; for although it is possible that the actual contact of the senses and the object will produce the knowledge of the particular object thus brought in contact, yet as there can never be such contact in the case of the past or the future, the universal proposition[15] which was to embrace the invariable connection of the middle and major terms in every case becomes impossible to be known. Nor may you maintain that this knowledge of the universal proposition has the general class as its object, because if so, there might arise a doubt as to the existence of the invariable connection in this particular case[16] [as, for instance, in this particular smoke as implying fire].

Nor is internal perception the means, since you cannot establish that the mind has any power to act independently towards an external object, since all allow that it is dependent on the external senses, as has been said by one of the logicians, "The eye, &c., have their objects as described; but mind externally is dependent on the others."

Nor can *inference* be the means of the knowledge of the universal proposition, since in the case of this inference we should also require another inference to establish it, and so on, and hence would arise the fallacy of an *ad infinitum* retrogression.

Nor can *testimony* be the means thereof, since we may either allege in reply, in accordance with the Vaiśeshika doctrine of Kaṇáda, that this is included in the topic of inference; or else we may hold that this fresh proof of testimony is unable to leap over the old barrier that stopped the progress of inference, since it depends itself on the recognition of a *sign* in the form of the language used in the child's presence by the old man;[17] and, moreover, there is no more reason for our believing on another's word that smoke and fire are invariably connected, than for our receiving the *ipse dixit* of Manu,& c. [which, of course, we Chárvákas reject].

And again, if testimony were to be accepted as the only means of the knowledge of the universal proposition, then in the case of a man to whom the fact of the invariable connection between the middle and major terms had not been pointed out by another person, there could be no inference of one thing [as fire] on seeing another thing [as smoke]; hence, on your own showing, the whole topic of inference for oneself[18] would have to end in mere idle words.

Then again *comparison*,[19] &c., must be utterly rejected as the means of the knowledge of the universal proposition, since it is impossible that they can produce the knowledge of the unconditioned connection [*i.e.*, the universal proposition], because their end is to produce the knowledge of quite another connection, viz., the relation of a name to something so named.

Again, this same absence of a condition,[20] which has been given as the definition of an invariable connection [*i.e.*, a universal proposition], can itself never be known; since it is impossible to establish that all conditions must be objects of perception; and therefore, although the absence of perceptible things may be itself perceptible, the absence of non-perceptible things must be itself non-perceptible; and thus, since we must here too have recourse to inference, &c., we cannot leap over the obstacle which has already been planted to bar them. Again, we must accept as the definition of the condition, "it is that which is reciprocal or equipollent in extension[21] with the major term though not constantly accompanying the middle." These three distinguishing clauses, "not constantly accompanying the middle term," "constantly accompanying the major term," and "being constantly accompanied by it" [*i.e.*, reciprocal], are needed in the full definition to stop respectively three such fallacious conditions, in the argument to prove the non-eternity of sound, as "being produced," "the nature of a jar," and "the not causing audition;"[22] wherefore the definition holds,—and again it is established by the śloka of the great Doctor beginning *samásama*.[23]

But since the knowledge of the condition must here precede the knowledge of the condition's absence, it is only when there is the knowledge of the condition, that the knowledge of the universality of the proposition is possible, *i.e.*, a knowledge in the form of such a connection between the middle term and major term as is distinguished by the absence of any such condition; and on the other hand, the knowledge of the condition depends upon the knowledge of the invariable connection. Thus we fasten on our opponents as with adamantine glue the thunderbolt-like fallacy of reasoning in a circle. Hence by the impossibility of knowing the universality of a proposition it becomes impossible to establish inference, &c.[24]

The step which the mind takes from the knowledge of smoke, &c., to the knowledge of fire, &c., can be accounted for by its being based on a former perception or by its being an error; and that in some cases this step is justified by the result, is accidental just like the coincidence of effects observed in the employment of gems, charms, drugs, &c.

From this it follows that fate, &c.,[25] do not exist, since these can only be proved by inference. But an opponent will say, if you thus do not allow adṛishṭa, the various phenomena of the world become destitute of any cause.

But we cannot accept this objection as valid, since these phenomena can all be produced spontaneously from the inherent nature of things. Thus it has been said—

The fire is hot, the water cold, refreshing cool the breeze of morn;
By whom came this variety? from their own nature was it born.

And all this has been also said by Bṛihaspati—

There is no heaven, no final liberation, nor any soul in another world,
Nor do the actions of the four castes, orders, &c., produce any real effect.
The Agnihotra, the three Vedas, the ascetic's three staves, and smearing one's self with ashes,
Were made by Nature as the livelihood of those destitute of knowledge and manliness.
If a beast slain in the Jyotishṭoma rite will itself go to heaven,
Why then does not the sacrificer forthwith offer his own father?[26]
If the Śráddha produces gratification to beings who are dead,
Then here, too, in the case of travellers when they start, it is needless to give provisions for the journey.
If beings in heaven are gratified by our offering the Śráddha here,
Then why not give the food down below to those who are standing on the housetop?
While life remains let a man live happily, let him feed on ghee even though he runs in debt;
When once the body becomes ashes, how can it ever return again?
If he who departs from the body goes to another world,

How is it that he comes not back again, restless for love of his kindred?
Hence it is only as a means of livelihood that Brahmans have established here
All these ceremonies for the dead,—there is no other fruit anywhere.
The three authors of the Vedas were buffoons, knaves, and demons.
All the well-known formulæ of the pandits, jarpharí, turpharí, &c.[27]
And all the obscene rites for the queen commanded in the Aśwamedha,
These were invented by buffoons, and so all the various kinds of presents to the priests,[28]
While the eating of flesh was similarly commanded by night-prowling demons.

Hence in kindness to the mass of living beings must we fly for refuge to the doctrine of Chárváka. Such is the pleasant consummation.

—E. B. C.

CHAPTER II.

THE BAUDDHA SYSTEM.

At this point the Buddhists remark: As for what you (Chárvákas) laid down as to the difficulty of ascertaining invariable concomitance, your position is unacceptable, inasmuch as invariable concomitance is easily cognisable by means of identity and causality. It has accordingly been said—

> "From the relation of cause and effect, or from identity as a determinant, results a law of invariable concomitance—not through the mere observation of the desired result in similar cases, nor through the non-observation of it in dissimilar cases."[29]

On the hypothesis (of the Naiyáyikas) that it is concomitance and non-concomitance (*e.g.*, A is where B is, A is not where B is not) that determine an invariable connection, the unconditional attendance of the major or the middle term would be unascertainable, it being impossible to exclude all doubt with regard to instances past and future, and present but unperceived. If one (a Naiyáyika) rejoin that uncertainty in regard to such instances is equally inevitable on our system, we reply: Say not so, for such a supposition as that an effect may be produced without any cause would destroy itself by putting a stop to activity of any kind; for such doubts alone are to be entertained, the entertainment of which does not implicate us in practical absurdity and the like, as it has been said, "Doubt terminates where there is a practical absurdity."[30]

1. By ascertainment of an effectuation, then, of that (viz., of the designate of the middle) is ascertained the invariable concomitance (of the major); and the ascertainment of such effectuation may arise from the well-known series of five causes, in the perceptive cognition or non-cognition of cause and effect. That fire and smoke, for instance, stand in the relation of cause and effect is ascertained by five indications, viz., (1.) That an effect is not cognised prior to its effectuation, that (2.) the cause being perceived (3.) the effect is perceived, and that after the effect is cognised (4.) there is its non-cognition, (5.) when the (material) cause is no longer cognised.

2. In like manner an invariable concomitance is ascertained by the ascertainment of identity (*e.g.*, a sisu-tree is a tree, or wherever we observe the attributes of a sisu we observe also the attribute arboreity), an absurdity attaching to the contrary opinion, inasmuch as if a sisu-tree should lose its arboreity it would lose its own self. But, on the other

hand, where there exists no absurdity, and where a (mere) concomitance is again and again observed, who can exclude all doubt of failure in the concomitance? An ascertainment of the identity of sisu and tree is competent in virtue of the reference to the same object (*i.e.*, predication),—This tree is a sisu. For reference to the same object (predication) is not competent where there is no difference whatever (*e.g.*, to say, "A jar is a jar," is no combination of diverse attributes in a common subject), because the two terms cannot, as being synonymous, be simultaneously employed; nor can reference to the same object take place where there is a reciprocal exclusion (of the two terms), inasmuch as we never find, for instance, horse and cow predicated the one of the other.

It has thus been evinced that an effect or a self-same supposes a cause or a self-same (as invariable concomitants).

If a man does not allow that inference is a form of evidence, *pramáṇa*, one may reply: You merely assert thus much, that inference is not a form of evidence: do you allege no proof of this, or do you allege any? The former alternative is not allowable according to the maxim that bare assertion is no proof of the matter asserted. Nor is the latter alternative any better, for if while you assert that inference is no form of evidence, you produce some truncated argument (to prove, *i.e.*, infer, that it is none), you will be involved in an absurdity, just as if you asserted your own mother to be barren. Besides, when you affirm that the establishment of a form of evidence and of the corresponding fallacious evidence results from their homogeneity, you yourself admit induction by identity. Again, when you affirm that the dissentiency of others is known by the symbolism of words, you yourself allow induction by causality. When you deny the existence of any object on the ground of its not being perceived, you yourself admit an inference of which non-perception is the middle term. Conformably it has been said by Tathágata—

> "The admission of a form of evidence in general results from its being present to the understanding of others.
>
> "The existence of a form of evidence also follows from its negation by a certain person."

All this has been fully handled by great authorities; and we desist for fear of an undue enlargement of our treatise.

These same Bauddhas discuss the highest end of man from four standpoints. Celebrated under the designations of Mádhyamika, Yogáchára, Sautrántika, and Vaibháshika, these Buddhists adopt respectively the doctrines of a universal void (nihilism), an external void (subjective idealism), the inferribility of external objects (representationism), and the perceptibility of external objects (presentationism).[31] Though the venerated Buddha be the only one teacher (his disciples) are fourfold in consequence of this diversity of views; just as when one has said, "The sun has set," the adulterer, the thief, the divinity student, and others understand that it is time to set about their assignations, their theft, their religious duties, and so forth, according to their several inclinations.

It is to be borne in mind that four points of view have been laid out, viz., (1.) All is momentary, momentary; (2.) all is pain, pain; (3.) all is like itself alone; (4.) all is void, void.

Of these points of view, the momentariness of fleeting things, blue and so forth (*i.e.*, whatever be their quality), is to be inferred from their existence; thus, whatever *is* is momentary (or fluxional) like a bank of clouds, and all these things *are*.[32] Nor may any one object that the middle term (existence) is unestablished; for an existence consisting of practical efficiency is established by perception to belong to the blue and other momentary things; and the exclusion of existence from that which is not momentary is established, provided that we exclude from it the non-momentary succession and simultaneity, according to the rule that exclusion of the continent is exclusion of the contained. Now this practical efficiency (here identified with existence) is contained under succession and simultaneity, and no medium is possible between succession and non-succession (or simultaneity); there being a manifest absurdity in thinking otherwise, according to the rule—

> "In a reciprocal contradiction there exists no ulterior alternative;
>
> "Nor is their unity in contradictories, there being a repugnance in the very statement."[33]

And this succession and simultaneity being excluded from the permanent, and also excluding from the permanent all practical efficiency, determine existence of the alternative of momentariness.—q.e.d.

Perhaps some one may ask: Why may not practical efficiency reside in the non-fluxional (or permanent)? If so, this is wrong, as obnoxious to the following dilemma. Has your "permanent" a power of past and future practical efficiency during its exertion of present practical efficiency or no? On the former alternative (if it has such power), it cannot evacuate such past and future efficiency, because we cannot deny that it has power, and because we infer the consequence, that which can at any time do anything does not fail to do that at that time, as, for instance, a complement of causes, and this entity is thus powerful. On the latter alternative (if the permanent has no such power of past and future agency), it will never do anything, because practical efficiency results from power only; what at any time does not do anything, that at that time is unable to do it, as, for instance, a piece of stone does not produce a germ; and this entity while exerting its present practical efficiency, does not exert its past and future practical efficiency. Such is the contradiction.

You will perhaps rejoin: By assuming successive subsidiaries, there is competent to the permanent entity a successive exertion of past and future practical efficiency. If so, we would ask you to explain: Do the subsidiaries assist the entity or not? If they do not, they are not required; for if they do nothing, they can have nothing to do with the successive exertion. If they do assist the thing, is this assistance (or supplementation) other than the thing or not? If it is other than the thing, then this adscititious (assistance) is the cause, and the non-momentary entity is not the cause: for the effect will then follow, by concomitance and non-concomitance, the adventitious supplementation. Thus it has been said:

> "What have rain and shine to do with the soul? Their effect is on the skin of man;
>
> "If the soul were like the skin, it would be non-permanent; and if the skin were like the soul, there could be no effect produced upon it."

Perhaps you will say: The entity produces its effect, *together with* its subsidiaries. Well, then (we reply), let the entity not give up its subsidiaries, but rather tie them lest they fly with a rope round their neck, and so produce the effect which it has to produce, and without forfeiting its own proper nature. Besides (we continue), does the additament (or supplementation) constituted by the subsidiaries give rise to another additament or not? In either case the afore-mentioned objections will come down upon you like a shower of stones. On the alternative that the additament takes on another additament, you will be embarrassed by a many-sided regress *in infinitum*. If when the additament is to be generated another auxiliary (or additament) be required, there will ensue an endless series of such additaments: this must be confessed to be one infinite regress. For example, let a seed be granted to be productive when an additament is given, consisting of a complement of objects such as water, wind, and the like, as subsidiaries; otherwise an additament would be manifested without subsidiaries. Now the seed in taking on the additament takes it on with the need of (ulterior) subsidiaries; otherwise, as there would always be subsidiaries, it would follow that a germ would always be arising from the seed. We shall now have to add to the seed another supplementation by subsidiaries themselves requiring an additament. If when this additament is given, the seed be productive only on condition of subsidiaries as before, there will be established an infinite regression of additaments to (or supplementations of) the seed, to be afforded by the subsidiaries.

Again, we ask, does the supplementation required for the production of the effect produce its effect independently of the seed and the like, or does it require the seed and the like? On the first alternative (if the supplementation works independently), it would ensue that the seed is in no way a cause. On the second (if the supplementation require the seed), the seed, or whatever it may be that is thus required, must take on a supplementation or additament, and thus there will be over and over again an endless series of additaments added to the additament constituted by the seed; and thus a second infinite regression is firmly set up.

In like manner the subsidiary which is required will add another subsidiary to the seed, or whatever it may be that is the subject of the additions, and thus there will be an endless succession of additaments added to the additaments to the seed which is supplemented by the subsidiaries; and so a third infinite regression will add to your embarrassment.

Now (or the other grand alternative), let it be granted that a supplementation identical with the entity (the seed, or whatever it may be) is taken on. If so, the former entity, that *minus* the supplementation, is no more, and a new entity identical with the supplementation, and designated (in the technology of Buddhism) *kurvad rúpa* (or effect-producing object), comes into being: and thus the tree of my desires (my doctrine of a universal flux) has borne its fruit.

Practical efficiency, therefore, in the non-momentary is inadmissible. Nor is practical efficiency possible apart from succession in time; for such a possibility is redargued by the following dilemma. Is this (permanent) entity (which you contend for) able to produce all its effects simultaneously, or does it continue to exist after production of effects? On the former alternative, it will result that the entity will produce its effects just as much at one time as at another; on the second alternative, the expectation of its permanency is as reasonable as expecting seed eaten by a mouse to germinate.

That to which contrary determinations are attributed is diverse, as heat and cold; but this thing is determined by contrary attributions. Such is the argumentation applied to the cloud (to prove that it has not a permanent but a fluxional existence). Nor is the middle term disallowable, for possession and privation of power and impotence are allowed in regard to the permanent (which you assert) at different times. The concomitance and non-concomitance already described (viz., That which can at any time do anything does not fail to do that at that time, and What at any time does not do anything, that at that time is unable to do it) are affirmed (by us) to prove the existence of such power. The negative rule is: What at any time is unable to produce anything, that at that time does not produce it, as a piece of stone, for example, does not produce a germ;

and this entity (the seed, or whatever it may be), while exerting a present practical efficiency, is incapable of past and future practical efficiencies. The contradiction violating this rule is: What at any time does anything, that at that time is able to do that thing, as a complement of causes is able to produce its effect; and this (permanent) entity exerts at time past and time future the practical efficiencies proper to those times.

(To recapitulate.) Existence is restricted to the momentary; there being observed in regard to existence a negative rule, that in regard to permanent succession and simultaneity being excluded, existence which contains succession and simultaneity is not cognisable; and there being observed in regard to existence a positive rule, in virtue of a concomitance observed (viz., that the existent is accompanied or "pervaded" by the momentary), and in virtue of a non-concomitance observed (viz., that the non-momentary is accompanied or "pervaded" by the non-existent). Therefore it has been said by Jñána-śrí—

> "What is is momentary, as a cloud, and as these existent things;
> "The power of existence is relative to practical efficiency, and belongs to the ideal; but this power exists not as eternal in things eternal (ether, &c.);
> "Nor is there only one form, otherwise one thing could do the work of another;
> "For two reasons, therefore (viz., succession and simultaneity), a momentary flux is congruous and remains true in regard to that which we have to prove."

Nor is it to be held, in acceptance of the hypothesis of the Vaiśeshikas and Naiyáyikas, that existence is a participation in the universal form existence; for were this the case, universality, particularity, and co-inhesion (which do not participate in the universal) could have no existence.

Nor is the ascription of existence to universality, particularity, and co-inhesion dependent on any *sui generis* existence of their own; for such an hypothesis is operose, requiring too many *sui generis*existences. Moreover, the existence of any universal is disproved by a dilemma regarding the presence or non-presence (of the one in the many); and there is not presented to us any one form running through all the diverse momentary things, mustard-seeds, mountains, and so forth, like the string running through the gems strung upon it. Moreover (we would ask), is the universal omnipresent or present everywhere in its subjicible subjects? If it is everywhere, all things in the universe will be confounded together (chaos will be eternal), and you will be involved in a tenet you reject, since Praśasta-páda has said, "Present in all its subjects." Again (if the universal is present only in its proper subjects), does the universal (the nature of a jar) residing in an already existing jar, on being attached to another jar now in making, come from the one to attach itself to the other, or not come from it? On the first alternative (if it comes), the universal must be a substance (for substances alone underlie qualities and motions); whereas, if it does not come, it cannot attach itself to the new jar. Again (we ask), when the jar ceases to exist, does the universal outlast it, or cease to exist, or go to another place? On the first supposition it will exist without a subject to inhere in; on the second, it will be improper to call it eternal (as you do); on the third, it will follow that it is a substance (or base of qualities and motions). Destroyed as it is by the malign influence of these and the like objections, the universal is unauthenticated.

Conformably it has been said—

> "Great is the dexterity of that which, existing in one place, engages without moving from that place in producing itself in another place.
>
> "This entity (universality) is not connected with that wherein it resides, and yet pervades that which occupies that place: great is this miracle.
>
> "It goes not away, nor was it there, nor is it subsequently divided, it quits not its former repository: what a series of difficulties!"

If you ask: On what does the assurance that the one exists in the many rest? You must be satisfied with the reply that we concede it to repose on difference from that which is different (or exclusion of heterogeneity). We dismiss further prolixity.

That all transmigratory existence is identical with pain is the common verdict of all the founders of institutes, else they would not be found desirous to put a stop to it and engaging in the method for bringing it to an end. We must, therefore, bear in mind that all is pain, and pain alone.

If you object: When it is asked, like what? you must quote an instance,—we reply: Not so, for momentary objects self-characterised being momentary, have no common characters, and therefore it is impossible to say that this is like that. We must therefore hold that all is like itself alone, like itself alone.

In like manner we must hold that all is void, and void alone. For we are conscious of a determinate negation. This silver or the like has not been seen by me in sleeping or waking. If what is seen were (really) existent, then reality would pertain to the corresponding act of vision, to the (nacre, &c.), which is the basis of its particular nature (or haecceity), to the silver, &c., illusorily superposed upon that basis, to the connection between them, to the co-inherence, and so forth: a supposition not entertained by any disputant. Nor is a semi-effete existence admissible. No one imagines that one-half of a fowl may be set apart for cooking, and the other half for laying eggs. The venerated Buddha, then, having taught that of the illusorily superposed (silver, &c.), the basis (nacre, &c.), the connection between them, the act of vision, and the *videns*, if one or more be unreal it will perforce ensue that all are unreal, all being equally objects of the negation; the Mádhyamikas excellently wise explain as follows, viz., that the doctrine of Buddha terminates in that of a total void (universal baselessness or nihilism) by a slow progression like the intrusive steps of a mendicant, through the position of a momentary flux, and through the (gradual) negation of the illusory assurances of pleasurable sensibility, of universality, and of reality.

The ultimate principle, then, is a void emancipated from four alternatives, viz., from reality, from unreality, from both (reality and unreality), and from neither (reality nor unreality). To exemplify this: If real existence were the nature of a water-pot and the like, the activity of its maker (the potter) would be superfluous.

If non-existence be its nature the same objection will accrue; as it is said—

> "Necessity of a cause befits not the existent, ether and the like, for instance;
>
> "No cause is efficacious of a non-existent effect, flowers of the sky and the like, for instance."

The two remaining alternatives, as self-contradictory, are inadmissible. It has accordingly been laid down by the venerated Buddha in the Alaṅkárávatára[34]—

> "Of things discriminated by intellect, no nature is ascertained;[35]
>
> "Those things are therefore shown to be inexplicable and natureless."

And again—

> "This matter perforce results, which the wise declare, No sooner are objects thought than they are dissipated."

That is to say, the objects are not determined by any one of the four alternatives. Hence it is that it has been said—

"A religious mendicant, an amorous man, and a dog have three views of a woman's person, respectively that it is a carcass, that it is a mistress, and that it is a prey."

In consequence, then, of these four points of view, when all ideas are come to an end, final extinction, which is a void, will result. Accordingly we have overtaken our end, and there is nothing to be taught to us. There consequently remain only two duties to the student—interrogation and acceptance. Of these, interrogation is the putting of questions in order to attain knowledge not yet attained. Acceptance is assent to the matters stated by the sacred teacher. These (Bauddha nihilists) are excellent in assenting to that which the religious teacher enounces, and defective in interrogation, whence their conventional designation of Mádhyamikas (or mediocre).

Certain other Buddhists are styled Yogácháras, because while they accept the four points of view proclaimed by the spiritual guide, and the void of external things, they make the interrogation: Why has a void of the internal (or baselessness of mental phenomena) been admitted? For their technology is as follows:—Self-subsistent cognition must be allowed, or it will follow that the whole universe is blind. It has conformably been proclaimed by Dharmakírti: "To one who disallows perception the vision of objects is not competent."

An external *percipibile* is not admissible in consequence of the following dilemma. Does the object cognitively apprehensible arise from an entity or not? It does not result from an entity, for that which is generated has no permanence. Nor is it non-resultant, for what has not come into being is non-existent. Or (we may proceed) do you hold that a past object is cognitively apprehensible, as begetting cognition? If so, this is childish nonsense, because it conflicts with the apparent presentness of the object, and because on such a supposition the sense organs (and other imperceptible things) might be apprehended. Further (we ask), Is the *percipibile* a simple atom or a complex body? The latter it cannot be, this alternative being ejected by the dilemma as to whether part or whole is perceived. The former alternative is equally impossible, an atom being supersensible, and it not being able to combine simultaneously with six others; as it has been said—

> "If an atom could simultaneously combine with six, it would have six surfaces;
>
> "And each of these being taken separately, there would be a body of atomic dimension."

Intellect, therefore, as having no other *percipibile* but itself, is shown to be itself its own *percipibile*, self-subsistent, luminous with its own light, like light. Therefore it has been said—

"There is naught to be objectified by intellect; there is no cognition ulterior thereto;

"There being no distinction between percept and percipient, intellect shines forth of itself alone."

The identity of percipient and percept is inferrible, thus: That which is cognised by any cognition is not other than that cognition, as soul, for instance, is not other than the cognition of soul; and blue and other momentary objects are cognised by cognitions. For if there were a difference (between percept and percipient), the object could not now have any connection with the cognition, there being no identity to determine a constancy of connection, and nothing to determine the rise of such a connection. As for the appearance of an interval between the object and subject consciousnesses, this is an illusion, like the appearance of two moons when there is only one. The cause of this illusion is ideation of difference in a stream without beginning and without interruption; as it has been said—

> "As invariably cognised together, the blue object and the cognition thereof are identical;
> "And the difference should be accounted for by illusory cognitions, as in the example of the single moon."

And again—

> "Though there is no division, the soul or intellect, by reason of illusory perceptions,
> "Appears to possess a duality of cognitions, of percepts and of percipient."

Nor must it be supposed that (on this hypothesis) the juice, the energy, and the digestion derivable from an imaginary and an actual sweetmeat will be the same; for it cannot be questioned that though the intellect be in strictness exempt from the modes of object and subject, yet there is competent to it a practical distinction in virtue of the succession of illusory ideas without beginning, by reason of its possessing diverse modes percept and percipient, conformably to its illusory supposition of practical agency, just as to those whose eyes are dim with some morbid affection a hair and another minute object may appear either diverse or identical; as it has been said—

> "As the intellect, not having object and subject modes, appears, by reason of illusory cognitions,
> "Illuded with the diverse forms of perception, percept and percipient;
> "So when the intellect has posited a diversity, as in the example of the differences of the cognition of a hair and the like,
> "Then it is not to be doubted that it is characterised as percipient and percept."

Thus it has been evinced that intellect, as affected by beginningless ideation, manifests itself under diverse forms.

When, therefore, by constancy of reflection (on the four points of view) aforesaid, all ideation has been interrupted, there arises knowledge purged from the illusions which take the form of objects, such illusions being now melted away; and this is technically called *Mahodaya* (the grand exaltation, emancipation).

Others again (the Sautrántikas) hold that the position that there is no external world is untenable, as wanting evidence. Nor (they contend) can it be maintained that invariability of simultaneous cognition is an evidence, for this simultaneous cognition which you accept as proof of the identity of subject and object is indecisive, being found in dubious and in contrary instances. If you rejoin (they proceed): Let there be a proof of this identity, and let this proof be invariability of simultaneous cognition,—we refuse this, because inasmuch as cognition must ultimately have some object, it is manifested in duality, and because such invariability of simultaneity as to time and place is impossible. Moreover (they continue), if the object, blue or whatever it be, were only a form of cognition, it should be presented as *Ego*, not as *Hoc aliquid*, because the cognition and the object would be identical. Perhaps you will say: A blue form consisting of cognition is illusorily presented as external and as other than self, and consequently the Ego is not suggested; and so it has been said—

> "This side of knowledge which appears external to the other portion,
> "This appearance of duality in the unity of cognition is an illusion."

And again—

> "The principle to be known as internal also manifests itself as if it were external."

To this we reply (say the Sautrántikas): This is untenable, for if there be no external objects, there being no genesis of such, the comparison "as if they were external" is illegitimate. No man in his senses would say, "Vasumitra looks like the son of a childless mother." Again, if the manifestation of identity be proved by the illusoriness of the presentment of duality, and the presentment of duality be proved illusory by the manifestation of identity, you are involved in a logical circle. Without controversy we observe that cognitions take external things, blue or whatever they may be, as their objects, and do not take merely internal modifications as such, and we see that men in their everyday life overlook their internal states. Thus this argument which you adduce to prove that there is difference between subject and object, turns out a mere absurdity, like milky food made of cow-dung. When then you say "as if it were external," you must already suppose an external *percipibile*, and your own arrow will return upon you and wound you.

If any one object that the externality of an object synchronous with the cognition is inadmissible, we (Sautrántikas) reply that this objection is inadmissible, inasmuch as the subject in juxtaposition to the sensory imposes its form upon the cognition then in production, and the object is inferrible from the form thus imposed. The interrogation and response on this point have been thus summarised—

> "If it be asked, How can there be a past *percipibile*? They recognise perceptibility,
> "And a competent inferribility of the individual thing is its imposition of its form."

To exemplify. As nourishment is inferred from a thriving look, as nationality is inferred from language, and as affection is inferred from flurried movements, so from the form of knowledge a knowable may be inferred. Therefore it has been said—

> "With half (of itself) the object moulds (the cognition) without losing the nature of a half;
> "The evidence, therefore, of the recognition of a knowable is the nature of the knowable."

For consciousness of the cognition cannot be the being of the cognition, for this consciousness is everywhere alike, and if indifference were to attach itself to this, it would reduce all things to indifference. Accordingly the formal argument for the existence of external things: Those things which while a thing exists appear only at times, all depend upon something else than that thing; as, for instance, if I do not wish to speak or to walk, presentments of speaking or walking must suppose others desirous of speaking or walking; and in like manner the presentments of activity under discussion, while there exists the recognition of a subject of them, are only at times manifested as blue and so forth. Of these, the recognition of a subject is the presentation of the Ego, the manifestation as blue and so forth is a presentment of activity, as it has been said—

> "That is a recognition of a subject which is conversant about the Ego:
> "That is a presentment of activity which manifests blue and the rest."

Over and above, therefore, the complement of subject-recognitions, let it be understood that there is an external object world perceptible, which is the cause of presentments of activity; and that this external world does not rise into being only from time to time on occasion of presentments resulting from ideation.

According to the view of the Sensationalists (*vijñánavádin*), ideation is a power of generating such and such sensations (or presentments of activity) in subject-recognitions which exist as a single stream. The maturescence of this power is its readiness to produce its effect; of this the result is a presentment (or sensation); the antecedent momentary object (sensation) in the mental train is accepted as the cause, no other mental train being admitted to exercise such causality. It must therefore be stated that all momentary objects (fleeting sensations) in the subject-consciousness are alike able to bring about that maturescence of ideation in the subject-consciousness, which maturescence is productive of presentments of activity. If any one (of these fleeting sensations) had not this power, none would possess it, all existing alike in the stream of subject-recognitions. On the supposition that they all have this power, the effects cannot be diversified, and therefore any intelligent man, however unwilling, if he has a clear understanding, must decide, without putting out of sight the testimony of his consciousness, that to account for the occasional nature (of sense percepts) the six cognitions of sound, touch, colour, taste, and smell, of pleasure, and so forth, are produced on occasion of four conditions. These four conditions are known as (1.) the data, (2.) the suggestion, (3.) the medium, and (4.) the dominant (organ). Of these, the form of blue or the like arises from the condition of blue data in the understanding in which there is a manifestation of blue or the like, which manifestation is styled a cognition. The resuscitation of forms or cognitions arises from suggestion as a condition. The restriction to the apprehension of this or that object arises from the medium, light, for instance, as a condition, and from the dominant, the eye, for example, as another condition. The eye, as determinant of one particular cognition (form) where taste, &c., might have been equally cognised, is able to become dominant; for in everyday life he who determines is regarded as dominant. We must thus recognise four causes of pleasure and the rest which constitute the understanding and its modifications.

So also the universe, which consists of mind and its modifications, is of five kinds, entitled (1.) the sensational, (2.) the perceptional, (3.) the affectional, (4.) the verbal, and (5.) the impressional. Of these, the sensible world (*rúpa-skandha*) is the sense organs and their objects, according to the etymology, viz., that objects are discriminated (*rúpyante*) by these. The perceptional world is the stream of subject-recognitions and of presentments of activity. The affectional world is the stream of feelings of pleasure and pain generated by the two aforesaid worlds. The verbal (or symbolical) world is the stream of cognitions conversant about words—the words "cow," and so forth. The impressional world is the miseries, as desire, aversion, &c., caused by the affectional world, the lesser miseries, as conceit, pride, &c., and merit and demerit.

Reflecting, therefore, that this universe is pain, an abode of pain, and an instrument of pain, a man should acquire a knowledge of the principles, the method of suppressing this pain. Hence it has been said—

> "The principles sanctioned by Buddha are to the saint the four methods of suppressing the aggregate of pain."[36]

In these words the sense of pain is known to every one; the "aggregate" means the cause of pain. This aggregate is twofold, as (1.) determined by concurrence; or (2.) determined by causation. Of these, there is an aphorism comprising the aggregate determined by concurrence, "which other causes resort to this effect;" the condition of these causes thus proceeding is concurrence; the concurrence of causes is the result of this only, and not of any conscious being,—such is the meaning of the aphorism. To exemplify this. A germ, caused by a seed, is generated by the concurrence of six elements. Of these, earth as an element produces hardness and smell in the germ; water as an element produces viscidity and moisture; light as an element produces colour and warmth; air as an element produces touch and motion; ether as an element produces expansion and sound; the season as an element produces a fitting soil, &c. The aphorism comprising the aggregate determined by causation is: "With the Tathágatas the nature of these conditions is fixed by production, or by non-production; there is continuance as a condition, and determination by a condition, and conformity of the production to the cause;" that is to say, according to the doctrine of the Tathágata Buddhas, the nature of these conditions, that is, the causal relation between the cause and effect, results from production or from non-production. That which comes into being, provided that something exists, is the effect of that as its cause; such is the explanation of the nature (or causal relation). Continuance as a condition is where the effect is not found without its cause. The (abstract) affix *tal* (in the word *sthititā*) has the sense of the concrete. Determination by a condition is the determination of the effect by the cause. Here some one might interpose the remark that the relation of cause and effect cannot exist apart from some conscious agent. For this reason it is added that there existing a cause, conformity of the genesis to that cause is the nature which is fixed in conditions (that is, in causes and effects); and in all this no intelligent designer is observed.[37] To illustrate this, the causal determination of a genesis to be gone through is as follows:—From the seed the germ, from the germ the stalk, from the stalk the hollow stem, from the hollow stem the bud, from the bud the spicules, from the spicules the blossom, from the blossom the fruit. In this external aggregate neither the cause, the seed and the rest, nor the effect, the germ and the rest, has any consciousness of bringing a germ into being, or of being brought into being by the seed. In like manner in mental facts two causes are to be recognised. There is a whole ocean of scientific matter before us, but we desist, apprehensive of making our treatise unduly prolix.

Emancipation is the suppression of these two causal aggregates, or the rise of pure cognition subsequent to such suppression. The method (path, road) is the mode of suppressing them. And this method is the knowledge of the principles, and this knowledge accrues from former ideas. Such is the highest mystery. The name Sautrántika arose from the fact that the venerated Buddha said to certain of his disciples who asked what was the ultimate purport (*anta*) of the aphorism (*sútra*), "As you have inquired the final purport of the aphorism, be Sautrántikas."

Certain Bauddhas, though there exist the external world, consisting of odours, &c., and the internal, consisting of colours, &c., in order to produce unbelief in these, declared the universe to be a void. These the venerated Buddha styled Práthamika (primary) disciples. A second school, attached to the apprehension of sensations only, maintain that sensation is the only reality. A third school, who contend that both are true (the internal and the external), and maintain that sensible objects are inferrible. Others hold all this to be absurd language (*viruddhá bháshá*), and are known under the designation of Vaibháshikas. Their technical language springs up as follows:—According to the doctrine of inferrible sensibles, there being no perceptible object, and consequently no object from which a universal rule can be attained, it will be impossible that any illation should take place, and therefore a contradiction will emerge to the consciousness of all mankind. Objects, therefore, are of two kinds, sensible and cogitable. Of these apprehension is a non-discriminative instrument of knowledge as other than mere representation; cognition which is discriminative is not a form of evidence, as being a merely ideal cognition. Therefore it has been said—

> "Apprehension, exempt from ideality and not illusory, is non-discriminative. Discrimination, as resulting from the appearances of things, is without controversy an illusion.
>
> "The perceptible evidence of things is perception: if it were aught else,
>
> "There could neither be things, nor evidence of things derived from verbal communication, inference, or sense."

Here some one may say: If discriminative cognition be unauthentic, how is the apprehension of real objects by one energising thereon and the universal consentiency of mankind to be accounted for? Let it be replied: This question does not concern us, for these may be accounted for by the possibility of an indirect apprehension of objects, just as if we suppose the light of a gem to be a gem (we may yet handle the gem, because it underlies the light, while if we were to take nacre for silver, we could not lay hold of any silver). The rest has been fully discussed in describing the Sautrántikas (cf. p. 27), and therefore need not here be further detailed.

It should not be contended that a diversity of instruction according to the disciples' modes of thought is not traditional (or orthodox); for it is said in the gloss on the Bodha-chitta—

> "The instructions of the leader of mankind (Buddha) accommodating themselves to the character and disposition (of those who are to be taught),
> "Are said to be diverse in many ways, according to a plurality of methods.
> "For as deep or superficial, and sometimes both deep and superficial,
> "Instructions are diverse, and diverse is the doctrine of a universal void which is a negation of duality."

It is well known in Buddhist doctrine that the worship of the twelve inner seats (*áyatana*) is conducive to felicity.

> "After acquiring wealth in abundance, the twelve inner seats
> "Are to be thoroughly reverenced; what use of reverencing aught else below?
> "The five organs of knowledge, the five organs of action,
> "The common sensory and the intellect have been described by the wise as the twelve inner seats."

The system of the Buddhists is described as follows in the Viveka-vilása:—

> "Of the Bauddhas Sugata (Buddha) is the deity, and the universe is momentarily fluxional;
> "The following four principles in order are to be known by the name of the noble truths:—
> "Pain, the inner seats, and from them an aggregate is held,[38]
> "And the path (method); of all this let the explication be heard in order.
> "Pain, and the *skandhas* of the embodied one, which are declared to be five,—
> "Sensation, consciousness, name, impression, and form.
> "The five organs of sense, the five objects of sense, sound and the rest, the common sensory,
> "And (the intellect) the abode of merit,—these are the twelve inner seats.
> "This should be the complement of desire and so forth, when it arises in the heart of man.
> "Under the name of soul's own nature, it should be the aggregate.
> "The fixed idea that all impressions are momentary,
> "This is to be known as the path, and is also styled emancipation.

"Furthermore, there are two instruments of science, perception and inference.

"The Bauddhas are well known to be divided into four sects, the Vaibháshikas and the rest.

"The Vaibháshika highly esteems an object concomitant to the cognition;

"The Sautrántika allows no external object apprehensible by perception;

"The Yogáchára admits only intellect accompanied with forms;

"The Mádhyamikas hold mere consciousness self-subsistent.

"All the four (sects of) Bauddhas proclaim the same emancipation,

"Arising from the extirpation of desire, &c., the stream of cognitions and impressions.

"The skin garment, the water-pot, the tonsure, the rags, the single meal in the forenoon,

"The congregation, and the red vesture, are adopted by the Bauddha mendicants."[39]

CHAPTER III.

THE ÁRHATA SYSTEM.

The Gymnosophists[40] (Jainas), rejecting these opinions of the Muktakachchhas,[41] and maintaining continued existence to a certain extent, overthrow the doctrine of the momentariness of everything. (They say): If no continuing soul is accepted, then even the arrangement of the means for attaining worldly fruit in this life will be useless. But surely this can never be imagined as possible—that one should act and another reap the consequences! Therefore as this conviction, "I who previously did the deed, am the person who now reap its consequences," establishes undoubtedly the existence of a continuing soul, which remains constant through the previous and the subsequent period, the discriminating Jaina Arhats reject as untenable the doctrine of momentary existence, *i.e.*, an existence which lasts only an instant, and has no previous or subsequent part.

But the opponent may maintain, "The unbroken stream (of momentary sensations) has been fairly proved by argument, so who can prevent it? In this way, since our tenet has been demonstrated by the argument, 'whatever is, is momentary, &c.,' it follows that in each parallel line of successive experiences the previous consciousness is the agent and the subsequent one reaps the fruit. Nor may you object that, 'if this were true, effects might extend beyond all bounds'—[*i.e.*, A might act, and B receive the punishment]—because there is an essentially controlling relation in the very nature of cause and effect. Thus we see that when mango seeds, after being steeped in sweet juices, are planted in prepared soil, there is a definite certainty that sweetness will be found in the shoot, the stalk, the stem, the branches, the peduncle, &c., and so on by an unbroken series to the fruit itself; or again, when cotton seeds have been sprinkled with lac juice, there will be a similar certainty of finding, through the same series of shoot, &c., an ultimate redness in the cotton. As it has been said—

"'In whatever series of successive states the original impression of the action was produced,

"'There verily accrues the result, just like the redness produced in cotton.

"'When lac juice, &c., are poured on the flower of the citron, &c.,

"'A certain capacity is produced in it,—do you not see it?'"

But all this is only a drowning man's catching at a straw, for it is overthrown by the following dilemma:—

In the example of the "cloud," &c. [*supra*, p. 15], was your favourite "momentariness" proved by this very proof or by some other? It could not be the former, because your alleged momentariness is not always directly visible in the cloud, and consequently, as your example is not an ascertained fact, your supposed inference falls to the ground. Nor can it be the latter—because you might always prove your doctrine of momentariness by this new proof (if you had it), and consequently your argument regarding all existence ["whatever is, is momentary," &c.] would become needless. If you take as your definition of "existence" "that which produces an effect," this will not hold, as it would include even the bite of a snake imagined in the rope, since this undoubtedly produces the effect [of fear]. Hence it has been said that the definition of an existence is "that which possesses an origin, an end, and an [intermediate] duration."

As for what was said [in p. 16] that "the momentariness of objects is proved by the fact that the contrary assumption leads to contradictory attributes of capacity and want of capacity existing contemporaneously,"*that* also is wrong—for the alleged contradiction is not proved, as the holders of the Syád-váda[42] doctrine [*vide infra*] willingly admit the indeterminateness of the action of causes. As for what was said of the example of the cotton, that is only mere words, since no proof is given, and we do not accept even in that instance a separate destruction [at each moment]. And again, your supposed continued series cannot be demonstrated without some subject to give it coherence, as has been said, "In individual things which are of the same class or successively produced or in mutual contact, there may be a continued series; and this series is held to be one [throughout all"].

Nor is our objection obviated by your supposed definite relation between causes and effects. For even on your own admission it would follow that something experienced by the teacher's mind might be remembered by that of the pupil whom he had formed, or the latter might experience the fruits of merit which the former had acquired; and thus we should have the twofold fault that the thing done passed away without result, and that the fruit of the thing not done was enjoyed. This has been said by the author of the Siddhasenávákya—

"The loss of the thing done,—the enjoyment of the fruit of a thing not done,—the dissolution of all existence,—and the abolition of memory,—bold indeed is the Buddhist antagonist, when, in the teeth of these four objections, he seeks to establish his doctrine of momentary destruction!"

Moreover, (on your supposition of momentary existence), as at the time of the perception (the second moment) the object (of the first moment) does not exist, and similarly at the time of the object's existence the perception does not exist, there can be no such things as a perceiver and a thing perceived, and consequently the whole course of the world would come to an end. Nor may you suppose that the object and the perception are simultaneous, because this would imply that, like the two horns of an animal, they did not stand in the relation of cause and effect [as this relation necessarily involves succession], and consequently the *Álambana*, or the object's data [*supra*, p. 29], would be abolished as one of the four concurrent causes (*pratyaya*).[43]

If you say that "the object may still be perceived, inasmuch as it will impress its form on the perception, even though the one may have existed in a different moment from the other," this too will not hold. For if you maintain that the knowledge acquired by perception has a certain form impressed upon it, you are met by the impossibility of explaining how a momentary perception can possess the power of impressing a form; and if you say that it has no form impressed upon it, you are equally met by the fact that, if we are to avoid incongruity, there must be some definite condition to determine the perception and knowledge in each several case. Thus by perception the abstract consciousness, which before existed uninfluenced by the external object, becomes modified under the form of a jar, &c., with a definite reference to each man's personality [*i.e.*, I see the jar], and it is not merely the passive recipient of a reflection like a mirror. Moreover, if the perception only reproduced the form of the object, there would be an end of using such words as "far," "near,"& c., of the objects.[44] Nor can you accept this conclusion, "as exactly in accordance with your own views," because, in spite of all our logic, the stubborn fact remains that we do use such phrases as "the mountain is nearer" or "further," "long" or "large." Nor may you say that "it is the object (which supplies the form) that really possesses these qualities of being 'further,' &c., and they are applied by a fashion of speech to the perception [though not really belonging to it]"—because we do not find that this is the case in a mirror [*i.e.*, it does not become a *far* reflection because it represents a far object.] And again, as the perception produced by an object follows it in assuming the form of blue, so too, if the object be insentient, it ought equally to assume its form and so become itself insentient. And thus, according to the proverb, "wishing to grow, you have destroyed your root," and your cause has fallen into hopeless difficulties.

If, in your wish to escape this difficulty, you assert that "the perception does not follow the object in being insentient," then there would be no perception that the object is insentient,[45] and so it is a case of the proverb, "While he looks for one thing which he has lost, another drops." "But what harm will it be if there is no perception of a thing's being insentient?" [We reply], that if its being insentient is not perceived, while its blue form is perceived, the two may be quite distinct [and as different from each other as a jar and cloth], or it may be a case of "indeterminateness" [so that the two may be only occasionally found together, as smoke with fire]. And again, if insentience is not perceived contemporaneously with the blue form, how could there then be conformity between them [so that both the blue and the insentience should together constitute the character of the thing?] We might just as well maintain that, on perceiving a post, the unperceived universe entered into it as also constituting its character.[46]

All this collection of topics for proof has been discussed at full length by the Jaina authors, Pratápachandra and others, in the *Prameyakamalamártaṇḍa*, &c., and is here omitted for fear of swelling the book too much.

Therefore those who wish for the *summum bonum* of man must not accept the doctrine of Buddha, but rather honour only the Árhata doctrine. The Arhat's nature has been thus described by Arhachchandrasúri,[47] in his *Áptaniśchayálaṅkára.*

"The divine Arhat is the supreme lord, the omniscient one, who has overcome all faults, desire, &c.,—adored by the three worlds, the declarer of things as they are."

But may it not be objected that no such omniscient soul can enter the path of proof, since none of the five affirmative proofs can be found to apply, as has been declared by Tautátita [Bhaṭṭa Kumárila[48]]?

1. "No omniscient being is seen by the sense here in this world by ourselves or others; nor is there any part of him seen which might help us as a sign to infer his existence.

2. "Nor is there any injunction (*vidhi*) of scripture which reveals an eternal omniscient one, nor can the meaning of the explanatory passages (*arthaváda*) be applied here.

3. "His existence is not declared by those passages which refer to quite other topics; and it cannot be contained in any emphatic repetitions (*anuváda*), as it had never been mentioned elsewhere before.

4. "An omniscient being who had a beginning can never be the subject of the eternal Veda; and how can he be established by a made and spurious Veda?

5. "Do you say that this omniscient one is accepted on his own word? How can you establish either when they thus both depend on reciprocal support?

6. "[If you say,] 'The saying is true because it was uttered by one omniscient, and this proves the Arhat's existence;' how can either point be established without some previously established foundation?

7. "But they who accept a [supposed] omniscient on the baseless word of a parviscient know nothing of the meaning of a real omniscient's words.

8. "And again, if we now could see anything like an omniscient being, we might have a chance of recognising him by the [well-known fourth] proof, comparison (*upamána*).

9. "And the teaching of Buddha [as well as that of Jina], which embraces virtue, vice, &c., would not be established as authoritative, if there were not in him the attribute of omniscience,[49] and so on."

We reply as follows:—As for the supposed contradiction of an Arhat's existence, derived from the failure of the five affirmative proofs,—this is untenable, because there *are* proofs, as inference,& c., which *do* establish[50] his existence. Thus any soul will become omniscient when, (its natural capacity for grasping all objects remaining the same), the hindrances to such knowledge are done away. Whatever thing has a natural capacity for knowing any object, will, when its hindrances to such knowledge are done away, actually know it, just as the sense of vision cognises form, directly the hindrances of darkness, &c., are removed. Now there *is* such a soul, which has its hindrances done away, its natural capacity for grasping all things remaining unchanged; therefore there is an omniscient being. Nor is the assertion unestablished that the soul has a natural capacity for grasping all things; for otherwise the Mímáṃsist could not maintain that a knowledge of all possible cases can be produced by the authoritative injunction of a text,[51]—nor could there otherwise be the knowledge of universal propositions, such as that in our favourite argument, "All things are indeterminate from the very fact of their existence" [and, of course, a follower of the Nyáya will grant that universal propositions can be known, though he will dispute the truth of this particular one]. Now it is clear that the teachers of the Púrva Mímáṃsá accept the thesis that the soul has a natural capacity for grasping all things; since they allow that a knowledge embracing all things can be produced by the discussion of injunctions and prohibitions, as is said [by Śabara in his commentary on the Sútras, i. 1, 2], "A precept makes known the past, the present, the future, the minute, the obstructed, the distant, &c." Nor can you say that "it is impossible to destroy the obstructions which hinder the soul's knowing all things," because we [Jainas] are convinced that there are certain special means to destroy these obstructions, viz., the three ["gems"], right intuition, &c. By this charm also, all inferior assaults of argument can be put to flight.

But the Naiyáyika may interpose, "You talk of the pure intelligence, which, after all hindrances are done away, sees all objects, having sense-perception at its height; but this is irrelevant, because there can be no hindrance to the omniscient, as from all eternity he has been always liberated." We reply that there is no proof of your eternally liberated being. There cannot be an omniscient who is eternally "liberated," from the very fact of his being "liberated," like other liberated persons,—since the use of the term "liberated" necessarily implies the having been previously bound; and if the latter is absent, the former must be too, as is seen in the case of the ether. "But is not this being's existence definitely proved by his being the maker of that eternal series of effects, the earth, &c.? according to the well-known argument, 'the earth, &c., must have had a maker, because they have the nature of effects, as a jar.'" This argument, however, will not hold, because you cannot prove that they have the nature of effects. You cannot establish this from the fact of their being composed of parts, because this supposition falls upon the horns of a dilemma. Does this "being composed of parts" mean (i.) the being in contact with the parts; or (ii.) "the being in intimate relation to the parts; or (iii.) the being produced from parts;" or (iv.) the being a substance in intimate relation; or (v.) the being the object of an idea involving the notion of parts?

Not *the first*, because it would apply too widely, as it would include ether [since this, though not itself composed of parts, is in contact with the parts of other things;] nor *the second*, because it would similarly include genus, &c. [as this resides in a substance by intimate relation, and yet itself is not composed of parts;] nor *the third*, because this involves a term ("produced") just as much disputed as the one directly in question;[52] nor *the fourth*, because its neck is caught in the pillory of the following alternative:—Do you mean by your phrase used above that it is to be a substance, and to have something else in intimate relation to itself,—or do you mean that it must have intimate relation to something else, in order to be valid for your argument? If you say the former, it will equally apply to ether, since this is a substance, and has its qualities resident in it by intimate relation; if you say the latter, your new position involves as much dispute as the original point, since you would have to prove the existence of intimate relation in the parts, or the so-called "intimate causes," which you mean by "something else." We use these terms in compliance with your terminology; but, of course, from our point of view, we do not allow such a thing as "intimate relation," as there is no proof of its existence.

Nor can *the fifth* alternative be allowed, because this would reach too far, as it would include soul, &c., since soul can be the object of an idea involving the notion of parts, and yet it is acknowledged to be not an effect.[53] Nor can you maintain that the soul may still be indiscerptible in itself, but by reason of its connection with something possessing parts may itself become metaphorically the object of an idea involving the notion of parts, because there is a mutual contradiction in the idea of that which has no parts and that which is all-pervading, just as the atom [which is indiscerptible but not all-pervading].

And, moreover, is there only one maker? Or, again, is he independent?

In the former case your position will apply too far, as it will extend erroneously to palaces, &c., where we see for ourselves the work of many different men, as carpenters, &c., and [in the second case] if all the world were produced by this one maker, all other agents would be superfluous. As it has been said in the *Vítarágastuti*, or "Praise of Jina"—

1. "There is one eternal maker for the world, all-pervading, independent, and true; they have none of these inextricable delusions, whose teacher art *thou*."

And again—

2. "There is here no maker acting by his own free will, else his influence would extend to the making of a mat. What would be the use of yourself or all the artisans, if Íśwara fabricates the three worlds?"

Therefore it is right to hold, as we do, that omniscience is produced when the hindrances are removed by the three means before alluded to.

Nor need the objection be made that "right intuition," &c., are impossible, as there is no other teacher to go to,—because this universal knowledge can be produced by the inspired works of former omniscient Jinas. Nor is our doctrine liable to the imputation of such faults as *Anyonyáśrayatá*,[54] &c., because we accept an eternal succession of revealed doctrines and omniscient teachers, like the endless series of seed springing from shoot and shoot from seed. So much for this preliminary discussion.

The well-known triad called the three gems, right intuition, &c., are thus described in the *Paramágamasára* (which is devoted to the exposition of the doctrines of the Arhats)—"Right intuition, right knowledge, right conduct are the path of liberation." This has been thus explained by Yogadeva:—

(*a.*) When the meaning of the predicaments, the soul, &c., has been declared by an Arhat in exact accordance with their reality, absolute faith in the teaching, *i.e.*, the entire absence of any contrary idea, is "right intuition." And to this effect runs the*Tattvártha-sútra*, "Faith in the predicaments[55] is right 'intuition.'" Or, as another definition gives it, "Acquiescence in the predicaments declared by a Jina is called 'right faith;'

it is produced either by natural character or by the guru's instruction." "Natural character" means the soul's own nature, independent of another's teaching; "instruction" is the knowledge produced by the teaching of another in the form of explanation, &c.

(*b.*) "Right knowledge" is a knowledge of the predicaments, soul, & c., according to their real nature, undisturbed by any illusion or doubt; as it has been said—

"That knowledge, which embraces concisely or in detail the predicaments as they actually are, is called 'right knowledge' by the wise."

This knowledge is fivefold as divided into *mati*, *śruta*, *avadhi*,*manas-paryáya*, and *kevala*; as it has been said, "*Mati*, *śruta*,*avadhi*, *manas-paryáya*, and *kevala*, these are knowledge." The meaning of this is as follows:—

1. *Mati* is that by which one cognises an object through the operation of the senses and the mind, all obstructions of knowledge being abolished.

2. *Śruta* is the clear knowledge produced by *mati*, all the obstructions of knowledge being abolished.

3. *Avadhi* is the knowledge of special objects caused by the abolition of hindrances, which is effected by "right intuition,"& c.[56]

4. *Manas-paryáya* is the clear definite knowledge of another's thoughts, produced by the abolition of all the obstructions of knowledge caused by the veil of envy.

5. *Kevala* is that pure unalloyed knowledge for the sake of which ascetics practise various kinds of penance.

The first of these (*mati*) is not self-cognised, the other four are. Thus it has been said—

"True knowledge is a proof which nothing can overthrow, and which manifests itself as well as its object; it is both supersensuous and itself an object of cognition, as the object is determined in two ways."

But the full account of the further minute divisions must be got from the authoritative treatise above-mentioned.

(*c.*) "Right conduct" is the abstaining from all actions tending to evil courses by one who possesses faith and knowledge, and who is diligent in cutting off the series of actions and their effects which constitutes mundane existence. This has been explained at length by the Arhat—

1. "Right conduct is described as the entire relinquishment of blamable impulses; this has been subjected to a fivefold division, as the 'five vows,' *ahiṃsá*, *súnṛita*, *asteya*, *brahmacharyá*, and*aparigraha*.[57]

2. "The 'vow' of *ahiṃsá* is the avoidance of injuring life by any act of thoughtlessness in any movable or immovable thing.

3. "A kind, salutary, and truthful speech is called the 'vow' of *súnṛita*. That truthful speech is not truthful, which is unkind to others and prejudicial.

4. "The not taking what is not given is declared to be the 'vow' of *asteya*; the external life is a man's property, and, when it is killed, it is killed by some one who seizes it.

5. "The 'vow' of *brahmacharyá* (chastity) is eighteen-fold, viz., the abandonment of all desires,[58] heavenly or earthly, in thought, word, and deed, and whether by one's own action or by one's consent, or by one's causing another to act.

6. "The 'vow' of *aparigraha* is the renouncing of all delusive interest in everything that exists not; since bewilderment of thought may arise from a delusive interest even in the unreal.

7. "When carried out by the five states of mind in a fivefold order, these great 'vows' of the world produce the eternal abode."

The full account of the five states of mind (*bhávaná*) has been given in the following passage [of which we only quote one śloka]—

"Let him carry out the 'vow' of *súnṛita* uninterruptedly by the abstinence from laughter, greed, fear, and anger, and by the deliberate avoidance of speech,"[59]—and so forth.

These three, right intuition, right knowledge, and right conduct, when united, produce liberation, but not severally; just as, in the case of an elixir, it is the knowledge of what it is, faith in its virtues, and the actual application of the medicine,,[60] united, which produce the elixir's effect, but not severally.

Here we may say concisely that the *tattvas* or predicaments are two, *jíva* and *ajíva*; the soul, *jíva*, is pure intelligence; the non-soul, *ajíva*, is pure non-intelligence. Padmanandin has thus said—

"The two highest predicaments are 'soul' and 'non-soul;' 'discrimination' is the power of discriminating these two, in one who pursues what is to be pursued, and rejects what is to be rejected. The affection, &c., of the agent are to be rejected; these are objects for the non-discriminating; the supreme light [of knowledge] is alone to be pursued, which is defined as *upayoga*."

Upayoga [or "the true employment of the soul's activities"] takes place when the vision of true knowledge recognises the manifestation of the soul's innate nature; but as long as the soul, by the bond of *pradeśa* and the mutual interpenetration of form which it produces [between the soul and the body], considers itself as identified with its actions [and the body which they produce], knowledge should rather be defined as "the cause of its recognising that it is other than these."[61]

Intelligence (*chaitanya*) is common to all souls, and is the real nature of the soul viewed as *pariṇata* [*i.e.*, as it is in itself]; but by the influence of *upaśamakshaya* and *kshayopaśama* it appears in the "mixed" form as possessing both,[62] or again, by the influence of actions as they arise, it assumes the appearance of foulness,& c.[63] As has been said by Váchakáchárya [in a sútra]—

"The *aupaśamika*, the *Ksháyika*, and the 'mixed' states are the nature of the soul, and also the *audayika* and the *Páriṇámika*."

1. The *aupaśamika* state of the soul arises when all the effects of past actions have ceased, and no new actions arise [to affect the future], as when water becomes temporarily pure through the defiling mud sinking to the bottom by the influence of the clearing nut-plant,[64] &c.

2. The *Ksháyika* state arises when there is the absolute abolition of actions and their effects, as in final liberation.

3. The "mixed" (*miśra*) state combines both these, as when water is partly pure.

4. The *audayika* state is when actions arise [exerting an inherent influence on the future]. The *Páriṇámika* state is the soul's innate condition, as pure intelligence, &c., and disregarding its apparent states, as (1), (2), (3), (4).[65] This nature, in one of the above-described varieties, is the character of every soul whether happy or unhappy. This is the meaning of the sútra quoted above.

This has been explained in the *Svarúpa-sambodhana*—

"Not different from knowledge, and yet not identical with it,—in some way both different and the same,—knowledge is its first and last; such is the soul described to be."

If you say that, "As difference and identity are mutually exclusive, we must have one or the other in the case of the soul, and its being equally both is absurd," we reply, that there is no evidence to support you when you characterise it as absurd. Only a valid non-perception[66] can thus preclude a suggestion as absurd; but this is not found in the present case, since (in the opinion of us, the advocates of the *Syád-váda*) it is perfectly notorious that all things present a mingled nature of many contradictory attributes.

Others lay down a different set of *tattvas* from the two mentioned above, *jíva* and *ajíva*; they hold that there are five *astikáyas*or categories,—*jíva*, *ákáśa*, *dharma*, *adharma*, and *pudgala*. To all these five we can apply the idea of "existence" (*asti*),[67] as connected with the three divisions of time, and we can similarly apply the idea of "body" (*káya*),[68] from their occupying several parts of space.

The *jívas* (souls) are divided into two, the "mundane" and the "released." The "mundane" pass from birth to birth; and these are also divided into two, as those possessing an internal sense (*samanaska*), and those destitute of it (*amanaska*). The former possesses *saṃjñá*, *i.e.*, the power of apprehension, talking, acting, and receiving instruction; the latter are those without this power. These latter are also divided into two, as "locomotive" (*trasa*), or "immovable" (*sthávara*).

The "locomotive" are those possessing at least two senses [touch and taste], as shell-fish, worms, &c., and are thus of four kinds [as possessing two, three, four, or five senses]; the "immovable" are earth, water, fire, air, and trees.[69] But here a distinction must be made. The dust of the road is properly "earth," but bricks, &c., are aggregated "bodies of earth," and that soul by whom this body is appropriated becomes "earthen-bodied," and that soul which will hereafter appropriate it is the "earth-soul." The same four divisions must also be applied to the others, water, &c. Now the souls which have appropriated or will appropriate the earth, &c., as their bodies, are reckoned as "immovable;" but earth, &c., and the "bodies of earth," &c., are not so reckoned, because they are inanimate.[70] These other immovable things, and such as only possess the one sense of touch, are considered as "released," since they are incapable of passing into any other state of existence.

Dharma, *adharma*, and *ákáśa* are singular categories [and not generic], and they have not the attribute of "action," but they are the causes of a substance's change of place.

Dharma, "merit," and *adharma*, "demerit," are well known. They assist souls in progressing or remaining stationary in the universally extended[71] sky [or ether] characterised by light, and also called Lokákáśa; hence the presence of the category "merit" is to be inferred from progress, that of "demerit" from stationariness. The effect of *ákáśa* is seen when one thing enters into the space previously occupied by another.

Pudgala, "body," possesses touch, taste, and colour. Bodies are of two kinds, atomic and compound. Atoms cannot be enjoyed;[72] the compounds are the binary and other combinations. Atoms are produced by the separation of these binary and other compounds, while these arise from the conjunction of atoms. Compounds sometimes arise from separation and conjunction [combined]; hence they are called *pudgalas*, because they "fill" (*púr*), and "dissolve" (*gal*). Although "time" is not properly an *astikáya*, because it does not occupy many separate parts of space [as mentioned in the definition], still it is a *dravya* [or *tattva*], as the definition will hold; "substance" (*dravya*) possesses "qualities and action."[73] Qualities reside in substance but do not themselves possess qualities, as the general qualities, knowledge, &c., of the *jíva*, form, &c., of the body, and the power of causing progress, stationariness, and motion into a place previously occupied, in the case respectively of "merit," "demerit," and *ákáśa*. "Action" (*paryáya*) has thus been defined; the actions (*paryáyáḥ*) of a substance are, as has been said, its existence, its production, its being what it is, its development, its course to the end, as, *e.g.*, in the *jíva*, the knowledge of objects, as of a jar, &c., happiness, pain, &c.; in the *pudgala*, the lump of clay, the jar, &c.; in merit and demerit, the special functions of progress, &c. Thus there are six substances or *tattvas* [*i.e.*, the five above mentioned and "time"].

Others reckon the *tattvas* as seven, as has been said—

"The *tattvas* are *jíva*, *ajíva*, *ásrava*, *bandha*, *saṃvara*, *nirjará*, and *moksha*." *Jíva* and *ajíva* have been already described.*Ásrava* is described as the movement of the soul called *yoga*,[74] through its participation in the movement of its various bodies,*audárika*, &c. As a door opening into the water is called *ásrava*, because it causes the stream to descend through it,[75] so this *yoga* is called *ásrava*, because by it as by a pipe actions and their consequences flow in upon the soul. Or, as a wet garment collects the dust brought to it from every side by the wind, so the soul, wet with previous sins, collects, by its manifold points of contact with the body, the actions which are brought to it by *yoga*. Or as, when water is thrown on a heated lump of iron, the iron absorbs the water altogether, so the *jíva*, heated by previous sins, receives from every side the actions which are brought by *yoga*. *Kasháya* ("sin," "defilement") is so called because it "hurts" (*kash*) the soul by leading it into evil states; it comprises anger, pride, delusion, and lust. *Ásrava* is twofold, as good or evil. Thus abstaining from doing injury is a good *yoga* of the body; speaking what is true, measured, and profitable is a good *yoga* of the speech.

These various subdivisions of *ásrava* have been described at length in several *Sútras*. "*Ásrava* is the impulse to action with body, speech, or mind, and it is good or evil as it produces merit or demerit," &c. Others, however, explain it thus:— "*Ásrava* is the action of the senses which impels the soul towards external objects; the light of the soul, coming in contact with external objects by means of the senses, becomes developed as the knowledge of form,& c."[76]

Bandha, "bondage," is when the soul, by the influence of "false intuition," "non-indifference," "carelessness," and "sin" (*kasháya*), and also by the force of *yoga*, assumes various bodies occupying many parts of space, which enter into its own subtile body, and which are suited to the bond of its previous actions. As has been said—

"Through the influence of sin the individual soul assumes bodies suitable to its past actions, this is, 'bondage.'"

In this quotation the word "sin" (*kasháya*) is used to include the other three causes of bondage as well as that properly so termed. Váchakácharya has thus enumerated the causes of bondage: "The causes of bondage are false intuition, non-indifference, carelessness, and sin."

(*a*) "False intuition" is twofold,—either innate from one's natural character, as when one disbelieves Jaina doctrines from the influence of former evil actions, irrespectively of another's teaching,—or derived, when learned by another's teaching.

(*b*) "Non-indifference" is the non-restraint of the five senses, and the internal organ from the set of six, earth, &c.

(*c*) "Carelessness" (*pramáda*) is a want of effort to practise the five kinds of *samiti*, *gupti*, &c.

(*d*) "Sin" consists of anger, &c. Here we must make the distinction that the four things, false intuition, &c., cause those kinds of bondage called *sthiti* and *anubháva*; *yoga* [or *ásrava*] causes those kinds called *prakṛiti* and *pradeśa*.

"Bondage" is fourfold, as has been said: "*Prakṛiti*, *sthiti*, *anubháva*, and *pradeśa* are its four kinds."

1. *Prakṛiti* means "the natural qualities," as bitterness or sweetness in the vimba plant or molasses. This may be subdivided into eight *múla-prakṛitis*.[77]

Thus obstructions (*ávaraṇa*)[78] cloud the knowledge and intuition, as a cloud obscures the sun or a shade the lamp. This is (*a*) *jnánávaraṇa*, or (*b*) *darśanávaraṇa*. (*c*) An object recognised as simultaneously existing or non-existing produces mingled pleasure and pain, as licking honey from a sword's edge,—this is *vedaníya*. (*d*) A delusion (*mohaníya*) in intuition produces want of faith in the Jaina categories, like association with the wicked; delusion in conduct produces want of self-restraint, like intoxication. (*e*) *Áyus* produces the bond of body, like a snare.[79] (*f*) *Náman*, or "the name," produces various individual appellations, as a painter paints his different pictures. (*g*) *Gotra* produces the idea of noble and ignoble, as the potter fashions his pots. (*h*) *Antaráya*produces obstacles to liberality, &c., as the treasurer hinders the king by considerations of economy.

Thus is the *prakṛiti-bandha* eightfold, being denominated as the eight *múla-prakṛitis*, with subdivisions according to the different actions of the various subject matter.

And thus has Umáswáti-váchakácharya[80] declared: "The first kind of *bandha* consists of obstructions of the knowledge and the intuition, *vedaníya*, *mohaníya*, *áyus*, *náman*, *gotra*, and *antaráya*;" and he has also reckoned up the respective subdivisions of each as five, nine, twenty-eight, four, two, forty, two, and fifteen. All this has been explained at full length in the *Vidyánanda* and other works, and here is omitted through fear of prolixity.

2. *Sthiti.* As the milk of the goat, cow, buffalo, &c., have continued unswerving from their sweet nature for so long a period, so the first three *múla-prakṛitis, jnánávaraṇa,* &c., and the last, *antaráya,* have not swerved from their respective natures even through the period described in the words, "*sthiti* lasts beyonds crores of crores of periods of time measured by thirty *ságaropamas*."[81] This continuance is *sthiti.*

3. *Anubháva.* As in the milk of goats, cows, buffaloes, &c., there exists, by its rich or poor nature, a special capacity for producing[82] its several effects, so in the different material bodies produced by our actions there exists a special capacity (*anubháva*) for producing their respective effects.

4. *Pradeśa.* The *bandha* called *pradeśa* is the entrance into the different parts of the soul by the masses, made up of an endless number of parts, of the various bodies which are developed by the consequences of actions.

Saṃvara is the stopping of *ásrava*—that by which the influence of past actions (*karman*) is stopped from entering into the soul. It is divided into *gupti*, *samiti*, &c. *Gupti* is the withdrawal of the soul from that "impulse" (*yoga*) which causes mundane existence,—it is threefold, as relating to body, speech, or mind. *Samiti* is the acting so as to avoid injury to all living beings. This is divided into five kinds, as *íryá*,[83] *bháshá*, &c., as has been explained by Hemachandra.

1. "In a public highway, kissed by the sun's rays, to walk circumspectly so as to avoid injuring living beings, this the good call *íryá*.

2. "Let him practise[84] a measured utterance in his intercourse with all people; this is called *bháshá-samiti*, dear to the restrainers of speech.

3. "The food which the sage takes, ever free from the forty-two faults which may accrue to alms, is called the *eshaṇá-samiti.*[85]

4. "Carefully looking at it and carefully seating himself upon it, let him take a seat, &c., set it down, and meditate,—this is called the *ádána-samiti.*

5. "That the good man should carefully perform his bodily evacuations in a spot free from all living creatures,[86]—this is the *utsarga-samiti.*[87] Hence *samvara* has been etymologically analysed as that which closes (*sam* + *vṛiṇoti*) the door of the stream of *ásrava,*[88] as has been said by the learned, '*Ásrava* is the cause of mundane existence, *saṃvara* is the cause of liberation;[89] this is the Árhat doctrine in a handful; all else is only the amplification of this.'"

Nirjará is the causing the fruit of past actions to decay by self-mortification, &c.; it destroys by the body the merit and demerit of all the previously performed actions, and the resulting happiness and misery; "self-mortification" means the plucking out of the hair,& c. This *nirjará* is twofold,[90] "temporary" (*yathákála*) and ancillary (*aupakramaṇika*). It is "temporary" as when a desire is dormant in consequence of the action having produced its fruit, and at that particular time, from this completion of the object aimed at, *nirjará* arises, being caused by the consumption of the desire, &c. But when, by the force of asceticism, the sage turns all actions into means for attaining his end (liberation), this is the *nirjará* of actions. Thus it has been said: "From the decaying of the actions which are the seeds of mundane existence, *nirjará* arises, which is twofold, *sakámá* and *akámá*. That called *sakámá* belongs to ascetics, the *akámá* to other embodied spirits."[91]

Moksha. Since at the moment of its attainment there is an entire absence of all future actions, as all the causes of bondage (false perception, &c.) are stopped,[92] and since all past actions are abolished in the presence of the causes of *nirjará*, there arises the absolute release from all actions,—this is *moksha*; as it has been said: "*Moksha* is the absolute release from all actions by the decay (*nirjará*) of the causes of bondage and of existence."

Then the soul rises upward to the end of the world. As a potter's wheel, whirled by the stick and hands, moves on even after these have stopped, until the impulse is exhausted, so the previous repeated contemplations of the embodied soul for the attainment of *moksha* exert their influence even after they have ceased, and bear the soul onward to the end of the world; or, as the gourd, encased with clay, sinks in the water, but rises to the surface when freed from its encumbrance, so the soul, delivered from works, rises upward by its isolation,[93] from the bursting of its bonds like the elastic seed of the castor-oil plant, or by its own native tendency like the flame.

"Bondage" is the condition of being unseparated, with a mutual interpenetration of parts [between the soul and the body]; *saṅga* is merely mutual contact. This has been declared as follows:—

"[Liberation] is unhindered, from the continuance of former impulses, from the absence of *saṅga*, from the cutting of all bonds, and from the natural development of the soul's own powers of motion, like the potter's wheel, the gourd with its clay removed, the seed of the castor-oil plant, or the flame of fire."

Hence they recite a śloka:—

> "However often they go away, the planets return, the sun, moon, and the rest;
>
> "But never to this day have returned any who have gone to Álokákáśa."

Others hold *moksha* to be the abiding in the highest regions, the soul being absorbed in bliss, with its knowledge unhindered and itself untainted by any pain or impression thereof.

Others hold nine *tattwas*, adding "merit" and "demerit" to the foregoing seven,—these two being the causes of pleasure and pain. This has been declared in the *Siddhánta*, "*Jíva, ajíva, puṇya, pápa, ásrava, saṃvara, nirjaraṇa, bandha*, and *moksha*, are the nine *tattwas*." As our object is only a summary, we desist here.

Here the Jainas everywhere introduce their favourite logic called the *sapta-bhaṅgí-naya*,[94] or the system of the seven paralogisms, "may be, it is," "may be, it is not," "may be, it is and it is not," "may be, it is not predicable," "may be, it is, and yet not predicable," "may be, it is not, and not predicable," "may be, it is and it is not, and not predicable." All this Anantavírya has thus laid down:—

> 1. "When you wish to establish a thing, the proper course is to say 'may be, it is;' when you wish to deny it, 'may be, it is not.'
>
> 2. "When you desire to establish each in turn, let your procedure likewise embrace both; when you wish to establish both at once, let it be declared 'indescribable' from the impossibility to describe it.
>
> 3. "The fifth process is enjoined when you wish to establish the first as well as its indescribableness; when the second as well as its indescribableness, the occasion for the sixth process arises.
>
> 4. "The seventh is required when all three characters are to be employed simultaneously."

Syát, "may be," is here an indeclinable particle in the form of a part of a verb, used to convey the idea of indeterminateness; as it has been said—

> "This particle *syát* is in the form of a verb, but, from its being connected with the sense, it denotes indeterminateness in sentences, and has a qualifying effect on the implied meaning."

If, again, the word *syát* denoted determinateness, then it would be needless in the phrase, "may be, it is;" but since it really denotes indeterminateness, "may be, it is," means "it is somehow;" *syát*, "may be," conveys the meaning of "somehow," *kathaṃchit*; and so it is not really useless. As one has said—

"The doctrine of the *syád-váda* arises from our everywhere rejecting the idea of the absolute;[95] it depends on the *sapta-bhaṅgí-naya*, and it lays down the distinction between what is to be avoided and to be accepted."

If a thing absolutely exists, it exists altogether, always, everywhere, and with everybody, and no one at any time or place would ever make an effort to obtain or avoid it, as it would be absurd to treat what is already present as an object to be obtained or avoided. But if it be relative (or indefinite), the wise will concede that at certain times and in certain places any one may seek or avoid it. Moreover, suppose that the question to be asked is this: "Is *being*or *non-being* the real nature of the thing?" The real nature of the thing cannot be *being*, for then you could not properly use the phrase, "It is a pot" (*ghaṭósti*), as the two words "is" and "pot" would be tautological; nor ought you to say, "It is not a pot," as the words thus used would imply a direct contradiction; and the same argument is to be used in other questions.[96] As it has been declared—

> "It must not be said 'It is a pot,' since the word 'pot' implies 'is;'
> "Nor may you say 'it is not a pot,' for existence and non-existence are mutually exclusive," &c.

The whole is thus to be summed up. Four classes of our opponents severally hold the doctrine of existence, non-existence, existence and non-existence successively, and the doctrine that everything is inexplicable (*anirvachaníyatá*);[97] three other classes hold one or other of the three first theories combined with the fourth.[98] Now, when they meet us with the scornful questions, "Does the thing exist?" & c., we have an answer always possible, "It exists in a certain way," & c., and our opponents are all abashed to silence, and victory accrues to the holder of the *Syád-váda*, which ascertains the entire meaning of all things. Thus said the teacher in the *Syádváda-mañjarí*—

"A thing of an entirely indeterminate nature is the object only of the omniscient; a thing partly determined is held to be the true object of scientific investigation.[99] When our reasonings based on one point proceed in the revealed way, it is called the revealed *Syád-váda*, which ascertains the entire meaning of all things."

"All other systems are full of jealousy from their mutual propositions and counter-propositions; it is only the doctrine of the Arhat which with no partiality equally favours all sects."

The Jaina doctrine has thus been summed up by Jinadatta-súri—

"The hindrances belonging to vigour, enjoyment, sensual pleasure, giving and receiving,—sleep, fear, ignorance, aversion, laughter, liking, disliking, love, hatred, want of indifference, desire, sorrow, deceit, these are the eighteen 'faults' (*dosha*) according to our system.[100] The divine Jina is our Guru, who declares the true knowledge of the *tattwas*. The path[101] of emancipation consists of knowledge, intuition, and conduct. There are two means of proof (*pramáṇa*) in the *Syád-váda* doctrine,—sense-perception and inference. All consists of the eternal and the non-eternal; there are nine or seven *tattwas*. The *jíva*, the *ajíva*, merit and demerit,*ásrava*, *saṃvara*, *bandha*, *nirjará*, *mukti*,—we will now explain each. *Jíva* is defined as intelligence; *ajíva* is all other than it; merit means bodies which arise from good actions, demerit the opposite; *ásrava* is the bondage of actions,[102] *nirjará* is the unloosing thereof; *moksha* arises from the destruction of the eight forms of *karman* or "action". But by some teachers "merit" is included in *saṃvara*,[103] and "demerit" in *ásrava*.

"Of the soul which has attained the four infinite things[104] and is hidden from the world, and whose eight actions are abolished, absolute liberation is declared by Jina. The Śwetámbaras are the destroyers of all defilement, they live by alms,[105] they pluck out their hair, they practise patience, they avoid all association, and are called the Jaina *Sádhus*. The Digambaras pluck out their hair, they carry peacocks' tails in their hands, they drink from their hands, and they eat upright in the giver's house,—these are the second class of the Jaina Ṛishis.

"A woman attains not the highest knowledge, she enters not Mukti,—so say the Digambaras; but there is a great division on this point between them and the Śwetámbaras."[106]

CHAPTER IV.

THE RÁMÁNUJA SYSTEM.

This doctrine of the Árhatas deserves a rational condemnation, for whereas there is only one thing really existent, the simultaneous co-existence of existence, non-existence and other modes in a plurality of really existing things is an impossibility. Nor should any one say: Granting the impossibility of the co-existence of existence and non-existence, which are reciprocally contradictory, why should there not be an alternation between existence and non-existence? there being the rule that it is action, not *Ens*, that alternates. Nor let it be supposed that the whole universe is multiform, in reliance upon the examples of the elephant-headed Gaṇeśa and of the incarnation of Vishṇu as half man, half lion; for the elephantine and the leonine nature existing in one part, and the human in another, and consequently there being no contradiction, those parts being different, these examples are inapplicable to the maintenance of a nature multiform as both existent and non-existent in one and the same part (or place). Again, if any one urge: Let there be existence in one form, and non-existence in another, and thus both will be compatible; we rejoin: Not so, for if you had said that at different times existence and non-existence may be the nature of anything, then indeed there would have been no vice in your procedure. Nor is it to be contended: Let the multiformity of the universe be like the length and shortness which pertain to the same thing (in different relations); for in these (in this length and shortness) there is no contrariety, inasmuch as they are contrasted with different objects. Therefore, for want of evidence, existence and non-existence as reciprocally contradictory cannot reside at the same time in the same thing. In a like manner may be understood the refutation of the other *bhaṅgas* (Árhata tenets).

Again, we ask, is this doctrine of the seven *bhaṅgas*, which lies at the base of all this, itself uniform (as excluding one contradictory), or multiform (as conciliating contradictories). If it is uniform, there will emerge a contradiction to your thesis that all things are multiform; if it is multiform, you have not proved what you wished to prove, a multiform statement (as both existent and non-existent) proving nothing.[107] In either case, there is rope for a noose for the neck of the Syád-Vádin.

An admirable author of institutes has the founder of the Árhata system, dear to the gods (uninquiring pietist), proved himself to be, when he has not ascertained whether his result is the settling of nine or of seven principles, nor the investigator who settles them, nor his organon, the modes of evidence, nor the matter to be evidenced, whether it be ninefold or not!

In like manner if it be admitted that the soul has (as the Árhatas say), an extension equal to that of the body, it will follow that in the case of the souls of ascetics, who by the efficacy of asceticism assume a plurality of bodies, there is a differentiation of the soul for each of those bodies. A soul of the size of a human body would not (in the course of its transmigrations) be able to occupy the whole body of an elephant; and again, when it laid aside its elephantine body to enter into that of an ant, it would lose its capacity of filling its former frame. And it cannot be supposed that the soul resides successively in the human, elephantine, and other bodies, like the light of a lamp which is capable of contraction and expansion, according as it occupies the interior of a little station on the road-side in which travellers are supplied with water, or the interior of a stately mansion; for it would follow (from such a supposition) that the soul being susceptible of modifications and consequently non-eternal, there would be a loss of merits and a fruition of good and evil unmerited.

As if then we had thrown their best wrestler, the redargution of the rest of their categories may be anticipated from this exposition of the manner in which their treatment of the soul has been vitiated.

Their doctrine, therefore, as repugnant to the eternal, infallible revelation, cannot be adopted. The venerated Vyása accordingly propounded the aphorism (ii. 2, 33), "Nay, because it is impossible in one;" and this same aphorism has been analysed by Rámánuja with the express purpose of shutting out the doctrine of the Jainas. The tenets of Rámánuja are as follows:—Three categories are established, as soul, not-soul, and Lord; or as subject, object, and supreme disposer. Thus it has been said—

> "Lord, soul, and not-soul are the triad of principles: Hari (Vishṇu)
> "Is Lord; individual spirits are souls; and the visible world is not-soul."

Others, again (the followers of Śaṅkaráchárya), maintain that pure intelligence, exempt from all differences, the absolute, alone is really existent; and that this absolute whose essence is eternal, pure, intelligent, and free, the identity of which with the individuated spirit is learnt from the "reference to the same object" (predication), "That art thou," undergoes bondage and emancipation. The universe of differences (or conditions) such as that of subject and object, is all illusorily imagined by illusion as in that (one reality), as is attested by a number of texts: Existent only, fair sir, was this in the beginning, One only without a second, and so forth. Maintaining this, and acknowledging a suppression of this beginningless illusion by knowledge of the unity (and identity) of individuated spirits and the undifferenced absolute, in conformity with hundreds of texts from the Upanishads, such as He that knows spirit passes beyond sorrow; rejecting also any real plurality of things, in conformity with the text condemnatory of duality, viz., Death after death he undergoes who looks upon this as manifold; and thinking themselves very wise, the Śáṅkaras will not tolerate this division (viz., the distribution of things into soul, not-soul, and Lord). To all this the following counterposition is laid down:—This might be all well enough if there were any proof of such illusion. But there is no such ignorance (or illusion), an unbeginning entity, suppressible by knowledge, testified in the perceptions, I am ignorant, I know not myself and other things. Thus it has been said (to explain the views of the Śáṅkara)—

> "Entitative from everlasting, which is dissolved by knowledge,
> "Such is illusion. This definition the wise enunciate."

This perception (they would further contend) is not conversant about the absence of knowledge. For who can maintain this, and to whom? One who leans on the arm of Prabhákara, or one to whom Kumárila-bhaṭṭa gives his hand? Not the former, for in the words—

> "By means of its own and of another's form, eternal in the existent and non-existent,
> "Thing is recognised something by some at certain times.
> "Non-entity is but another entity by some kind of relation. Non-entity is but another entity, naught else, for naught else is observed."

They deny any non-entity ulterior to entity. Non-entity being cognisable by the sixth instrument of knowledge (*anupalabdhi*), and knowledge being always an object of inference, the absence of knowledge cannot be an object of perception. If, again, any one who maintains non-entity to be perceptible should employ the above argument (from the perceptions, I am ignorant, I know not myself, and other things); it may be replied: "Is there, or is there not, in the consciousness, I am ignorant, an apprehension of self as characterised by an absence, and of knowledge as the thing absent or non-existent? If there is such apprehension, consciousness of the absence of knowledge will be impossible, as involving a contradiction. If there is not, consciousness of the absence of knowledge, which consciousness presupposes a knowledge of the subject and of the thing absent, will not readily become possible." Inasmuch (the Śáṅkaras continue) as the foregoing difficulties do not occur if ignorance (or illusion) be entitative, this consciousness (I am ignorant, I know not myself, and other things) must be admitted to be conversant about an entitative ignorance.

All this (the Rámánuja replies) is about as profitable as it would be for a ruminant animal to ruminate upon ether; for an entitative ignorance is not more supposable than an absence of knowledge. For (we would ask), is any self-conscious principle presented as an object and as a subject (of ignorance) as distinct from cognition? If it is presented, how, since ignorance of a thing is terminable by knowledge of its essence, can the ignorance continue? If none such is presented, how can we be conscious of an ignorance which has no subject and no object? If you say: A pure manifestation of the spiritual essence is revealed only by the cognition opposed to ignorance (or illusion), and thus there is no absurdity in the consciousness of ignorance accompanied with a consciousness of its subject and object; then we rejoin:—Unfortunately for you, this (consciousness of subject) must arise equally in the absence of knowledge (for such we define illusion to be), notwithstanding your assertion to the contrary. It must, therefore, be acknowledged that the cognition, I am ignorant, I know not myself and other things, is conversant about an absence of cognition allowed by us both.

Well, then (the Śáṅkaras may contend), let the form of cognition evidentiary of illusion, which is under disputation, be inference, as follows:—Right knowledge must have had for its antecedent another entity (*sc.* illusion), an entity different from mere prior non-existence of knowledge, which envelops the objects of knowledge, which is terminable by knowledge, which occupies the place of knowledge, inasmuch as it (the right knowledge) illuminates an object not before illuminated, like the light of a lamp springing up for the first time in the darkness. This argument (we reply) will not stand grinding (in the dialectic mill); for to prove the (antecedent) illusion, you will require an ulterior illusion which you do not admit, and a violation of your own tenets will ensue, while if you do not so prove it, it may or may not exist; and, moreover, the example is incompatible with the argument, for it cannot be the lamp that illumines the hitherto unillumined object, since it is knowledge only that illumines; and an illumination of objects may be effected by knowledge even without the lamp, while the light of the lamp is only ancillary to the visual organ which effectuates the cognition, ancillary mediately through the dispulsion of the obstruent darkness. We dismiss further prolixity.

The counterposition (of the Rámánujas) is as follows:—The illusion under dispute does not reside in Brahman, who is pure knowledge, because it is an illusion, like the illusion about nacre, &c. If any one ask: Has not the self-conscious entity that underlies the illusion about nacre, &c., knowledge only for its nature? they reply: Do not start such difficulties; for we suppose that consciousness by its bare existence has the nature of creating conformity to the usage about (*i.e.*, the name and notion of) some object; and such consciousness, also called knowledge, apprehension, comprehension, intelligence, &c., constitutes the soul, or knowledge, of that which acts and knows. If any one ask: How can the soul, if it consists of cognition, have cognition as a quality? they reply: This question is futile; for as a gem, the sun, and other luminous things, existing in the form of light, are substances in which light as a quality inheres—for light, as existing elsewhere than in its usual receptacle, and as being a mode of things though a substance, is still styled and accounted a quality derived from determination by that substance,—so this soul, while it exists as a self-luminous intelligence, has also intelligence as its quality. Accordingly the Vedic texts: A lump of salt is always within and without one entire mass of taste, so also this soul is within and without an entire mass of knowledge; Herein this person is itself a light; Of the knowledge of that which knows there is no suspension; He who knows, smells this; and so also, This is the soul which, consisting of knowledge, is the light within the heart; For this person is the seer, the hearer, the taster, the smeller, the thinker, the understander, the doer; The person is knowledge, and the like texts.

It is not to be supposed that the Veda also affords evidence of the existence of the cosmical illusion, in the text, Enveloped in untruth (*anṛita*); for the word untruth (*anṛita*) denotes that which is other than truth (*ṛita*). The word *ṛita* has a passive sense, as appears from the words, Drinking *ṛita*. *Ṛita* means works done without desire of fruit; having as its reward the attainment of the bliss of the Supreme Spirit through his propitiation. In the text in question, untruth (*anṛita*) designates the scanty fruit enjoyed during transmigratory existence as opposed to that (which results from propitiation of the Supreme Spirit), which temporal fruit is obstructive to the attainment of supreme existence (*brahman*); the entire text (when the context is supplied) being: They who find not this supreme sphere (*brahma-loka*) are enveloped in untruth. In such texts, again, as Let him know illusion (*máyá*) to be the primary emanative cause (*prakṛiti*), the term (*máyá*) designates the emanative cause, consisting of the three "cords" (*guṇa*), and creative of the diversified universe. It does not designate the inexplicable illusion (for which the Śáṅkaras contend).

In such passages as, By him the defender of the body of the child, moving rapidly, the thousand illusions (*máyá*) of the barbarian were swooped upon as by a hawk, we observe that the word "illusion" (*máyá*) designates the really existent weapon of a Titan, capable of projective diversified creation. The Veda, then, never sets out an inexplicable illusion. Nor (is the cosmical illusion to be inferred from the "grand text," That art thou), inasmuch as the words, That art thou, being incompetent to teach unity, and indicating a conditionate Supreme Spirit, we cannot understand by them the essential unity of the mutually exclusive supreme and individual spirits; for such a supposition (as that they are identical) would violate the law of excluded middle. To explain this. The term That denotes the Supreme Spirit exempt from all imperfections, of illimitable excellence, a repository of innumerable auspicious attributes, to whom the emanation, sustentation, retractation of the universe is a pastime;[108] such being the Supreme Spirit, spoken of in such texts as, That desired, let me be many, let me bring forth. Perhaps the word Thou, referring to the same object (as the word That), denotes the Supreme Spirit characterised by consciousness, having all individual spirits as his body; for a "reference to the same object" designates one thing determined by two modes. Here, perhaps, an Advaita-vádin may reply: Why may not the purport of the reference to the same object in the words, That art thou, be undifferenced essence, the unity of souls, these words (That and thou) having a (reciprocally) implicate power by abandonment of opposite portions of their meaning; as is the case in the phrase, This is that Devadatta. In the words, This is that Devadatta, we understand by the word That, a person in relation to a different time and place, and by the word This, a person in relation to the present time and place. That both are one and the same is understood by the form of predication ("reference to the same object"). Now as one and the same thing cannot at the same time be known as in different times and places, the two words (This and That) must refer to the essence (and not to the accidents of time and place), and unity of essence can be understood. Similarly in the text, That art thou, there is implicated an indivisible essence by abandonment of the contradictory portions (of the denotation), viz., finite cognition (which belongs to the individual soul or Thou), and infinite cognition (which belongs to the real or unindividual soul). This suggestion (the Rámánujas reply) is unsatisfactory, for there is no opposition (between This and That) in the example (This is that Devadatta), and consequently not the smallest particle of "implication" (*lakshaṇá*, both This and That being used in their denotative capacity). The connection of one object with two times past and present involves no contradiction. And any contradiction supposed to arise from relation to different places may be avoided by a supposed difference of time, the existence in the distant place being past, and the existence in the near being present. Even if we concede to you the "implication," the (supposed) contradiction being avoidable by supposing one term (either That or Thou) to be implicative, it is unnecessary to admit that both words are implicative. Otherwise (if we admit that both words are implicative), if it be granted that the one thing may be recognised, with the concomitant assurance that it differs as this and as that, permanence in things will be inadmissible, and the Buddhist assertor of a momentary flux of things will be triumphant.

We have, therefore (the Rámánujas continue), laid it down in this question that there is no contradiction in the identity of the individual and the Supreme Spirit, the individual spirits being the body and the Supreme Spirit the soul. For the individual spirit as the body, and therefore a form, of the Supreme Spirit, is identical with the Supreme Spirit, according to another text, Who abiding in the soul, is the controller of the soul, who knows the soul, of whom soul is the body.

Your statement of the matter, therefore, is too narrow. All words are designatory of the Supreme Spirit. They are not all synonymous, a variety of media being possible; thus as all organised bodies, divine, human, &c., are forms of individual spirits, so all things (are the body of Supreme Spirit), all things are identical with Supreme Spirit. Hence—

God, Man, Yaksha, Piśácha, serpent, Rákshasa, bird, tree, creeper, wood, stone, grass, jar, cloth,—these and all other words, be they what they may, which are current among mankind as denotative by means of their base and its suffixes, as denoting those things, in denoting things of this or that apparent constitution, really denote the individual souls which assumed to them such body, and the whole complexus of things terminating in the Supreme Spirit ruling within. That God and all other words whatsoever ultimately denote the Supreme Spirit is stated in the Tattva-muktávalí and in the Chaturantara—

> "God, and all other words, designate the soul, none else than That, called the established entity,
>
> "Of this there is much significant and undoubted exemplification in common speech and in the Veda;
>
> "Existence when dissociated from spirit is unknown; in the form of gods, mortals, and the rest
>
> "When pervading the individual spirit, the infinite has made a diversity of names and forms in the world."

In these words the author, setting forth that all words, God, and the rest, designate the body, and showing in the words, "No unity in systems," &c., the characteristic of body, and showing in the words, "By words which are substitutes for the essence of things," &c., that it is established that nothing is different from the universal Lord, lays down in the verses, Significant of the essence, &c., that all words ultimately designate the Supreme Spirit. All this may be ascertained from that work. The same matter has been enforced by Rámánuja in the Vedártha-saṅgraha, when analysing the Vedic text about names and forms.

Moreover, every form of evidence having some determinate object, there can be no evidence of an undetermined (unconditionate) reality.

Even in non-discriminative perception it is a determinate (or conditioned) thing that is cognised. Else in discriminative perception there could not be shown to be a cognition characterised by an already presented form. Again, that text, That art thou, is not sublative of the universe as rooted in illusion, like a sentence declaratory that what was illusorily presented, as a snake is a piece of rope; nor does knowledge of the unity of the absolute and the soul bring (this illusory universe) to an end; for we have already demonstrated that there is no proof of these positions.

Nor is there an absurdity (as the Śáṅkaras would say), on the hypothesis enunciatory of the reality of the universe, in affirming that by a cognition of one there is a cognition of all things: for it is easily evinced that the mundane egg, consisting of the primary cause (*prakṛiti*), intellect, self-position, the rudimentary elements, the gross elements, the organs (of sense and of action), and the fourteen worlds, and the gods, animals, men, immovable things, and so forth, that exist within it, constituting a complex of all forms, is all an effect, and that from the single cognition of absolute spirit as its (emanative) cause, when we recognise that all this is absolute spirit (there being a tautology between cause and effect), there arises cognition of all things, and thus by cognition of one cognition of all. Besides, if all else than absolute spirit were unreal, then all being non-existent, it would follow that by one cognition all cognition would be sublated.

It is laid down (by the Rámánujas) that retractation into the universe (*pralaya*) is when the universe, the body whereof consists of souls and the originant (*prakṛiti*), returns to its imperceptible state, unsusceptible of division by names and forms, existing as absolute spirit the emanative cause; and that creation (or emanation) is the gross or perceptible condition of absolute spirit, the body whereof is soul and not soul divided by diversity of names and forms, in the condition of the (emanative) effect of absolute spirit. In this way the identity of cause and effect laid down in the aphorism (of Vyása) treating of origination, is easily explicable. The statements that the Supreme Spirit is void of attributes, are intended (it is shown) to deny thereof phenomenal qualities which are to be escaped from by those that desire emancipation. The texts which deny plurality are explained as allowed to be employed for the denial of the real existence of things apart from the Supreme Spirit, which is identical with all things, it being Supreme Spirit which subsists under all forms as the soul of all, all things sentient and unsentient being forms as being the body of absolute Spirit.[109]

What is the principle here involved, pluralism or monism, or a universe both one and more than one? Of these alternatives monism is admitted in saying that Supreme Spirit alone subsists in all forms as all is its body; both unity and plurality are admitted in saying that one only Supreme Spirit subsists under a plurality of forms diverse as soul and not-soul; and plurality is admitted in saying that the essential natures of soul, not-soul, and the Lord, are different, and not to be confounded.

Of these (soul, not-soul, and the Lord), individual spirits, or souls, consisting of uncontracted and unlimited pure knowledge, but enveloped in illusion, that is, in works from all eternity, undergo contraction and expansion of knowledge according to the degrees of their merits. Soul experiences fruition, and after reaping pleasures and pains proportionate to merits and demerits, there ensues knowledge of the Lord, or attainment of the sphere of the Lord. Of things which are not-soul, and which are objects of fruition (or experience of pleasure and pain), unconsciousness, unconduciveness to the end of man, susceptibility of modification, and the like, are the properties. Of the Supreme Lord the attributes are subsistence, as the internal controller (or animator) of both the subjects and the objects of fruition; the boundless glory of illimitable knowledge, dominion, majesty, power, brightness, and the like, the countless multitude of auspicious qualities; the generation at will of all things other than himself, whether spiritual or non-spiritual; various and infinite adornment with unsurpassable excellence, singular, uniform, and divine.

Veṅkaṭa-nátha has given the following distribution of things:—

> "Those who know it have declared the principle to be twofold, substance and non-substance;
>
> "Substance is dichotomised as unsentient and sentient; the former being the unevolved (*avyakta*), and time.
>
> "The latter is the 'near' (*pratyak*) and the 'distant' (*parák*); the 'near' being twofold, as either soul or the Lord;
>
> "The 'distant' is eternal glory and intelligence; the other principle some have called the unsentient primary."

Of these—

> "Substance undergoes a plurality of conditions; the originant is possessed of goodness and the other cords;
>
> "Time has the form of years, &c.; soul is atomic and cognisant; the other spirit is the Lord;
>
> "Eternal bliss has been declared as transcending the three cords (or modes of phenomenal existence), and also as characterised by goodness;
>
> "The cognisable manifestation of the cognisant is intelligence; thus are the characteristics of substance summarily recounted."

Of these (soul, not-soul, and the Lord), individual spirits, called souls, are different from the Supreme Spirit and eternal. Thus the text: Two birds, companions, friends, &c. (Rig-Veda, i. 164, 20). Accordingly it is stated (in the aphorisms of Kaṇáda, iii. 2, 20), Souls are diverse by reason of diversity of conditions. The eternity of souls is often spoken of in revelation—

> "The soul is neither born, nor dies, nor having been shall it again cease to be;
> "Unborn, unchanging, eternal, this ancient of days is not killed when the body is killed" (Bhagavad-gítá, ii. 20).

Otherwise (were the soul not eternal) there would follow a failure of requital and a fruition (of pleasures and pains) unmerited. It has accordingly been said (in the aphorisms of Gautaṃa, iii. 25): Because no birth is seen of one who is devoid of desire. That the soul is atomic is well known from revelation—

> "If the hundredth part of a hair be imagined to be divided a hundred times,
> "The soul may be supposed a part of that, and yet it is capable of infinity."

And again—

> "Soul is of the size of the extremity of the spoke of a wheel. Spirit is to be recognised by the intelligence as atomic."

The visible, unsentient world, designated by the term not-soul, is divided into three, as the object, the instrument, or the site of fruition. Of this world the efficient and substantial cause is the Deity, known under the names Purushottama (best of spirits), Vásudeva (a patronymic of Kṛishṇa), and the like.

> "Vásudeva is the supreme absolute spirit, endowed with auspicious attributes,
> "The substantial cause, the efficient of the worlds, the animator of spirits."

This same Vásudeva, infinitely compassionate, tender to those devoted to him, the Supreme Spirit, with the purpose of bestowing various rewards apportioned to the deserts of his votaries in consequence of pastime, exists under five modes, distinguished as "adoration" (*archá*), "emanation" (*vibhava*), "manifestation" (*vyúha*), "the subtile" (*súkshma*), and the "internal controller." (1.) "Adoration" is images, and so forth. (2.) "Emanation" is his incarnation, as Ráma, and so forth. (3.) His "manifestation" is fourfold, as Vásudeva, Saṅkarshaṇa, Pradyumna, and Aniruddha. (4.) "The subtile" is the entire Supreme Spirit, with six attributes, called Vásudeva. His attributes are exemption from sin, and the rest. That he is exempt from sin is attested in the Vedic text: Passionless, deathless, without sorrow, without hunger, desiring truth, true in purpose. (5.) The "internal controller," the actuator of all spirits, according to the text: Who abiding in the soul, rules the soul within. When by worshipping each former embodiment a mass of sins inimical to the end of the soul (*i.e.*, emancipation) have been destroyed, the votary becomes entitled to practise the worship of each latter embodiment. It has, therefore, been said—

> "Vásudeva, in his tenderness to his votaries, gives, as desired by each,
> "According to the merits of his qualified worshippers, large recompense.
> "For that end, in pastime he makes to himself his five embodiments;
> "Images and the like are 'adoration;' his incarnations are 'emanations;'
> "As Saṅkarshaṅa, Vásudeva, Pradyumna, Aniruddha, his manifestation is to be known to be fourfold; 'the subtile' is the entire six attributes;
> "That self-same called Vásudeva is styled the Supreme Spirit;
> "The internal controller is declared as residing in the soul, the actuator of the soul,
> "Described in a multitude of texts of the Upanishads, such as 'Who abiding in the soul.'
> "By the worship of 'adoration,' a man casting off his defilement becomes a qualified votary;
> "By the subsequent worship of 'emanation,' he becomes qualified for the worship of 'manifestation;' next,
> "By the worship thereafter of 'the subtile,' he becomes able to behold the 'internal controller.'"

The worship of the Deity is described in the Pañcha-rátra as consisting of five elements, viz., (1.) the access, (2.) the preparation, (3.) oblation, (4.) recitation, (5.) devotion. Of these, access is the sweeping, smearing, and so forth, of the way to the temple. The preparation is the provision of perfumes, flowers, and the like appliances of worship. Oblation is worship of the deities. Recitation is the muttered ejaculation of sacred texts, with attention to what they mean, the rehearsal of hymns and lauds of Vishṇu, the commemoration of his names, and study of institutes which set forth the truth. Devotion is meditation on the Deity. When the vision of the visible world has been brought to a close by knowledge accumulated by the merit of such worship, the infinitely compassionate Supreme Spirit, tender to his votaries, bestows upon the votary devoted to his lord and absorbed in his lord, his own sphere infinite and endless, marked by consciousness of being like him, from which there is no future return (to the sorrows of transmigratory existence). So the traditionary text—

"When they have come to me, the high-souled no longer undergo future birth, a receptacle of pain, transitory, having attained to the supreme consummation.

"Vásudeva, having found his votary, bestows upon him his own mansion, blissful, undecaying, from whence there is no more return."

After laying up all this in his heart, leaning upon the teaching of the great Upanishad, and finding the gloss on the Vedánta aphorisms by the venerated Bodháyanachárya too prolix, Rámánuja composed a commentary on the Śárírakamímánsá (or Vedánta theosophy). In this the sense of the first aphorism, "Then hence the absolute must be desired to be known," is given as follows:—The word *then* in this aphorism means, after understanding the hitherto-current sacred rites. Thus the glossator writes: "After learning the sacred rites," he desires to know the absolute. The word *hence* states the reason, viz., because one who has read the Veda and its appendages and understands its meaning is averse from sacred rites, their recompense being perishable. The wish to know the absolute springs up in one who longs for permanent liberation, as being the means of such liberation. By the word *absolute* is designated the Supreme Spirit, from whom are essentially excluded all imperfections, who is of illimitable excellence, and of innumerable auspicious attributes. Since then the knowledge of sacred rites and the performance of those rites is mediately through engendering dispassionateness, and through putting away the defilement of the understanding, an instrument of the knowledge of the absolute; and knowledge of sacred rites and knowledge of the absolute being consequently cause and effect, the former and the latter Mímánsá constitute one system of institutes. On this account the glossator has described this system as one with the sixteenfold system of Jaimini. That the fruit of sacred rites is perishable, and that of the knowledge of the absolute imperishable, has been laid down in virtue of Vedic texts, such as: Scanning the spheres gained by rites, let him become passionless; Not wrought by the rite performed, accompanied with inference and disjunctive reasoning. Revelation, by censuring each when unaccompanied by the other, shows that it is knowledge together with works that is efficacious of emancipation, in the words: Blind darkness they enter who prefer illusion, and a greater darkness still do they enter who delight in knowledge only; knowledge and illusion, he who knows these both, he passing beyond death together with illusion, tastes immortality by knowledge. Conformably it is said in the Pañcharátra-rahasya—

"That ocean of compassion, the Lord, tender to his votaries,
"For his worshipper's sake takes five embodiments upon him.
"These are styled Adoration, Emanation, Manifestation, the Subtile, the Internal Controller,

"Resorting whereto souls attain to successive stages of knowledge.
"As a man's sins are worn away by each successive worship,
"He becomes qualified for the worship of each next embodiment.
"Thus day by day, according to religion, revealed and traditional,
"By the aforesaid worship Vásudeva becomes propitious to mankind.
"Hari, when propitiated by devotion in the form of meditation,
"At once brings to a close that illusion which is the aggregate of works.
"Then in souls the essential attributes, from which transmigration has vanished,
"Are manifested, auspicious, omniscience, and the rest.
"These qualities are common to the emancipated spirits and the Lord,
"Universal efficiency alone among them is peculiar to the Deity.
"Emancipated spirits are ulterior to the infinite absolute, which is unsusceptible of aught ulterior;
"They enjoy all beatitudes together with that Spirit."

It is therefore stated that those who suffer the three kinds of pain must, for the attainment of immortality, investigate the absolute spirit known under such appellations as the Highest Being. According to the maxim: The base and the suffix convey the meaning conjointly, and of these the meaning of the suffix takes the lead, the notion of desire is predominant (in the word *jijñásitavya*), and desired knowledge is the predicate (in the aphorism, Then hence the absolute must be desired to be known). Knowledge is cognition designated by such terms as meditation, devotion; not the merely superficial knowledge derived from verbal communication, such being competent to any one who hears a number of words and understands the force of each, even without any predication; in conformity with such Vedic texts as: Self indeed it is that is to be seen, to be heard, to be thought, to be pondered; He should meditate that it is self alone; Having known, let him acquire excellent wisdom; He should know that which is beyond knowledge. In these texts "to be heard" is explanatory, hearing being understood (but not enounced) in the text about sacred study (viz.,*shaḍaṅgena vedo 'dhyeyo jñeyaścha*, the Veda, with its six appendages, is to be studied and known); so that a man who has studied the Veda must of his own accord, in acquiring the Veda and its appendages, engage in "hearing," in order to ascertain the sense by examining it and the occasion of its enouncement. The term "to be thought" (or "to be inferred") is also explanatory, cogitation (or inference) being understood as the complementary meaning of hearing, according to the aphorism: Before its signification is attained the system is significant. Meditation is a reminiscence consisting of an unbroken succession of reminiscences like a stream of oil, it being revealed in the text, in continuity of reminiscence there is a solution of all knots,—that it is unintermittent reminiscence that is the means of emancipation. And this reminiscence is tantamount to intuition.

"Cut is his heart's knot, solved are all his doubts,

"And exhausted are all his works, when he has seen the Highest and Lowest,"

because he becomes one with that Supreme. So also in the words, Self indeed is to be seen, it is predicated of this reminiscence that it is an intuition. Reminiscence becomes intuitional through the vivacity of the representations. The author of the Vákya has treated of all this in detail in the passage beginning Cognition is meditation. The characters of this meditation are laid out in the text: This soul is not attainable by exposition, nor by wisdom, nor by much learning; Whom God chooses by him God may be attained. To him this self unfolds its own nature. For it is that which is dearest which is choice-worthy, and as the soul finds itself most dear, so the Lord is of Himself most dear, as was declared by the Lord Himself—

"To them always devoted, who worship me with love,
"I give the devotion of understanding whereby they come to me."
And again—
"That Supreme Spirit, Arjuna, is attainable by faith unwavering."

But devotion (or faith) is a kind of cognition which admits no other motive than the illimitable beatitude, and is free from all other desires; and the attainment of this devotion is by discrimination and other means. As is said by the author of the Vákya: Attainment thereof results from discrimination (*viveka*), exemption (*vimoka*), practice (*abhyása*), observance (*kriyá*), excellence (*kalyáṇa*), freedom from despondency (*anavasáda*), satisfaction (*anuddharsha*), according to the equivalence (of the definition), and the explication (of these terms). Of these means, discrimination is purity of nature, resultant from eating undefiled food, and the explication (of discrimination) is From purity of diet, purity of understanding, and by purity of understanding the unintermittent reminiscence. Exemption is non-attachment to sensuous desires; the explication being, Let the quietist meditate. Practice is reiteration; and of this a traditionary explication is quoted (from the Bhagavad-gítá) by (Rámánuja) the author of the commentary: For ever modified by the modes thereof. Observance is the performance of rites enjoined in revelation and tradition according to one's ability; the explication being (the Vedic text), He who has performed rites is the best of those that know the supreme. The excellences are veracity, integrity, clemency, charity (alms-giving), and the like; the explication being, It is attained by veracity. Freedom from despondency is the contrary of dejection; the explication being, This soul is not attained by the faint-hearted. Satisfaction is the contentment which arises from the contrary of dejection; the explication being, Quiescent, self-subdued. It has thus been shown that by the devotion of one in whom the darkness has been dispelled by the grace of the Supreme Spirit, propitiated by certain rites and observances, which devotion is meditation transformed into a presentative manifestation of soul, without ulterior motive, as incessantly and illimitably desired, the sphere of the Supreme Spirit (Vaikuṇṭha) is attained. Thus Yámuna says: Attainable by the final and absolute devotion of faith in one internally purified by both (works and knowledge); that is, in one whose internal organ is rectified by the devotion of works and knowledge.

In anticipation of the inquiry, But what absolute is to be desired to be known? the definition is given (in the second aphorism). From which the genesis, and so forth, of this. The genesis, and so forth, the creation (emanation), sustentation, and retractation (of the universe). The purport of the aphorism is that the emanation, sustentation, and retractation of this universe, inconceivably multiform in its structure, and interspersed with souls, from Brahmá to a tuft of grass, of determinate place, time, and fruition, is from this same universal Lord, whose essence is contrary to all qualities which should be escaped from, of illimitable excellences, such as indefeasible volition, and of innumerable auspicious attributes, omniscient, and omnipotent.

In anticipation of the further inquiry, What proof is there of an absolute of this nature? It is stated that the system of institutes itself is the evidence (in the third aphorism): Because it has its source from the system. To have its source from the system is to be that whereof the cause or evidence is the system. The system, then, is the source (or evidence) of the absolute, as being the cause of knowing the self, which is the cause of knowing the absolute. Nor is the suspicion possible that the absolute may be reached by some other form of evidence. For perception can have no conversancy about the absolute since it is supersensible. Nor can inference, for the illation, the ocean, and the rest, must have a maker, because it is an effect like a water-pot, is worth about as much as a rotten pumpkin. It is evinced that it is such texts as, Whence also these elements, that prove the existence of the absolute thus described.

Though the absolute (it may be objected) be unsusceptible of any other kind of proof, the system, did it not refer to activity and cessation of activity, could not posit the absolute aforesaid. To avoid by anticipation any queries on this point, it is stated (in the fourth aphorism): But that is from the construction. This is intended to exclude the doubt anticipated. The evidence, then, of the system is the only evidence that can be given of the absolute. Why? Because of the construction, that is because the absolute, that is, the highest end for man, is construed as the subject (of the first aphorism, viz., Then thence the absolute is to be desired to be known). Moreover, a sentence which has nothing to do either with activity or with cessation of activity is not therefore void of purpose, for we observe that sentences merely declaratory of the nature of things, such as, A son is born to you, This is not a snake, convey a purpose, viz., the cessation of joy or of fear. Thus there is nothing unaccounted for. We have here given only a general indication. The details may be learnt from the original (viz., Rámánuja's Bháshya on the Vedánta aphorisms); we therefore decline a further treatment, apprehensive of prolixity; and thus all is clear.[110]

CHAPTER V.

THE SYSTEM OF PURNA-PRAJNA.

Ánanda-tírtha (Púrṇa-prajña, or Madhva) rejected this same Rámánuja system, because, though like his own views, it teaches the atomic size of the soul, the servitude of the soul, the existence of the Veda without any personal author, the authenticity of the Veda, the self-evidence of the instruments of knowledge, the triad of evidences, dependency upon the Pañcha-rátra, the reality of plurality in the universe, and so forth,—yet, in accepting three hypotheses as to reciprocally contradictory divisions, &c., it coincides with the tenets of the Jainas. Showing that He is soul, That art thou, and a number of other texts of the Upanishads bear a different import under a different explanation, he set up a new system under the guise of a new explication of the Brahma-Mímáṇsá (or Vedánta).

For in his doctrine ultimate principles are dichotomised into independent and dependent; as it is stated in the Tattva-viveka:—

> "Independent and dependent, two principles are received;
>
> "The independent is Vishṇu the Lord, exempt from imperfections, and of inexhaustible excellences."

Here it will be urged (by the Advaita-vádins): Why predicate of the absolute these inexhaustible excellences in the teeth of the Upanishads, which lay down that the absolute principle is void of homogeneity and heterogeneity, and of all plurality in itself? To this be it replied: Not so, for these texts of the Upanishads, as contradictory of many proofs positive of duality, cannot afford proof of universal unity; perception, for example, in the consciousness, This is different from that, pronounces a difference between things, blue and yellow, and so forth. The opponent will rejoin: Do you hold that perception is cognisant of a perceptional difference, or of a difference constituted by the thing and its opposite? The former alternative will not hold: for without a cognition of the thing and its opposite, the recognition of the difference, which presupposes such a cognition, will be impossible. On the latter alternative it must be asked, Is the apprehension of the difference preceded by an apprehension of the thing and its contrary, or are all the three (the thing, its contrary, and the contrariety) simultaneously apprehended? It cannot be thus preceded, for the operation of the intellect is without delay (or without successive steps), and there would also result a logical seesaw (apprehension of the difference presupposing apprehension of the thing and its contrary, and apprehension of the thing and its contrary presupposing apprehension of the difference). Nor can there be a simultaneous apprehension (of the thing, its contrary, and the difference); for cognitions related as cause and effect cannot be simultaneous, and the cognition of the thing is the cause of the recognition of the difference; the causal relation between the two being recognised by a concomitance and non-concomitance (mutual exclusion), the difference not being cognised even when the thing is present, without a cognition of its absent contrary. The perception of difference, therefore (the opponent concludes), is not easily admissible. To this let the reply be as follows:—Are these objections proclaimed against one who maintains a difference identical with the things themselves, or against one who maintains a difference between things as the subjects of attributes? In the former case, you will be, as the saying runs, punishing a respectable Bráhman for the offence of a thief, the objections you adduce being irrelevant. If it be urged that if it is the essence of the thing that is the difference, then it will no longer require a contrary counterpart; but if difference presuppose a contrary counterpart, it will exist everywhere; this statement must be disallowed, for while the essence of a thing is first known as different from everything else, the determinate usage (name and notion) may be shown to depend upon a contrary counterpart; for example, the essence of a thing so far as constituted by its dimensions is first cognised, and afterwards it becomes the object of some determinate judgment, as long or short in relation to some particular counterpart (or contrasted object). Accordingly, it is said in the Vishṇu-tattva-nirṇaya: "Difference is not proved to exist by the relation of determinant and determinate; for this relation of determinant and determinate (or predicate and subject) presupposes difference; and if difference were proved to depend upon the thing and its counterpart, and the thing and its counterpart to presuppose difference, difference as involving a logical circle could not be accounted for; but difference is itself a real predicament (or ultimate entity). For this reason (viz., because difference is a *thing*) it is that men in quest of a cow do not act (as if they had found her) when they see a gayal, and do not recall the word *cow*. Nor let it be objected that (if difference be a real entity and as such perceived) on seeing a mixture of milk and water, there would be a presentation of difference; for the absence of any manifestation of, and judgment about, the difference, may be accounted for by the force of (the same) obstructives (as hinder the perception of other things), viz., aggregation of similars and the rest." Thus it has been said (in the Sáṅkhya-káriká, v. vii.)—

"From too great remoteness, from too great nearness, from defect in the organs, from instability of the common sensory,

"From subtilty, from interposition, from being overpowered, and from aggregation of similars."

There is no perception respectively of a tree and the like on the peak of a mountain, because of its too great remoteness; of collyrium applied to the eyes, and so forth, because of too great proximity; of lightning and the like, because of a defect in the organs; of a jar or the like in broad daylight, by one whose common sensory is bewildered by lust and other passions, because of instability of the common sensory; of an atom and the like, because of their subtility; of things behind a wall, and so forth, because of interposition; of the light of a lamp and the like, in the day-time, because of its being overpowered; of milk and water, because of the aggregation of similars.

Or let the hypothesis of difference in qualities be granted, and no harm is done; for given the apprehension of a subject of attributes and of its contrary, the presentation of difference in their modes is possible. Nor let it be supposed that on the hypothesis of difference in the modes of things, as each difference must be different from some ulterior difference, there will result an embarrassing progression to infinity, there being no occasion for the occurrence of the said ulterior difference, inasmuch as we do not observe that men think and say that two things are different as differenced from the different. Nor can an ulterior difference be inferred from the first difference, for there being no difference to serve as the example in such inference, there cannot but be a non-occurrence of inference. And thus it must be allowed that in raising the objection you have begged for a little oil-cake, and have had to give us gallons of oil. If there be no difference for the example the inference cannot emerge. The bride is not married for the destruction of the bridegroom. There being, then, no fundamental difficulty, this infinite progression presents no trouble.

Difference (duality) is also ascertained by inference. Thus the Supreme Lord differs from the individual soul as the object of its obedience; and he who is to be obeyed by any person differs from that person, a king, for instance, from his attendant. For men, desiring as they do the end of man, Let me have pleasure, let me not have the slightest pain, if they covet the position of their lord, do not become objects of his favour, nay, rather, they become recipients of all kinds of evil. He who asserts his own inferiority and the excellence of his superior, he it is who is to be commended; and the gratified superior grants his eulogist his desire. Therefore it has been said:—

> "Kings destroy those who assert themselves to be kings,
> "And grant to those who proclaim their kingly pre-eminence all that they desire."

Thus the statement of those (Advaita-vádins) in their thirst to be one with the Supreme Lord, that the supreme excellence of Vishṇu is like a mirage, is as if they were to cut off their tongues in trying to get a fine plantain, since it results that through offending this supreme Vishṇu they must enter into the hell of blind darkness (*andha-tamasa*). The same thing is laid down by Madhya-mandira in the Mahábhárata-tátparya-nirṇaya:—

"O Daityas, enemies of the eternal, Vishṇu's anger is waxed great;
"He hurls the Daityas into the blind darkness, because they decide blindly."

This service (or obedience of which we have spoken) is trichotomised into (1.) stigmatisation, (2.) imposition of names, (3.) worship.

Of these, (1.) stigmatisation is (the branding upon oneself) of the weapons of Náráyaṇa (or Vishṇu) as a memorial of him, and as a means of attaining the end which is needful (emancipation). Thus the sequel of the Sákalya-samhitá:—

"The man who bears branded in him the discus of the immortal Vishṇu, which is the might of the gods,
"He, shaking off his guilt, goes to the heaven (Vaikuṇṭha) which ascetics, whose desires are passed away, enter into:
"The discus Sudarśana by which, uplifted in his arm, the gods entered that heaven;
"Marked wherewith the Manus projected the emanation of the world, that weapon Bráhmans wear (stamped upon them);
"Stigmatised wherewith they go to the supreme sphere of Vishṇu;
"Marked with the stigmas of the wide-striding (Vishṇu), let us become beatified."

Again, the Taittiríyaka Upanishad says: "He whose body is not branded, is raw, and tastes it not: votaries bearing it attain thereto." The particular parts to be branded are specified in the Ágneya-puráṇa:—

"On his right hand let the Bráhman wear Sudarśana,
"On his left the conch-shell: thus have those who know the Veda declared."

In another passage is given the invocation to be recited on being branded with the discus:—

"Sudarśana, brightly blazing, effulgent as ten million suns,
"Show unto me, blind with ignorance, the everlasting way of Vishṇu.
"Thou aforetime sprangest from the sea, brandished in the hand of Vishṇu,
"Adored by all the gods; O Páńchajanya, to thee be adoration."

(2.) Imposition of names is the appellation of sons and others by such names as Keśava, as a continual memorial of the name of the Supreme Lord.

(3.) Worship is of ten kinds, viz., with the voice, (1.) veracity, (2.) usefulness, (3.) kindliness, (4.) sacred study; with the body, (5.) alms-giving, (6.) defence, (7.) protection; with the common sensory, (8.) mercy, (9.) longing, and (10.) faith. Worship is the dedication to Náráyaṇa of each of these as it is realised. Thus it has been said:—

"Stigmatisation, imposition of names, worship; the last is of ten kinds."

Difference (or duality between the Supreme Being and the universe) may also be inferred from cognisability and other marks. So also difference (or duality) may be understood from revelation, from texts setting out duality in emancipation and beatitude, such as: "All rejoice over truth attained; truthful, and celebrating the gift of the divine Indra, they recount his glory;" "Sarva, among those that know the truth, O Bráhman, is in the universe, true spirit; true is individual spirit; truth is duality, truth is duality, in me is illusion, in me illusion, in me illusion."

Again:—

"After attaining this knowledge, becoming like unto me,
"In creation they are not born again, in retractation they perish not" (Bhagavad-gítá, xiv. 2).

According also to such aphorisms as, "Excepting cosmical operation because of occasion, and because of non-proximity."

Nor should suggestion be made that individual spirit is God in virtue of the text, He that knows the absolute becomes the absolute; for this text is hyperbolically eulogistic, like the text, Worshipping a Bráhman devoutly a Śúdra becomes a Bráhman, *i.e.*, becomes exalted.

If any one urge that according to the text:—

"If the universe existed it would doubtless come to an end,"

this duality is merely illusory, and in reality a unity, and that duality is learnt to be illusorily imagined; it may be replied: What you say is true, but you do not understand its meaning; for the real meaning is, If this world had been produced, it would, without doubt, come to an end; therefore this universe is from everlasting, a fivefold dual universe; and it is not non-existent, because it is mere illusion. Illusion is defined to be the will of the Lord, in virtue of the testimony of many such passages as:—

"The great illusion, ignorance, necessity, the bewilderment,

"The originant, ideation,—thus is thy will called, O Infinite.

"The originant, because it originates greatly; ideation, because it produces ideas;

"The illusion of Hari, who is called *a*, is termed (*avidyá*) ignorance:

"Styled (*máyá*) illusion, because it is pre-eminent, for the name *máyá* is used of the pre-eminent;

"The excellent knowledge of Vishṇu is called, though one only, by these names;

"For Hari is excellent knowledge, and this is characterised by spontaneous beatitude."

That in which this excellent knowledge produces knowledge and effects sustentation thereof, that is pure illusion, as known and sustained, therefore by the Supreme Lord duality is not illusorily imagined. For in the Lord illusory imagination of the universe is not possible, illusory imagination arising from non-perception of differences (which as an imperfection is inconsistent with the divine nature).

If it be asked how then that (illusory duality) is predicated, the answer is that in reality there is a non-duality, that is in reality, Vishṇu being better than all else, has no equal and no superior. Accordingly, the grand revelation:—

"A difference between soul and the Lord, a difference between the unsentient and the Lord,

"A difference among souls, and a difference of the unsentient and the soul each from the other.

"Also the difference of unsentient things from one another, the world with its five divisions.

"This same is real and from all eternity; if it had had a beginning it would have an end:

"Whereas it does not come to an end; and it is not illusorily imagined:

"For if it were imagined it would cease, but it never ceases.

"That there is no duality is therefore the doctrine of those that lack knowledge;

"For this the doctrine of those that have knowledge is known and sustained by Vishṇu."

The purpose, then, of all revelations is to set out the supreme excellence of Vishṇu. With this in view the Lord declared:—

"Two are these persons in the universe, the perishable and the imperishable;

"The perishable is all the elements, the imperishable is the unmodified.

"The other, the most excellent person, called the Supreme Spirit,

"Is the undecaying Lord, who pervading sustains the three worlds.

"Since transcending the perishable, I am more excellent than the imperishable (soul),

"Hence I am celebrated among men and in the Veda as the best of persons (*Purushottama*);

"He who uninfatuated knows me thus the best of persons, he all-knowing worships me in every wise.

"Thus this most mysterious institute is declared, blameless (Arjuna):

"Knowing this a man may be wise, and may have done what he has to do, O Bhárata" (Bhagavad-gítá, xv. 16-20).

So in the Mahá-varáha—

"The primary purport of all the Vedas relates to the supreme spouse of Śrī;

"Its purport regarding the excellence of any other deity must be subordinate."

It is reasonable that the primary purport should regard the supreme excellence of Vishṇu. For emancipation is the highest end of all men, according to the text of the Bhállaveya Upanishad: While merit, wealth, and enjoyment are transitory, emancipation is eternal; therefore a wise man should strive unceasingly to attain thereto. And emancipation is not won without the grace of Vishṇu, according to the text of the Náráyaṇa Upanishad: Through whose grace is the highest state, through whose essence he is liberated from transmigration, while inferior men propitiating the divinities are not emancipated; the supreme object of discernment to those who desire to be liberated from this snare of works. According also to the words of the Vishṇu-puráṇa—

"If he be propitiated, what may not here be won? Enough of all wealth and enjoyments. These are scanty enough. On climbing the tree of the supreme essence, without doubt a man attains to the fruit of emancipation."

And it is declared that the grace of Vishṇu is won only through the knowledge of his excellence, not through the knowledge of non-duality. Nor is there in this doctrine any confliction with texts declaratory of the identity (of personal and impersonal spirit) such as, That art thou (for this pretended identity) is mere babbling from ignorance of the real purport.

"The word That, when undetermined, designates the eternally unknown,
"The word Thou designates a knowable entity; how can these be one?"

And this text (That art thou) indicates similarity (not identity) like the text, The sun is the sacrificial post. Thus the grand revelation:—

"The ultimate unity of the individual soul is either similarity of cognition,

"Or entrance into the same place, or in relation to the place of the individual;

"Not essential unity, for even when it is emancipated it is different,

"The difference being independence and completeness (in the Supreme Spirit), and smallness and dependence (in the individual spirit)."

Or to propose another explanation of the text, *Átmá tat tvam asi*, That art thou, it may be divided, *átmá tat tvam asi*. He alone is soul as possessing independence and other attributes, and thou art not-that (*atat*) as wanting those attributes; and thus the doctrine of unity is utterly expelled. Thus it has been said:—

"Or the division may be *Atat tvam*, and thus unity will be well got rid of."

According, therefore, to the Tattva-váda-rahasya, the words in the nine examples (in the Chhándogya Upanishad), He like a bird tied with a string, &c., teach unity with the view of giving an example of non-duality. Accordingly the Mahopanishad:—

"Like a bird and the string; like the juices of various trees;

"Like rivers and the sea; like fresh and salt water;

"Like a robber and the robbed; like a man and his energy;

"So are soul and the Lord diverse, for ever different.

"Nevertheless from subtilty (or imperceptibility) of form, the supreme Hari

"Is not seen by the dim-sighted to be other than the individual spirit, though he is its actuator;

"On knowing their diversity a man is emancipated: otherwise he is bound."

And again—

"Brahmá, Śiva, and the greatest of the gods decay with the decay of their bodies;

"Greater than these is Hari, undecaying, because his body is for the sustentation of Lakshmí.

"By reason of all his attributes, independence, power, knowledge, pleasure, and the rest,

"All they, all the deities, are in unlimited obedience to him."

And again:—

"Knowing Vishṇu, full of all excellences, the soul, exempted from transmigration,

"Rejoices in his presence for ever, enjoying painless bliss.

"Vishṇu is the refuge of liberated souls, and their supreme ruler.

> "Obedient to him are they for ever; he is the Lord."

That by knowledge of one thing there is knowledge of all things may be evinced from its supremacy and causality, not from the falsity of all things. For knowledge of the false cannot be brought about by knowledge of real existence. As we see the current assurance and expression that by knowing or not knowing its chief men a village is known or not known; and as when the father the cause is known, a man knows the son; (so by knowing the supreme and the cause, the inferior and the effect is known). Otherwise (on the doctrine of the Advaita-vádins that the world is false and illusory) the words *one* and *lump* in the text, By one lump of clay, fair sir, all that is made of clay is recognised, would be used to no purpose, for the text must be completed by supplying the words, By reason of clay recognised. For the text, Utterance with the voice, modification, name, clay (or other determinate object),—these alone are real, cannot be assumed to impart the falsity of things made; the reality of these being admitted, for what is meant is, that of which utterance with the voice is a modification, is unmodified, eternal; and a name such as clay, such speech is true. Otherwise it would result that the words *name* and *alone* would be otiose. There is no proof anywhere, then, that the world is unreal. Besides (we would ask) is the statement that the world is false itself true or false. If the statement is true, there is a violation of a real non-duality. If the statement is untrue, it follows that the world is true.

Perhaps it may be objected that this dilemma is a kind of fallacious reasoning, like the dilemma: Is transitoriness permanent or transitory? There is a difficulty in either case. As it is said by the author of the Nyáya-nirváṇa: The proof of the permanence of the transitory, as being both permanent and transitory, is a paralogism. And in the Tárkika-rakshá—

> "When a mode cannot be evinced to be either such and such, or not such and such,
>
> "The denial of a subject characterised by such a mode is called Nitya-sama."

With the implied mention of this same technical expression it is stated in the Prabodha-siddhi: Equality of characteristic modes results from significancy. If it be said, This then is a valid rejoinder, we reply, This is a mere scaring of the uninstructed, for the source of fallacy has not been pointed out. This is twofold, general and particular: of these, the former is self-destructive, and the latter is of three kinds, defect of a requisite element, excess of an element not requisite, and residence in that which is not the subjicible subject. Of these (two forms of the fallacy), the general form is not suspected, no self-pervasion being observed in the dilemma in question (viz., Is the statement that the world is unreal itself true or false? &c.) So likewise the particular; for if a water-jar be said to be non-existent, the affirmation of its non-existence is equally applicable to the water-jar as that of its existence.

If you reply: We accept the unreality (or falsity) of the world, not its non-existence; this reply is about as wise as the procedure of the carter who will lose his head rather than pay a hundred pieces of money, but will at once give five score; for falsity and non-existence are synonymous. We dismiss further prolixity.

The meaning of the first aphorism, viz., Then hence the absolute is to be desired to be known, is as follows:—The word *then* is allowed to purport auspiciousness, and to designate subsequency to the qualification (of the aspirant). The word *hence* indicates a reason.

Accordingly it is stated in the Gáruḍa-puráṇa:—

> "All the aphorisms begin with the words Then and Hence regularly; what then is the reason of this?
>
> "And what is the sense of those words, O sage? Why are those the most excellent?
>
> "Tell me this, Brahmá, that I may know it truly."

Thus addressed by Nárada, the most excellent Brahmá replied:—

> "The word Then is used of subsequency and of competency, and in an auspicious sense,
>
> "And the word Thence is employed to indicate the reason."

It is laid down that we must institute inquiries about the absolute, because emancipation is not attained without the grace of Náráyana, and his grace is not attained without knowledge. The absolute, about which the inquiry is to be instituted, is described in the words (of the second aphorism): From which the genesis, and so forth, of this. The meaning of the sentence is that the absolute is that from which result emanation, sustentation, and retractation; according to the words of the Skanda-puráṇa—

> "He is Hari the sole ruler, the spirit from whom are emanation, sustentation, retractation, necessity, knowledge, involution (in illusion), and bondage and liberation;"

and according to such Vedic texts, From which are these. The evidence adducible for this is described (in the third aphorism): Because it has its source from the system. That the absolute should be reached by way of inference is rejected by such texts as, He that knows not the Veda cogitates not that mighty one; Him described in the Upanishads. Inference, moreover, is not by itself authoritative, as is said in the Kaurma-puráṇa—

> "Inference, unaccompanied by revelation, in no case
> "Can definitely prove a matter, nor can any other form of evidence;
> "Whatsoever other form of evidence, companioned by revelation and tradition,
> "Acquires the rank of probation, about this there can be no hesitation."

What a Śástra (or system of sacred institutes) is, has been stated in the Skanda-puráṇa:—

> "The Rig-veda, the Yajur-veda, the Sáma-veda, the Atharva-veda, the Mahábhárata, the Pañcha-rátra, and the original Rámáyaṇa, are called Śástras.
> "That also which is conformable to these is called Śástra.
> "Any aggregate of composition other than this is a heterodoxy."

According, then, to the rule that the sense of the sacred institutes is not to be taken from other sources than these, the Monist view, viz., that the purport of the texts of the Veda relates not to the duality learnt from those but to non-duality, is rejected: for as there is no proof of a God from inference, so there is no proof of the duality between God and other things from inference. Therefore there can be in these texts no mere explanation of such duality, and the texts must be understood to indicate the duality. Hence it is that it has said:—

> "I ever laud Náráyaṇa, the one being to be known from genuine revelation, who transcends the perishable and the imperishable, without imperfections, and of inexhaustible excellences."

It has thus been evinced that the sacred institutes are the evidence of (the existence of) this (ultimate reality, *Brahman*). (The fourth aphorism is): But that is from the construction. In regard to this, the commencement and other elements are stated to be the marks of the construction, in the Bṛihat-saṃhitá:—

> "Commencement, conclusion, reiteration, novelty, profit, eulogy, and demonstration, are the marks by which the purport is ascertained."

It is thus stated that in accordance with the purport of the Upanishads the absolute is to be apprehended only from the sacred institutes. We have here given merely a general indication. What remains may be sought from the Ánandatírtha-bháshya-vyákhyána (or exposition of the Commentary of Ánanda-tírtha). We desist for fear of giving an undue prolixity to our treatise. This mystery was promulgated by Púrṇa-prajña Madhya-mandira, who esteemed himself the third incarnation of Váyu:—

> "The first was Hanumat, the second Bhíma,
> "The third Púrṇa-prajña, the worker of the work of the Lord."

After expressing the same idea in various passages, he has written the following stanza at the conclusion of his work:—

> "That whereof the three divine forms are declared in the text of the Veda, sufficiently
> "Has that been set forth; this is the whole majesty in the splendour of the Veda;
> "The first incarnation of the Wind-god was he that bowed to the words of Ráma (Hanumat); the second was Bhíma;
> "By this Madhva, who is the third, this book has been composed in regard to Keśava."

The import of this stanza may be learnt by considering various Vedic texts.

The purport of this is that Vishṇu is the principle above all others in every system of sacred institutes. Thus all is clear.[111]

CHAPTER VI.

THE PÁŚUPATA SYSTEM OF NAKULÍŚA.

Certain Máheśvaras disapprove of this doctrine of the Vaishṇavas known by its technicalities of the servitude of souls and the like, inasmuch as bringing with it the pains of dependence upon another, it cannot be a means of cessation of pain and other desired ends. They recognise as stringent such arguments as, Those depending on another and longing for independence do not become emancipated, because they still depend upon another, being destitute of independence like ourselves and others; and, Liberated spirits possess the attributes of the Supreme Deity, because at the same time, that they are spirits they are free from the germ of every pain as the Supreme Deity is. Recognising these arguments, these Máheśvaras adopt the Páśupata system, which is conversant about the exposition of five categories, as the means to the highest end of man. In this system the first aphorism is: Now then we shall expound the Páśupata union and rites of Paśupati. The meaning is as follows:—The word *now* refers to something antecedent, and this something antecedent is the disciple's interrogation of the spiritual teacher. The nature of a spiritual teacher is explicated in the Gaṇakáriká:—

> "But there are eight pentads to be known, and a group, one with three factors;
> "He that knows this ninefold aggregate is a self-purifier, a spiritual guide.
> "The acquisitions, the impurities, the expedients, the localities, the perseverance, the purifications,
> "The initiations, and the powers, are the eight pentads; and there are three functions."

The employment in the above line of the neuter numeral three (*tríṇi*), instead of the feminine three (*tisraḥ*), is a Vedic construction.

(*a.*) Acquisition is the fruit of an expedient while realising, and is divided into five members, viz., knowledge, penance, permanence of the body, constancy, and purity. Thus Haradattácharya says: Knowledge, penance, permanence, constancy, and purity as the fifth.

(*b.*) Impurity is an evil condition pertaining to the soul. This is of five kinds, false conception and the rest. Thus Haradatta also says:—

> "False conception, demerit, attachment, interestedness, and falling,
> "These five, the root of bondage, are in this system especially to be shunned."

(*c.*) An expedient is a means of purifying the aspirant to liberation. These expedients are of five kinds, use of habitation, and the rest. Thus he also says:—

"Use of habitation, pious muttering, meditation, constant recollection of Rudra,
"And apprehension, are determined to be the five expedients of acquirements."

(*d.*) Locality is that by which, after studying the categories, the aspirant attains increase of knowledge and austerity, viz., spiritual teachers and the rest. Thus he says:—

"The spiritual teachers, a cavern, a special place, the burning-ground, and Rudra only."

(*e.*) Perseverance is the endurance in one or other of these pentads until the attainment of the desired end, and is distributed into the differenced and the rest. Thus it is said:—

"The differenced, the undifferenced, muttering, acceptance, and devotion as the fifth."

(*f.*) Purification is the putting away, once for all, of false conception and the other four impurities. It is distributed into five species according to the five things to be put away. Thus it is said—

"The loss of ignorance, of demerit, of attachment, of interestedness,
"And of falling, is declared to be the fivefold purification of the state of bondage."

(*g.*) The five initiations are thus enumerated:—

"The material, the proper time, the rite, the image, and the spiritual guide as the fifth."

(*h.*) The five powers are as follow:—

"Devotion to the spiritual guide, clearness of intellect, conquest of pleasure and pain,
"Merit and carefulness, are declared the five heads of power."

The three functions are the modes of earning daily food consistent with propriety, for the diminution of the five impurities, viz., mendicancy, living upon alms, and living upon what chance supplies. All the rest is to be found in the standard words of this sect.

In the first aphorism above recited, the word *now* serves to introduce the exposition of the termination of pain (or emancipation), that being the object of the interrogation about the putting away of pain personal, physical, and hyperphysical. By the word *paśu* we are to understand the effect (or created world), the word designating that which is dependent on something ulterior. By the word *pati* we are to understand the cause (or *principium*), the word designating the Lord, who is the cause of the universe, the *pati*, or ruler. The meaning of the words sacrifices and rites every one knows.

In this system the cessation of pain is of two kinds, impersonal and personal. Of these, the impersonal consists in the absolute extirpation of all pains; the personal in supremacy consisting of the visual and active powers. Of these two powers the visual, while only one power, is, according to its diversity of objects, indirectly describable as of five kinds, vision, audition, cogitation, discrimination, and omniscience. Of these five, vision is cognition of every kind of visual, tactual, and other sensible objects, though imperceptible, intercepted, or remote. Audition is cognition of principles, conversant about all articulate sounds. Cogitation is cognition of principles, conversant about all kinds of thoughts. Discrimination is cognition of principles conversant about the whole system of institutes, according to the text and according to its significance. Omniscience is cognition of principles ever arising and pervaded by truth, relative to all matters declared or not declared, summary or in detail, classified and specialised. Such is this intellectual power.

The active power, though one only, is indirectly describable as of three kinds, the possession of the swiftness of thought, the power of assuming forms at will, and the faculty of expatiation. Of these, the possession of the swiftness of thought is ability to act with unsurpassable celerity. The power of assuming forms at will is the faculty of employing at pleasure, and irrespective of the efficacy of works, the organs similar and dissimilar of an infinity of organisms. The faculty of expatiation is the possession of transcendent supremacy even when such organs are not employed. Such is this active power.

All that is effected or educed, depending on something ulterior, it is threefold, sentiency, the insentient, and the sentient. Of these, sentiency is the attribute of the sentients. It is of two degrees according to its nature as cognitive or incognitive. Cognitive sentiency is dichotomised as proceeding discriminately and as proceeding indiscriminately. The discriminate procedure, manifestable by the instruments of knowledge, is called the cogitative. For by the cogitant organ every sentient being is cognisant of objects in general, discriminated or not discriminated, when irradiated by the light which is identical with the external things. The incognitive sentiency, again, is either characterised or not characterised by the objects of the sentient soul.

The insentient, which while unconscious is dependent on the conscious, is of two kinds, as styled the effect and as styled the cause. The insentient, styled the effect, is of ten kinds, viz., the earth and the other four elements, and their qualities, colour, and the rest. The insentient, called the causal insentient, is of thirteen kinds, viz., the five organs of cognition, the five organs of action, and the three internal organs, intellect, the egoising principle, and the cogitant principle, which have for their respective functions ascertainment, the illusive identification of self with not-self, and determination.

The sentient spirit, that to which transmigratory conditions pertain, is also of two kinds, the appetent and non-appetent. The appetent is the spirit associated with an organism and organs; the non-appetent is the spirit apart from organism and organs. The details of all this are to be found in the Pañchártha-bháshyadípiká and other works. The cause is that which retracts into itself and evolves the whole creation. This though one is said to be divided according to a difference of attributes and actions (into Maheśvara, Vishṇu, &c.) The Lord is the possessor of infinite, visual, and active power. He is absolutely first as connected eternally with this lordship or supremacy, as possessing a supremacy not adventitious or contingent. This is expounded by the author of the Ádarśa, and other institutional authorities.

Union is a conjunction of the soul with God through the intellect, and is of two degrees, that characterised by action, and that characterised by cessation of action. Of these, union characterised by action consists of pious muttering, meditation, and so forth; union characterised by cessation of action is called consciousness, &c.

Rite or ritual is activity efficacious of merit as its end. It is of two orders, the principal and the subsidiary. Of these, the principal is the direct means of merit, religious exercise. Religious exercise is of two kinds, acts of piety and postures. The acts of piety are bathing with sand, lying upon sand, oblations, mutterings, and devotional perambulation. Thus the revered Nakulíśa says:—

> "He should bathe thrice a day, he should lie upon the dust. Oblation is an observance divided into six members."

Thus the author of the aphorisms says:—

> "He should worship with the six kinds of oblations, viz., laughter, song, dance, muttering *hum*, adoration, and pious ejaculation."

Laughter is a loud laugh, Aha, Aha, by dilatation of the throat and lips. Song is a celebration of the qualities, glories, &c., of Maheśvara, according to the conventions of the Gandharva-śástra, or art of music. The dance also is to be employed according to the *ars saltatoria*, accompanied with gesticulations with hands and feet, and with motions of the limbs, and with outward indications of internal sentiment. The ejaculation *hum* is a sacred utterance, like the bellowing of a bull, accomplished by a contact of the tongue with the palate, an imitation of the sound *hudung*, ascribed to a bull, like the exclamation Vashat. Where the uninitiated are, all this should be gone through in secret. Other details are too familiar to require exposition.

The postures are snoring, trembling, limping, wooing, acting absurdly, talking nonsensically. Snoring is showing all the signs of being asleep while really awake. Trembling is a convulsive movement of the joints as if under an attack of rheumatism. Limping is walking as if the legs were disabled. Wooing is simulating the gestures of an *innamorato* on seeing a young and pretty woman. Acting absurdly is doing acts which every one dislikes, as if bereft of all sense of what should and what should not be done. Talking nonsensically is the utterance of words which contradict each other, or which have no meaning, and the like.

The subsidiary religious exercise is purificatory subsequent ablution for putting an end to the sense of unfitness from begging, living on broken food, &c. Thus it is said by the author of the aphorisms: Bearing the marks of purity by after-bathing.

(It has been stated above that omniscience, a form of the cognitive power, is cognition of principles ever arising and pervaded by truth, relative to all matters declared or not declared, summary, or in detail). The summary is the enouncement of the subjects of attributes generally. This is accomplished in the first aphorism: (Now then we shall expound the Páśupata union and rites of Paśupati). Detail is the fivefold enouncement of the five categories according to the instruments of true knowledge. This is to be found in the Ráśíkara-bháshya. Distribution is the distinct enouncement of these categories, as far as possible according to definitions. It is an enumeration of these according to their prevailing characters, different from that of other recognised systems. For example, the cessation of pain (or emancipation) is in other systems (as in the Sānkhya) the mere termination of miseries, but in this system it is the attainment of supremacy or of the divine perfections. In other systems the create is that which has become, and that which shall become, but in this system it is eternal, the spirits, and so forth, the sentient and insentient. In other systems the *principium* is determined in its evolution or creative activity by the efficacy of works, whereas in this system the *principium* is the Lord not thus determined. In other institutes union results in isolation, &c., while in these institutes it results in cessation of pains by attainment of the divine perfections. In other systems paradise and similar spheres involve a return to metempsychosis, but in this system they result in nearness to the Supreme Being, either followed or not followed by such return to transmigratory experiences.

Great, indeed, an opponent may say, is this aggregate of illusions, since if God's causality be irrespective of the efficacy of works, then merits will be fruitless, and all created things will be simultaneously evolved (there being no reason why this should be created at one time, and that at another), and thus there will emerge two difficulties. Think not so, replies the Páśupata, for your supposition is baseless. If the Lord, irrespective of the efficacy of works, be the cause of all, and thus the efficacy of works be without results, what follows? If you rejoin that an absence of motives will follow, in whom, we ask, will this absence of motives follow? If the efficacy of works be without result, will causality belong to the doer of the works as to the Lord? It cannot belong to the doer of the works, for it is allowed that the efficacy of works is fruitful only when furthered by the will of the creator, and the efficacy so furthered may sometimes be fruitless, as in the case of the works of Yayáti, and others. From this it will by no means follow that no one will engage in works, for they will engage in them as the husbandman engages in husbandry, though the crop be uncertain. Again, sentient creatures engage in works because they depend on the will of the creator. Nor does the causality pertain to the Lord alone, for as all his desires are already satisfied, he cannot be actuated by motives to be realised by works. As for your statement, continues the Páśupata, that all things will be simultaneously evolved, this is unreasonable, inasmuch as we hold that causal efficiency resides in the unobstructed active power which conforms itself to the will of the Lord, whose power is inconceivable. It has accordingly been said by those versed in sacred tradition:—

> "Since he, acting according to his will, is not atuated by the efficacy of works,
>
> "For this reason is he in this system the cause of all causes."

Some one may urge: In another system emancipation is attained through a knowledge of God, where does the difference lie? Say not so, replies the Páśupata, for you will be caught in a trilemma. Is the mere knowledge of God the cause of emancipation, or the presentation, or the accurate characterisation, of God? Not the mere knowledge, for then it would follow that the study of any system would be superfluous, inasmuch as without any institutional system one might, like the uninstructed, attain emancipation by the bare cognition that Mahádeva is the lord of the gods. Nor is presentation or intuition of the deity the cause of emancipation, for no intuition of the deity is competent to sentient creatures burdened with an accumulation of various impurities, and able to see only with the eyes of the flesh. On the third alternative, viz., that the cause of emancipation is an accurate characterisation of the deity, you will be obliged to consent to our doctrine, inasmuch as such accurate characterisation cannot be realised apart from the system of the Páśupatas. Therefore it is that our great teacher has said:—

> "If by mere knowledge, it is not according to any system, but intuition is unattainable;
>
> "There is no accurate characterisation of principles otherwise than by the five categories."

Therefore those excellent persons who aspire to the highest end of man must adopt the system of the Páśupatas, which undertakes the exposition of the five categories.

—A. E. G.

CHAPTER VII.

THE ŚAIVA-DARŚANA.

[The seventh system in Mádhava's Sarva-darśana-saṅgraha is theŚaiva-darśana. This sect is very prevalent in the South of India, especially in the Tamil country; it is said to have arisen there about the eleventh century a.d. Several valuable contributions have been lately made to our knowledge of its tenets in the publications of the Rev. H. R. Hoisington and the Rev. T. Foulkes. The former especially, by his excellent articles in the American Oriental Society's Journal, has performed a great service to the students of Hindu philosophy. He has there translated the Tattuva-Kaṭṭalei, or law of the Tattwas, theŚiva-Gnánapotham, or instruction in the knowledge of God, and the Śiva-Pirakásam, or light of Śiva, and the three works shed immense light on the outline as given by Mádhava. One great use of the latter is to enable us to recognise the original Sanskrit names in their Tamil disguise, no easy matter occasionally, as *aṛul* for *anugraha* and *tíḍchei* for *díkshá* may testify.

The Śaivas have considerable resemblance to the Theistic Sánkhya; they hold that God, souls, and matter are from eternity distinct entities, and the object of philosophy is to disunite the soul from matter and gradually to unite it to God. Śiva is the chief deity of the system, and the relation between the three is quaintly expressed by the allegory of a beast, its fetters, and its owner. Paśupati is a well-known name of Śiva, as the master or creator of all things.

There seem to be three different sets of so-called Saiva sútras. One is in five books, called by Colebrooke the Paśupati-śástra, which is probably the work quoted by Mádhava in his account of the Nakulíśa Páśupatas; another is in three books, with a commentary by Kshemarája, with its first sútra, *chaítanyam átmá*. The third was commented on by Abhinava-gupta, and opens with the śloka given in the Sarva-Darśana-Saṅgraha, p. 91, lines 1-4. The MS. which I consulted in Calcutta read the first words—

Kathañchid ásádya Maheśvarasya dásyam.

None of these works, however, appear to be the authority of the present sect. They seem chiefly to have relied on the twenty-eight Ágamas and some of the Puráṇas. A list of the Ágamas is given in Mr. Foulkes' "Catechism of the Śaiva Religion;" and of these the Kiraṇa and Karaṇa are quoted in the following treatise.]

THE ŚAIVA-DARŚANA.

Certain, however, of the Máheśvara sect receiving the system of truth authoritatively laid down in the Śaiva Ágama,[112] reject the foregoing opinion that "the Supreme Being is a cause as independent of our actions, &c.," on the ground of its being liable to the imputation of partiality and cruelty. They, on the contrary, hold the opinion that "the Supreme Being is a cause in dependence on our actions, &c.;" and they maintain that there are three categories distinguished as the Lord, the soul, and the world (or literally "the master," "the cattle," and "the fetter"). As has been said by those well versed in the Tantra doctrines—

> "The Guru of the world, having first condensed in one sútra the great tantra, possessed of three categories and four feet, has again declared the same at full length."

The meaning of this is as follows:—Its three categories are the three before mentioned; its four feet are learning, ceremonial action, meditation, and morality, hence it is called the great Tantra, possessed of three categories and four feet. Now the "souls" are not independent, and the "fetters" are unintelligent, hence the Lord, as being different from these, is first declared; next follows the account of the souls as they agree with him in possessing intelligence; lastly follow the "fetters" or matter, such is the order of the arrangement.[113] Since the ceremony of initiation is the means to the highest human end, and this cannot be accomplished without knowledge which establishes the undoubted greatness of the hymns, the Lords of the hymns, &c., and is a means for the ascertainment of the real nature of the "cattle," the "fetter," and the "master," we place as first the "foot" of *knowledge* (*jñána*) which makes known all this unto us.[114] Next follows the "foot" of *ceremonial action* (*kriyá*) which declares the various rules of initiation with the divers component parts thereof. Without meditation the end cannot be attained, hence the "foot" of *meditation* (*yoga*) follows next, which declares the various kinds of *yoga* with their several parts. And as meditation is worthless without practice, *i.e.*, the fulfilling what is enjoined and the abstaining from what is forbidden, lastly follows the fourth "foot" of practical duty (*charyá*), which includes all this.

Now Śiva is held to be the Lord (or master). Although participation in the divine nature of Śiva belongs to liberated souls and to such beings as Vidyeśvara, &c., yet these are not independent, since they depend on the Supreme Being; and the nature of an effect is recognised to belong to the worlds, &c., which resemble him, from the very fact of the orderly arrangement of their parts. And from their thus being effects we infer that they must have been caused by an intelligent being. By the strength of this inference is the universal acknowledgment of a Supreme Being confirmed.

"But may we not object that it is not proved that the body is thus an effect? for certainly none has ever, at any time or place, seen a body being made by any one." We grant it: yet it is not proper to deny that a body has some maker on the ground that its being made has not been seen by any one, since this can be established from inference [if not from actual perception]. Bodies, &c., must be effects, because they possess an orderly arrangement of parts, or because they are destructible, as jars, &c.; and from their being effects it is easy to infer that they must have been caused by an intelligent being. Thus the subject in the argument [sc. bodies, &c.] must have had a maker, from the fact that it is an effect, like jars, &c.; that which has the afore-mentioned middle term (*sádhana*) must have the afore-mentioned major (*sádhya*); and that which has not the former will not have the latter, as the soul, &c.[115] The argument which establishes the authority of the original inference to prove a Supreme Being has been given elsewhere, so we refrain from giving it at length here. In fact, that God is the universal agent, but not irrespective of the actions done by living beings, is proved by the current verse[116]—

> "This ignorant *jívátman*, incapable of its own true pleasures or pains, if it were only under God's direction [and its own merits not taken into account], would always go to heaven or always to hell."[117]

Nor can you object that this opinion violates God's independence, since it does not really violate an agent's independence to allow that he does not act irrespectively of means; just as we say that the king's bounty shows itself in gifts, but these are not irrespective of his treasurer. As has been said by the Siddha Guru—

> "It belongs to independence to be uncontrolled and itself to employ means, &c.;
>
> "This is an agent's true independence, and not the acting irrespectively of works, &c."

And thus we conclude that inference (as well as Śruti) establishes the existence of an agent who knows the various fruits [of action], their means, material causes, &c., according to the laws of the various individual merits. This has been thus declared by the venerable Bṛihaspati—

> "He who knows the fruits to be enjoyed, their means and material causes,—
>
> "Apart from him this world knows not how the desert that resides in accumulated actions should ripen."—

"The universe is the subject of our argument, and it must have had an intelligent maker,

"This we maintain from its being an effect, just as we see in any other effect, as jars, &c."

God's omniscience also is proved from his being identical with everything, and also from the fact that an ignorant being cannot produce a thing.[118] This has been said by the illustrious Mṛigendra[119]—

"He is omniscient from his being the maker of all things: for it is an established principle

"That he only can make a thing who knows it with its means, parts, and end."

"Well," our opponents may say, "we concede that God is an independent maker, but then he has no body.[120] Now experience shows that all effects, as jars, &c., are produced by beings possessed of bodies, as potters, &c.; but if God were possessed of a body, then he would be like us subject to trouble, and no longer be omniscient or omnipotent." We, however, deny this, for we see that the incorporeal soul does still produce motion, &c., in its associated body; moreover, even though we conceded that God *did* possess a body, we should still maintain that the alleged defects would not necessarily ensue. The Supreme Being, as he has no possible connection with the fetters of matter, such as *mala*,[121] action, &c., cannot have a material body, but only a body of pure energy (Sákta),[122] since we know that his body is composed of the five hymns which are forms of Śakti, according to the well-known text: "The Supreme has the *Iśána* as his head, the *Tatpurusha* as his mouth, the *Aghora* as his heart, the *Vámedeva*as his secret parts, and the *Sadyojáta* as his feet."[123] And this body, created according to his own will, is not like our bodies, but is the cause of the five operations of the Supreme, which are respectively grace, obscuration, destruction, preservation, and production.[124] This has been said in the Śrímat Mṛigendra—

"From the impossibility of its possessing *mala*, &c., the body of the Supreme is of pure energy, and not like ours."

And it has also been said elsewhere—

"His body is composed of the five mantras which are subservient to the five operations,

"And his head, &c., are formed out of the Ísa, Tatpurusha, Aghora, Váma, and other hymns."

If you object to this view that "such passages in the Ágamas as 'He is five-faced and fifteen-eyed,' assert prominently the fact that the Supreme Being is endowed with a body, organs, &c.," we concede what you say, but we maintain that there is no contradiction in his assuming such forms to show his mercy to his devoted servants, since meditation, worship, &c., are impossible towards a Being entirely destitute of form. This has been said in the Paushkara—

> "This form of his is mentioned for the preservation of the devotee."

And similarly elsewhere—

> "Thou art to be worshipped according to rule as possessed of form;
> "For the understanding cannot reach to a formless object."

Bhojarája[125] has thus detailed the five operations—

> "Fivefold are his operations, creation, preservation, destruction, and obscuration,
> "And to these must be added the active grace of him who is eternally exalted."

Now these five operations, in the view of the pure Path, are held to be performed directly by Śiva, but in that of the toilsome Path they are ascribed to Ananta,[126] as is declared in the Śrímat Karaṇa[127]—

> "In the Pure Path Śiva is declared to be the only agent, but Ananta in that which is opposed to the One Supreme."

It must here be understood that the word Śiva includes in its proper meaning "the Lord," all those who have attained to the state of Śiva, as the Lords of the Mantras, Maheśwara, the emancipated souls who have become Śivas, and the inspired teachers (*váchakas*), together with all the various means, as initiation, &c., for obtaining the state ofŚiva. Thus has been explained the first category, the Lord (*pati*).

We now proceed to explain the second category, the soul (*paśu*). The individual soul which is also known by such synonyms as the non-atomic,[128] the *Kshetrajña*, or knower of the body,[129] &c., is the *Paśu*. For we must not say with the Chárvákas that it is the same as the body, since on this view we could not account for memory, as there is a proverb that one man cannot remember what another has seen. Nor may we say with the Naiyáyikas that it is cognisable by perception,[130] as this would involve an *ad infinitum* regressus. As has been said—

> "If the soul were cognisable, there would need to be again a second knower;[131]

"And this would require another still, if the second were itself to be known."

Nor must we hold it non-pervading with the Jainas, nor momentary with the Bauddhas, since it is not limited by space or time. As has been said—

"That object which is unlimited in its nature by space or time,
"They hold to be eternal and pervading,—hence the soul's all-pervadingness and eternity."

Nor may we say with the Vedántin that it is only one, since the apportionment of different fruits proves that there are many individual souls; nor with the Sánkhyas that it is devoid of action, since, when all the various "fetters" are removed, Śruti informs us of a state of identity with Śiva, which consists in intelligence in the form of an eternal and infinite vision and action.[132] This has been declared in the Śrímat Mṛigendra—

"It is revealed that identity with Śiva results when all fetters are removed."

And again—

"Intelligence consists in vision and action, and since in his soul
"This exists always and on every side, therefore, after liberation, Śruti calls it that which faces every way."

It is also said in the Tattva-prakáśa—

"The liberated souls are themselves Śivas, but these are liberated by his favour;
"He is to be known as the one eternally liberated, whose body is the five Mantras."

Now the souls are threefold, as denominated *vijñánákaláḥ*, *pralayákaláḥ*, and *sakaláḥ*.[133] (*a.*) The first are those who are under the influence of *mala* only, since their actions are cancelled by receiving their proper fruits, or by abstraction, contemplation, and knowledge, and since they have no "fetters" in the form of enjoyments, such as *kalá*, &c. (which fetters would, however, be the cause of cancelling actions by bringing about their proper fruit). (*b.*) The second are those who are under the influence of *mala* and *karman*, since in their case *kalá*, &c., are destroyed by mundane destructions, hence their name *pralayákala*. (*c.*) The third are those who are bound in the three fetters of *mala*, *máyá*, and *karman*, hence their name *sakala*. The first class are again subdivided into *samápta-kalusháḥ* and*asamápta-kalusháḥ*, according as their inherent corruption is perfectly exhausted or not. The former,—having received the mature penalties of their corruptions,—are now, as foremost of men and worthy of the privilege, raised by Śiva's favour to the rank of the Lords of Knowledge (the Vidyeśvaras), Ananta, and the rest. This ogdoad of the Lords of Knowledge is described in the Bahudaivatya—

> "Ananta, and Súkshma, and Śivottama,
> "Ekanetra, and again Ekarudra and Trimúrttika,
> "Śríkaṇṭha and Śikhaṇḍin,—these are declared to be the Vidyeśvaras."

The latter Śiva, in his mercy, raises to the rank of the seventy million Mantras.[134] All this is explained in the Tattva-prakáśa.[135] Similarly Soma-Śambhu has said—

> "One class is named *vijñánákala,* the second *pralayákala,*
> "The third *sakala,*—these are the three whom the Śástra regards as objects of mercy.
> "The first is united to *mala* alone, the second to *mala* and *karma,*
> "The third are united to all the tattvas beginning with *kalá* and ending with 'earth.'"[136]

The *Pralayákaláḥ* are also twofold, as being *pakvapáśadvaya* or not,*i.e.*, those in whom the two remaining fetters are matured, and those in whom they are not. The former attain liberation, but the latter, by the power of *karman*, are endowed with the *puryashṭaka*[137] body, and pass through various births. As has been said in the Tattva-prakáśa—

> "Those among the Pralayákalas whose *karman* and *mala* are immature,
> "Go, united with the *puryashṭaka* body, into many births by the power of *karman.*"

The *puryashṭaka* is also thus described in the same work—

> "The *puryashṭaka* is composed of the internal organ, thought (*dhí*), *karman*, and the instruments."

This is thus explained by Aghora Śiva Áchárya, "the *puryashṭaka* is a subtile body apportioned to each individual soul, which continues from the creation until the close of the kalpa, or until liberation: it is composed of the thirty[138] tattvas beginning with 'earth' and ending with *kalá*." As has been said in the Tattva-sangraha—

> "This set of tattvas, commencing with 'earth' and ending with *kalá*, is assigned to each soul,
> "And wanders by the law of *karman* through all the bodies produced by the world."

The following is the full meaning of this passage:—The word "*internal organ,*" which properly includes "mind," "intelligence," "egoism," and "reason,"[139] includes also the seven tattvas which enter into the production of enjoyment [or experience], viz., those called *kalá*, time, fate, knowledge, concupiscence, nature, and quality:[140] the words "*thought*" (*dhí*) and *karman* signify the five cognisable gross elements, and their originators, the subtile rudiments. By the word "*instruments*" are comprehended the ten organs of sense and action.

"But is it not declared in the Śrímat Kálottara that 'The set of five, sound, touch, form, taste and smell, intelligence, mind and egoism, these constitute the *puryashṭaka*?'"

How, then, can any different account be maintained? We grant this, and hence the venerable Ráma Kaṇṭha has explained that sútra in its literal meaning [*i. e*., as *puryashṭaka*, is derived from *ashṭa*, "eight"], so why should we be prolix in the discussion? Still, if you ask how we can reconcile our account with the strict nominal definition of *puryashṭaka*, we reply that there is really no contradiction, as we maintain that it is composed of a set of eight in the following manner:—(1.) The five elements; (2.) the five rudiments; (3.) the five organs of knowledge; (4.) those of action; (5.) the fourfold internal organ; (6.) their instrument;[141] (7.) nature [prakṛiti]; and (8.) the class composed of the five, beginning with *kalá*, which form a kind of case.[142]

Now in the case of some of those souls who are joined to the *puryashṭaka* body, Maheśvara Ananta having compassionated them as possessed of peculiar merit, constitutes them here as lords of the world; as has been said—

> "Maheśvara pities some and grants them to be lords of the world."

The class called *sakala* is also divided into two, as *pakvakalusha* and *apakvakalusha*. As for the former, the Supreme Being, in conformity with their maturity (*paripáka*), puts forth a power agreeable thereto, and transfers them to the position of the hundred and eighteen Lords of the Mantras, signified by the words Maṇḍalí,& c., as has been said—

> "The rest are denominated *sakala*, from their connection with *Kalá*, &c., seized by time whose mouths are days;
>
> "The Supreme of his own will makes one hundred and eighteen of these the Lords of the Mantras.
>
> "Eight of these are called *Maṇḍalins*; eight again are Krodha, &c.;
>
> "Víreśa, Śríkaṇṭha, and the hundred Rudras,—these together are the hundred and eighteen."

In their case again, the Supreme, having assumed the form of a teacher, stops the continued accession of maturity and contracts his manifested power, and ultimately grants to them liberation by the process of initiation; as has been said—

> "These creatures whose *mala* is matured, by putting forth a healing power,
> "He, assuming the form of a teacher, unites by initiation to the highest principle."

It is also said in the Srímad Mṛigendra—

> "He removes from that infinitesimal soul all the bonds which previously exerted a contrary influence over it."[143]

All this has been explained at great length by Náráyaṇa-Kaṇṭha, and there it is to be studied; but we are obliged to pass on through fear of prolixity.

But as for the second class, or those called *apakvakalusha*, the Supreme Being, as impelled by the desert of their respective actions, appoints them, as bound and endued with infinitesimal bodies, to enjoy the rewards of their previous actions.[144] As has been said—

> "The other souls, bound [in their material bonds] he appoints to enjoy their various deserts,
> "According to their respective actions: such are the various kinds of souls."

We now proceed to describe the third category, matter (or *páśa*). This is fourfold, *mala*, *karman*, *máyá*, and *rodha-śakti*.[145] But it may be objected, "Is it not said in the Śaiva Ágamas that the chief things are the Lord, souls, and matter? Now the Lord has been shown to mean Śiva, 'souls' mean atoms (or beings endowed with atomic bodies), and matter (or 'bond') is said to be the pentad,[146] hence matter will be fivefold. How then is it now reckoned to be only fourfold?" To this we reply as follows:—Although the *vindu* or nasal dot, which is the germinal atom of *máyá*, and is called aŚiva-tattva, may be well regarded as material in comparison with the highest liberation as defined by the attainment of the state of Śiva, still it cannot really be considered as matter when we remember that it is a secondary kind of liberation as causing the attainment of the state of such deities as Vidyeśvara, &c. Thus we see there is no contradiction. Hence it has been said in the Tattva-prakáśa—

> "The bonds of matter will be fourfold."

And again in the Srímad Mṛigendra—

"The enveloper-controller (*mala*), the overpowerer (*rodha*), action, and the work of Máyá,

"These are the four 'bonds,' and they are collectively called by the name of 'merit.'"

The following is the meaning of this couplet:—

(1.) "Enveloping," because *mala* exceedingly obscures and veils the soul's powers of vision and action; "controlling," because *mala*, a natural impurity, controls the soul by its independent influence. As has been said—

"*Mala*, though itself one, by manifold influence interrupts the soul's vision and action;

"It is to be regarded as the husk in rice or rust on copper."[147]

(2.) The "overpowerer" is the obscuring power; this is called a "bond" [or matter] in a metaphorical sense, since this energy of Śiva obscures the soul by superintending matter [rather than by itself partaking of the nature of matter].

Thus it has been said—

"Of these I am the chief energy, and the gracious friend of all,

"I am metaphorically called *páśa*,[148] because I follow desert."

(3.) Action [or rather its consequences, *karman*] as being performed by those who desire the fruit. It is in the form of merit or demerit, like the seed and shoot, and it is eternal in a never-beginning series. As has been said in the Śrímat Kiraṇa—

"As *Mala* has no beginning, its least actions are beginningless:

"If an eternal character is thus established, then what cause could produce any change therein?"

(4.) "*Máyá*," because herein as an energy of the Divine Being all the world is potentially contained (*máti*) at a mundane destruction, and again at a creation it all comes (*yáti*) into manifestation, hence the derivation of the name. This has been said in the Śrímat Saurabheya—

"The effects, as a form of the Divine energy, are absorbed therein at a mundane destruction,

"And again at a renovation it is manifested anew in the form of effects as *kalá*, &c."[149]

Although much more might be added on this topic, yet we stop here through fear of extending this treatise too far. Thus have the three categories been declared,—the Lord, the soul, and matter.

A different mode of treating the subject is found in the Jñánaratnávalí, &c., in such lines as—

> "The Lord, knowledge, ignorance, the soul, matter, and the cause
> "Of the cessation thereof,—these are collectively the six categories."

But our readers must seek for full information from the work itself. Thus our account of the system is complete.

—E. B. C.

CHAPTER VIII.

THE PRATYABHIJNA-DARSANA, OR RECOGNITIVE SYSTEM.

Other Máheśvaras are dissatisfied with the views set out in the Śaiva system as erroneous in attributing to motiveless and insentient things causality (in regard to the bondage and liberation of transmigrating spirits). They therefore seek another system, and proclaim that the construction of the world (or series of environments of those spirits) is by the mere will of the Supreme Lord. They pronounce that this Supreme Lord, who is at once other than and the same with the several cognitions and *cognita*, who is identical with the transcendent self posited by one's own consciousness, by rational proof, and by revelation, and who possesses independence, that is, the power of witnessing all things without reference to aught ulterior, gives manifestation, in the mirror of one's own soul, to all entities[150] as if they were images reflected upon it. Thus looking upon recognition as a new method for the attainment of ends and of the highest end, available to all men alike, without any the slightest trouble and exertion, such as external and internal worship, suppression of the breath, and the like, these Máheśvaras set forth the system of recognition (*pratyabhijñá*). The extent of this system is thus described by one of their authorities—

> "The aphorisms, the commentary, the gloss, the two explications, the greater and the less,
> "The five topics, and the expositions,—such is the system of recognition."

The first aphorism in their text-book is as follows:[151]—

> "Having reached somehow or other the condition of a slave of Maheśvara, and wishing also to help mankind,
> "I set forth the recognition of Maheśvara, as the method of attaining all felicity."

[This aphorism may be developed as follows]:—

"Somehow or other," by a propitiation, effected by God, of the lotus feet of a spiritual director identical with God, "having reached," having fully attained, this condition, having made it the unintercepted object of fruition to myself. Thus knowing that which has to be known, he is qualified to construct a system for others: otherwise the system would be a mere imposture.

Maheśvara is the reality of unintermitted self-luminousness, beatitude, and independence, by portions of whose divine essence Vishṇu, Viriñchi, and other deities are deities, who, though they transcend the fictitious world, are yet implicated in the infinite illusion.

The condition of being a slave to Maheśvara is the being a recipient of that independence or absoluteness which is the essence of the divine nature, a slave being one to whom his lord grants all things according to his will and pleasure (*i.e.*, *dásya*, from *dá*).

The word *mankind* imports that there is no restriction of the doctrine to previously qualified students. Whoever he may be to whom this exposition of the divine nature is made, he reaps its highest reward, the emanatory *principium* itself operating to the highest end of the transmigrating souls. It has been accordingly laid down in theŚiva-dṛishṭi by that supreme guide the revered Sománandanátha—

> "When once the nature of Śiva that resides in all things has been known with tenacious recognition, whether by proof or by instruction in the words of a spiritual director,
>
> "There is no further need of doing aught, or of any further reflection. When he knows Suvarṇa (or Śiva) a man may cease to act and to reflect."

The word *also* excludes the supposition that there is room in self which has recognised the nature of Maheśvara, and which manifests to itself its own identity with him, and is therefore fully satisfied, for any other motive than felicity for others. The well-being of others is a motive, whatever may be said, for the definition of a motive applies to it: for there is no such divine curse laid upon man that self-regard should be his sole motive to the exclusion of a regard for others. Thus Akshapáda (i. 24) defines a motive: A motive is that object towards which a man energises.

The preposition *upa* in *upapádayami* (I set forth) indicates proximity: the result is the bringing of mankind near unto God.

Hence the word *all* in the phrase *the method of attaining all felicities*. For when the nature of the Supreme Being is attained, all felicities, which are but the efflux thereof, are overtaken, as if a man acquired the mountain Rohaṇa (Adam's Peak), he would acquire all the treasures it contains. If a man acquire the divine nature, what else is there that he can ask for? Accordingly Utpaláchárya says—

> "What more can they ask who are rich in the wealth of devotion? What else can they ask who are poor in this?"

We have thus explained the motive expressed in the words *the method of attaining all felicities*, on the supposition that the compound term is a

Tatpurusha genitively constructed. Let it be taken as a Bahuvríhi or relative compound. Then the recognition of Maheśvara, the knowing him through vicarious idols, has for its motive the full attainment, the manifestation, of all felicities, of every external and internal permanent happiness in their proper nature. In the language of everyday life, recognition is a cognition relative to an object represented in memory: for example, This (perceived) is the same (as the remembered) Chaitra. In the recognition propounded in this system,—there being a God whose omnipotence is learnt from the accredited legendaries, from accepted revelation, and from argumentation,—there arises in relation to my presented personal self the cognition that I am that very God,—in virtue of my recollection of the powers of that God.

This same recognition I set forth. To set forth is to enforce. I establish this recognition by a stringent process which renders it convincing. [Such is the articulate development of the first aphorism of the Recognitive Institutes.]

Here it may be asked: If soul is manifested only as consubstantial with God, why this laboured effort to exhibit the recognition? The answer is this:—The recognition is thus exhibited, because though the soul is, as you contend, continually manifested as self-luminous (and therefore identical with God), it is nevertheless under the influence of the cosmothetic illusion manifested as partial, and therefore the recognition must be exhibited by an expansion of the cognitive and active powers in order to achieve the manifestation of the soul as total (the self being to the natural man a part, to the man of insight the whole, of the divine pleroma). Thus, then, the syllogism: This self must be God, because it possesses cognitive and active powers; for so far forth as any one is cognitive and active, to that extent he is a lord, like a lord in the world of everyday life, or like a king, therefore the soul is God. The five-membered syllogism is here employed, because so long as we deal with the illusory order of things, the teaching of the Naiyáyikas may be accepted. It has thus been said by the son of Udayákara—

> "What self-luminous self can affirm or deny that self-active and cognitive is Maheśvara the primal being?
>
> "Such recognition must be effected by an expansion of the powers, the self being cognised under illusion, and imperfectly discerned."

And again—

> "The continuance of all living creatures in this transmigratory world lasts as long as their respiratory *involucrum*; knowledge and action are accounted the life of living creatures.

"Of these, knowledge is spontaneously developed, and action (or ritual), which is best at Káśi,

"Is indicated by others also: different from these is real knowledge."

And also—

"The knowledge of these things follows the sequence of those things:

"The knower, whose essence is beatitude and knowledge without succession, is Maheśvara."

Sománandanátha also says—

"He always knows by identity with Śiva: he always knows by identity with the real."

Again at the end of the section on knowledge—

"Unless there were this unity with Śiva, cognitions could not exist as facts of daily life:

"Unity with God is proved by the unity of light. He is the one knower (or illuminator of cognitions).

"He is Maheśvara, the great Lord, by reason of the unbroken continuity of objects:

"Pure knowledge and action are the playful activity of the deity."

The following is an explanation of Abhinava-gupta:—The text, "After that as it shines shines the all of things, by the light of that shines diversely this All," teaches that God illumines the whole round of things by the glory of His luminous intelligence, and that the diversity or plurality of the object world, whereby the light which irradiates objects is a blue, a yellow light, and the like, arises from diversity of tint cast upon the light by the object. In reality, God is without plurality or difference, as transcending all limitations of space, time, and figure. He is pure intelligence, self-luminousness, the manifester; and thus we may read in the Śaiva aphorisms, "Self is intelligence." His synonymous titles are Intelligential Essence, Unintermitted Cognition, Irrespective Intuition, Existence as a mass of Beatitude, Supreme Domination. This self-same existing self is knowledge.

By pure knowledge and action (in the passage of Sománandanátha cited above) are meant real or transcendent cognition and activity. Of these, the cognition is self-luminousness, the activity is energy constructive of the world or series of spheres of transmigratory experience. This is described in the section on activity—

"He by his power of bliss gives light unto these objects, through the efficacy of his will: this activity is creativeness."

And at the close of the same section—

> "The mere will of God, when he wills to become the world under its forms of jar, of cloth, and other objects, is his activity worked out by motive and agent.
>
> "This process of essence into emanation, whereby if this be that comes to be, cannot be attributed to motiveless, insentient things."

According to these principles, causality not pertaining either to the insentient or to the non-divine intelligence, the mere will of Maheśvara, the absolute Lord, when he wills to emanate into thousands of forms, as this or that difference, this or that action, this or that modification of entity, of birth, continuance, and the like, in the series of transmigratory environments,—his mere will is his progressively higher and higher activity, that is to say, his universal creativeness.

How he creates the world by his will alone is clearly exhibited in the following illustration—

> "The tree or jar produced by the mere will of thaumaturgists, without clay, without seed, continues to serve its proper purpose as tree or jar."

If clay and similar materials were really the substantial cause of the jar and the rest, how could they be produced by the mere volition of the thaumaturgist? If you say: Some jars and some plants are made of clay, and spring from seeds, while others arise from the bare volition of the thaumaturgist; then we should inform you that it is a fact notorious to all the world that *different* things must emanate from different materials.

As for those who say that a jar or the like cannot be made without materials to make it of, and that when a thaumaturgist makes one he does so by putting atoms in motion by his will, and so composing it: they may be informed that unless there is to be a palpable violation of the causal relation, *all* the co-efficients, without exception, must be desiderated; to make the jar there must be the clay, the potter's staff, the potter's wheel, and all the rest of it; to make a body there must be the congress of the male and female, and the successive results of that congress. Now, if that be the case, the genesis of a jar, a body, or the like, upon the mere volition of the thaumaturgist, would be hardly possible.

On the other hand, there is no difficulty in supposing that Mahádeva, amply free to remain within or to over-step any limit whatever, the Lord, manifold in his operancy, the intelligent principle, thus operates. Thus it is that Vasuguptácharya says—

> "To him that painted this world-picture without materials, without appliances, without a wall to paint it on,—to him be glory, to him resplendent with the lunar digit, to him that bears the trident."

It may be asked: If the supersensible self be no other than God, how comes this implication in successive transmigratory conditions? The answer is given in the section treating of accredited institution—

> "This agent of cognition, blinded by illusion, transmigrates through the fatality of works:
>
> "Taught his divine nature by science, as pure intelligence, he is enfranchised."

It may be asked: If the subject and the object are identical, what difference can there be between the self bound and the self liberated in regard to the objects cognisable by each? The answer to this question is given in a section of the Tattvártha-Saṅgraha—

> "Self liberated cognises all that is cognisable as identical with itself, like Maheśvara free from bondage: the other (or unliberated) self has in it infinite plurality."

An objection may be raised: If the divine nature is essential to the soul, there can be no occasion to seek for this recognition; for if all requisites be supplied, the seed does not fail to germinate because it is unrecognised. Why, then, this toilsome effort for the recognition of the soul? To such an objection we reply: Only listen to the secret we shall tell you. All activity about objects is of two degrees, being either external, as the activity of the seed in developing the plant, or internal, as the activity which determines felicity, which consists in an intuition which terminates in the conscious self. The first degree of activity presupposes no such recognition as the system proposes, the second does presuppose it. In the Recognitive System the peculiar activity is the exertion of the power of unifying personal and impersonal spirit, a power which is the attainment of the highest and of mediate ends, the activity consisting in the intuition I am God. To this activity a recognition of the essential nature of the soul is a pre-requisite.

It may be urged that peculiar activity terminating in the conscious self is observed independent of recognition. To this it is replied: A certain damsel, hearing of the many good qualities of a particular gallant, fell in love with him before she had seen him, and agitated by her passion and unable to suffer the pain of not seeing him, wrote to him a love-letter descriptive of her condition. He at once came to her, but when she saw him she did not recognise in him the qualities she had heard about; he appeared much the same as any other man, and she found no gratification in his society. So soon, however, as she recognised those qualities in him as her companions now pointed them out, she was fully gratified. In like manner, though the personal self be manifested as identical with the universal soul, its manifestation effects no complete satisfaction so long as there is no recognition of those attributes; but as soon as it is taught by a spiritual director to recognise in itself the perfections of Maheśvara, his omniscience, omnipotence, and other attributes, it attains the whole pleroma of being.

It is therefore said in the fourth section—

> "As the gallant standing before the damsel is disdained as like all other men, so long as he is unrecognised, though he humble himself before her with all manner of importunities: In like manner the personal self of mankind, though it be the universal soul, in which there is no perfection unrealised, attains not its own glorious nature; and therefore this recognition thereof must come into play."

This system has been treated in detail by Abhinava-gupta and other teachers, but as we have in hand a summary exposition of systems, we cannot extend the discussion of it any further lest our work become too prolix. This then may suffice.[152]

—A. E. G.

CHAPTER IX.

THE RASEŚVARA-DARŚANA OR MERCURIAL SYSTEM.[153]

Other Máheśvaras there are who, while they hold the identity of self with God, insist upon the tenet that the liberation in this life taught in all the systems depends upon the stability of the bodily frame, and therefore celebrate the virtues of mercury or quicksilver as a means of strengthening the system. Mercury is called *párada*, because it is a means of conveyance beyond the series of transmigratory states. Thus it has been said—

"It gives the farther shore of metempsychosis: it is called *párada*."

And again in the Rasárṇava—

"It is styled *párada* because it is employed for the highest end by the best votaries.

"Since this in sleep identical with me, goddess, arises from my members, and is the exudation of my body, it is called *rasa*."

It may be urged that the literal interpretation of these words is incorrect, the liberation in this life being explicable in another manner. This objection is not allowable, liberation being set out in the six systems as subsequent to the death of the body, and upon this there can be no reliance, and consequently no activity to attain to it free from misgivings. This is also laid down in the same treatise—

"Liberation is declared in the six systems to follow the death of the body.

"Such liberation is not cognised in perception like an emblic myrobalan fruit in the hand.

"Therefore a man should preserve that body by means of mercury and of medicaments."

Govinda-bhagavat also says—

"Holding that the enjoyments of wealth and of the body are not permanent, one should strive

"After emancipation; but emancipation results from knowledge, knowledge from study, and study is only possible in a healthy body."

The body, some one may say, is seen to be perishable, how can its permanency be effected? Think not so, it is replied, for though the body, as a complexus of six sheaths or wrappers of the soul, is dissoluble, yet the body, as created by Hara and Gaurí under the names of mercury and mica, may be perdurable. Thus it is said in the Rasahṛidaya—

> "They who, without quitting the body, have attained to a new body, the creation of Hara and Gaurí,
> "They are to be lauded, perfected by mercury, at whose service is the aggregate of magic texts."

The ascetic, therefore, who aspires to liberation in this life should first make to himself a glorified body. And inasmuch as mercury is produced by the creative conjunction of Hara and Gaurí, and mica is produced from Gaurí, mercury and mica are severally identified with Hara and Gaurí in the verse—

> "Mica is thy seed, and mercury is my seed;
> "The combination of the two, O goddess, is destructive of death and poverty."

This is very little to say about the matter. In the Raseśvara-siddhánta many among the gods, the Daityas, the Munis, and mankind, are declared to have attained to liberation in this life by acquiring a divine body through the efficacy of quicksilver.

> "Certain of the gods, Maheśa and others; certain Daityas,Śukra and others;
> "Certain Munis, the Bálakhilyas and others; certain kings, Someśvara and others;
> "Govinda-bhagavat, Govinda-náyaka,
> "Charvaṭi, Kapila, Vyáli, Kápáli, Kandaláyana,
> "These and many others proceed perfected, liberated while alive,
> "Having attained to a mercurial body, and therewith identified."

The meaning of this, as explicated by Parameśvara to Parameśvarí, is as follows:—

> "By the method of works is attained, O supreme of goddesses, the preservation of the body;
> "And the method of works is said to be twofold, mercury and air,
> "Mercury and air swooning carry off diseases, dead they restore to life,
> "Bound they give the power of flying about."

The swooning state of mercury is thus described—

> "They say quicksilver to be swooning when it is perceived, as characterised thus—
> "Of various colours, and free from excessive volatility.

"A man should regard that quicksilver as dead, in which the following marks are seen—

"Wetness, thickness, brightness, heaviness, mobility."

The bound condition is described in another place as follows:—

"The character of bound quicksilver is that it is—

"Continuous, fluent, luminous, pure, heavy, and that it parts asunder under friction."

Some one may urge: If the creation of mercury by Hara and Gaurí were proved, it might be allowed that the body could be made permanent; but how can that be proved? The objection is not allowable, inasmuch as that *can* be proved by the eighteen modes of elaboration. Thus it is stated by the authorities—

"Eighteen modes of elaboration are to be carefully discriminated,

"In the first place, as pure in every process, for perfecting the adepts."

And these modes of elaboration are enumerated thus—

"Sweating, rubbing, swooning, fixing, dropping, coercion, restraining,

"Kindling, going, falling into globules, pulverising, covering,

"Internal flux, external flux, burning, colouring, and pouring,

"And eating it by parting and piercing it,—are the eighteen modes of treating quicksilver."

These treatments have been described at length by Govinda-bhagavat, Sarvajña-rámeśvara and the other ancient authorities, and are here omitted to avoid prolixity.

The mercurial system is not to be looked upon as merely eulogistic of the metal, it being immediately, through the conservation of the body, a means to the highest end, liberation. Thus it is said in the Rasárṇava—

"Declare to me, O god, that supremely efficacious destruction of the blood, that destruction of the body, imparted by thee, whereby it attained the power of flying about in the sky. Goddess (he replied), quicksilver is to be applied both to the blood and to the body. This makes the appearance of body and blood alike. A man should first try it upon the blood, and then apply it to the body."

It will be asked: Why should we make this effort to acquire a celestial body, seeing that liberation is effected by the self-manifestation of the supreme principle, existence, intelligence, and beatitude? We reply: This is no objection, such liberation being inaccessible unless we acquire a healthy body. Thus it is said in the Rasahṛidaya—

"That intelligence and bliss set forth in all the systems in which a multitude of uncertainties are melted away,

"Though it manifest itself, what can it effect for beings whose bodies are unglorified?

"He who is worn out with decrepitude, though he be free from cough, from asthma, and similar infirmities,

"He is not qualified for meditation in whom the activities of the cognitive organs are obstructed.

"A youth of sixteen addicted to the last degree to the enjoyment of sensual pleasures,

"An old man in his dotage, how should either of these attain to emancipation?"

Some one will object: It is the nature of the personal soul to pass through a series of embodiments, and to be liberated is to be extricated from that series of embodiments; how, then, can these two mutually exclusive conditions pertain to the same bodily tenement? The objection is invalid, as unable to stand before the following dilemmatic argument:—Is this extrication, as to the nature of which all the founders of institutes are at one, to be held as cognisable or as incognisable? If it is incognisable, it is a pure chimera; if it is cognisable, we cannot dispense with life, for that which is not alive cannot be cognisant of it. Thus it is said in the Rasasiddhánta—

"The liberation of the personal soul is declared in the mercurial system, O subtile thinker.

"In the tenets of other schools which repose on a diversity of argument,

"Know that this knowledge and knowable is allowed in all sacred texts;

"One not living cannot know the knowable, and therefore there is and must be life."

And this is not to be supposed to be unprecedented, for the adherents of the doctrine of Vishṇu-svámin maintain the eternity of the body of Vishṇu half-man and half-lion. Thus it is said in the Sákára-siddhi—

"I glorify the man-lion set forth by Vishṇu-svámin,

"Whose only body is existence, intelligence, and eternal and inconceivably perfect beatitude."

If the objection be raised that the body of the man-lion, which appears as composite and as coloured, is incompatible with real existence, it may be replied: How can the body of the man-lion be otherwise than really existent, proved as it is by three kinds of proof: (1.) by the intuition of Śanaka and others; (2.) by Vedic texts such as, A thousand heads has Purusha; and (3.) by Puráṇic texts such as, That wondrous child, lotus-eyed, four-armed, armed with the conch-shell, the club, and other weapons? Real existence and other like predicates are affirmed also by Śríkánta-miśra, the devoted adherent of Vishṇu-svámin. Let, then, those who aspire to the highest end of personal souls be assured that the eternity of the body which we are setting forth is by no means a mere innovation. It has thus been said—

"What higher beatitude is there than a body undecaying, immortal,
"The repository of sciences, the root of merit, riches, pleasure, liberation?"

It is mercury alone that can make the body undecaying and immortal, as it is said—

"Only this supreme medicament can make the body undecaying and imperishable."

Why describe the efficacy of this metal? Its value is proved even by seeing it, and by touching it, as it is said in the Rasárṇava—

"From seeing it, from touching it, from eating it, from merely remembering it,
"From worshipping it, from tasting it, from imparting it, appear its six virtues.
"Equal merit accrues from seeing mercury as accrues from seeing all the phallic emblems
"On earth, those at Kedára, and all others whatsoever."

In another place we read—

"The adoration of the sacred quicksilver is more beatific than the worship of all the phallic emblems at Káśi and elsewhere,
"Inasmuch as there is attained thereby enjoyment, health, exemption from decay, and immortality."

The sin of disparaging mercury is also set out—

"The adept on hearing quicksilver heedlessly disparaged should recall quicksilver to mind.
"He should at once shun the blasphemer, who is by his blasphemy for ever filled with sin."

The attainment, then, of the highest end of the personal soul takes place by an intuition of the highest principle by means of the practice of union (ἕνωσις after the acquisition of a divine body in the manner we have described. Thereafter—

"The light of pure intelligence shines forth unto certain men of holy vision,

"Which, seated between the two eyebrows, illumines the universe, like fire, or lightning, or the sun:

"Perfect beatitude, unalloyed, absolute, the essence whereof is luminousness, undifferenced,

"From which all troubles are fallen away, knowable, tranquil, self-recognised:

"Fixing the internal organ upon that, seeing the whole universe manifested, made of pure intelligence,

"The aspirant even in this life attains to the absolute, his bondage to works annulled."

A Vedic text also declares: That is Rasa (mercury), having obtained this he becomes beatitude.

Thus, then, it has been shown that mercury alone is the means of passing beyond the burden of transmigratory pains. And conformably we have a verse which sets forth the identity between mercury and the supreme self—

"May that mercury, which is the very self, preserve us from dejection and from the terrors of metempsychosis,

"Which is naturally to be applied again and again by those that aspire to liberation from the enveloping illusion,

"Which perfected endures, which plays not again when the soul awakes,

"Which, when it arises, pains no other soul, which shines forth by itself from itself."

—A. E. G.

CHAPTER X.

THE VAIŚESHIKA OR AULÚKYA DARŚANA.[154]

Whoso wishes to escape the reality of pain, which is established by the consciousness of every soul through its being felt to be essentially contrary to every rational being, and wishes therefore to know the means of such escape,—learns that the knowledge of the Supreme Being is the true means thereof, from the authority of such passages as these (*Śvetáśvatara Upan*. vi. 20)—

> "When men shall roll up the sky as a piece of leather,
> "Then shall there be an end of pain without the knowledge ofŚiva."

Now the knowledge of the Supreme is to be gained by hearing (*śravaṇa*), thought (*manana*), and reflection (*bhávaná*), as it has been said—

> "By scripture, by inference, and by the force of repeated meditation,—
> "By these three methods producing knowledge, he gains the highest union (*yoga*)."

Here thought depends on inference, and inference depends on the knowledge of the *vyápti* (or universal proposition), and the knowledge of the *vyápti* follows the right understanding of the categories,—hence the saint Kaṇáda[155] establishes the six categories in his tenfold treatise, commencing with the words, "Now, therefore, we shall explain duty."

In the first book, consisting of two daily lessons, he describes all the categories which are capable of intimate relation. In the first*áhnika* he defines those which possess "genus" (*játi*), in the second "genus" (or "generality") itself and "particularity." In the similarly divided second book he discusses "substance," giving in the first *áhnika* the characteristics of the five elements, and in the second he establishes the existence of space and time. In the third book he defines the soul and the internal sense, the former in the first *áhnika*, the latter in the second. In the fourth book he discusses the body and its adjuncts, the latter in the first *áhnika*, and the former in the second. In the fifth book he investigates action; in the first *áhnika* he considers action as connected with the body, in the second as belonging to the mind. In the sixth book he examines merit and demerit as revealed in Śruti; in the first *áhnika* he discusses the merit of giving, receiving gifts, &c., in the second the duties of the four periods of religious life. In the seventh book he discusses quality and intimate relation; in the first *áhnika* he considers the qualities independent of thought, in the second those qualities which are related to it, and also intimate relation. In the eighth book he examines "indeterminate" and "determinate" perception, and means of proof. In the ninth book he discusses the characteristics of intellect. In the tenth book he establishes the different kinds of inference.[156]

The method of this system is said to be threefold, "enunciation," "definition," and "investigation."[157] "But," it may be objected, "ought we not to include 'division,' and so make the method fourfold, not threefold?" We demur to this, because "division" is really included in a particular kind of enunciation. Thus when we declare that substance, quality, action, generality, particularity, and intimate relation are the only six positive categories,—this is an example of enunciation. If you ask "What is the reason for this definite order of the categories?" we answer as follows:—Since "substance" is the chief, as being the substratum of all the categories, we enounce this first; next "quality," since it resides in its generic character in all substances [though different substances have different qualities]; then "action," as it agrees with "substance" and "quality" in possessing "generality;"[158] then "generality," as residing in these three; then "particularity," inasmuch as it possesses "intimate relation;"[159] lastly, "intimate relation" itself; such is the principle of arrangement.

If you ask, "Why do you say that there are only six categories since 'non-existence' is also one?" we answer: Because we wish to speak of the six as positive categories, *i.e.*, as being the objects of conceptions which do not involve a negative idea. "Still," the objector may retort, "how do you establish this definite number 'only six'? for either horn of the alternative fails. For, we ask, is the thing to be thus excluded already thoroughly ascertained or not? If it is thoroughly ascertained, why do you exclude it? and still more so, if it is not thoroughly ascertained? What sensible man, pray, spends his strength in denying that a mouse has horns? Thus your definite number 'only six' fails as being inapplicable." This, however, we cannot admit; if darkness, &c., are allowed to form certainly a seventh category (as "non-existence"), we thus (by our definite number) deny it to be one of the six *positive* categories,—and if others attempt to include "capacity," "number," &c., which we allow to be certainly positive existences, we thus deny that they make a *seventh* category. But enough of this long discussion.

Substantiality, &c. (*dravyatvádi*), *i.e.*, the genera of substance, quality, and action, are the definition of the triad substance, quality, and action respectively. The genus of substance (*dravyatva*) is that which, while it alike exists with intimate relation in the (eternal) sky and the (transitory) lotus, is itself eternal,[160] and does not exist with intimate relation in smell.[161]

The genus of quality (*guṇatva*) is that which is immediately subordinate to the genus existence, and exists with intimate relation in whatever is not an intimate or mediate cause.[162] The genus of action (*karmatva*) is that which is immediately subordinate to the genus existence, and is not found with intimate relation in anything eternal.[163] Generality (or genus, *sámánya*) is that which is found in many things with intimate relation, and can never be the counter-entity to emergent non-existence.[164] Particularity[165] (*viśesha*) exists with intimate relation, but it is destitute of generality, which stops mutual non-existence.[166] Intimate relation (*samaváya*) is that connection which itself has not intimate relation.[167] Such are the definitions of the six categories.

Substance is ninefold,—earth, water, fire, air, ether, time, space, soul, and mind. The genera of earth, &c. (*pṛithivítva*), are the definitions of the first four. The genus of earth is that generality which is immediately subordinate to substance, and resides in the same subject with colour produced by baking.[168]

The genus of water is that generality which is found with intimate relation in water, being also found in intimate relation in river and sea. The genus of fire is that generality which is found with intimate relation in fire, being also found with intimate relation in the moon and gold. The genus of air is that which is immediately subordinate to substance, and is found with intimate relation in the organ of the skin.[169]

As ether, space, and time, from their being single, cannot be subordinate genera, their several names stand respectively for their technical appellations. Ether is the abode of particularity, and is found in the same subject with the non-eternal (*janya*) special quality which is not produced by contact.[170]

Time is that which, being a pervading substance, is the abode of the mediate cause[171] of that idea of remoteness (*paratva*) which is not found with intimate relation in space;[172] while space is that pervading substance which possesses no special qualities and yet is not time.[173] The general terms *átmatva* and *manastva* are the respective definitions of soul (*átman*) and mind (*manas*). The general idea of soul is that which is subordinate to substance, being also found with intimate relation in that which is without form[174] (*amúrtta*). The general idea of mind is that which is subordinate to substance, being also found existing with intimate relation in an atom, but [unlike other atoms] not the intimate cause of any substance. There are twenty-four qualities; seventeen are mentioned directly in Kaṇáda's Sútras (i. 1, 6), "colour, taste, smell, touch, number, quantity, severalty, conjunction, disjunction, remoteness, proximity, intelligence, pleasure, pain, desire, aversion, and effort;" and, besides these, seven others are understood in the word "*and*," viz., gravity, fluidity, viscidity, faculty, merit, demerit, and sound. Their respective genera (*rúpatva*, &c.) are their several definitions. The class or genus of "colour" is that which is subordinate to quality and exists with intimate relation in blue. In the same way may be formed the definitions of the rest.

"Action" is fivefold, according to the distinction of throwing upwards, throwing downwards, contracting, expanding, and going: revolution, evacuating, &c., being included under "going." The genus of throwing upwards, &c., will be their respective definitions. The genus of throwing upwards is a subordinate genus to action; it exists with intimate relation, and is to be known as the mediate cause of conjunction with a higher place. In the same manner are to be made the definitions of throwing downwards, &c. Generality (or genus) is twofold, extensive and non-extensive; existence is extensive as found with intimate connection in substance and quality, or in quality and action; substance, &c., are non-extensive. The definition of generality has been given before. Particularity and intimate relation cannot be divided,—in the former case in consequence of the infinite number of separate particularities, in the latter from intimate relation being but one; their definitions have been given before.

There is a popular proverb—

"Duality, change produced by baking, and disjunction produced by disjunction,—he whose mind vacillates not in these three is the true Vaiśeshika;" and therefore we will now show the manner of the production of duality, &c.

There is here first the contact of the organ of sense with the object; thence there arises the knowledge of the genus unity; then the distinguishing perception *apekshábuddhi* [by which we apprehend "this is one," "this is one," &c.]; then the production of duality, *dvitva*(in the object);[175] then the knowledge of the abstract genus of duality (*dvitvatva*); then the knowledge of the quality duality as it exists in the two things; then imagination[176] (*saṃskára*).[177]

But it may here be asked what is the proof of duality, &c., being thus produced from *apekshábuddhi*? The great doctor (Udayana) maintained that *apekshábuddhi* must be the producer of duality, &c., because duality is never found separated from it, while, at the same time, we cannot hold *apekshábuddhi* as the cause only of its being known [and therefore it follows that it must be the cause of its being produced[178]], just as contact is with regard to sound. We, however, maintain the same opinion by a different argument; duality, &c., cannot be held to be made known (*jñápya*) by that non-eternal apprehension whose object is two or more individual unities (*i.e.,apekshábuddhi*), because these are qualities which reside in a plurality of subjects [and not in any one individual[179]] just as "severalty" does [and, therefore, as *apekshábuddhi* is not their*jñápaka*, it must be their *janaka*].

Next we will describe the order of the successive destructions. From *apekshábuddhi* arises, simultaneously with the production of duality (*dvitva*), the destruction of the knowledge of the genus of unity; next from the knowledge of the genus of duality (*dvitvatva*) arises, simultaneously with the knowledge of the quality duality, the destruction of *apekshábuddhi*; next from the destruction of*apekshábuddhi* arises, simultaneously with the knowledge of the two substances, the destruction of the duality; next from the knowledge of the two substances arises, simultaneously with the production of imagination (*saṃskára*), the destruction of the knowledge of the quality; and next from imagination arises the destruction of the knowledge of the substances.

The evidence for the destruction of one kind of knowledge by another, and for the destruction of another knowledge by imagination, is to be found in the following argument; these knowledges themselves which are the subjects of the discussion *are* successively destroyed by the rise of others produced from them, because knowledge, like sound, is a special quality of an all-pervading substance, and of momentary duration.[180] I may briefly add, that when you have the knowledge of the genus of unity simultaneously with an action in one of the two things themselves, producing that separation which is the opposite to the conjunction that produced the whole, in that case you have the subsequent destruction of duality produced by the destruction of its abiding-place (the two things); but where you have this separate action taking place simultaneously with the rise of *apekshábuddhi*, there you have the destruction of duality produced by the united influence of both.[181]

Apekshábuddhi is to be considered as that operation of the mind which is the counter-entity to that emergent non-existence (*i.e.*, destruction) which itself causes a subsequent destruction.[182]

Next we will inquire in how many moments, commencing with the destruction of the compound of two atoms (the *dvyaṇuka*), another compound of two atoms is produced, having colour, &c. In the course of this investigation the mode of production will be explained. First, the compound of two atoms is gradually destroyed by the series of steps commencing with the contact of fire;[183] secondly, from the conjunction of fire arises the destruction of the qualities black,& c., in the single atom; thirdly, from another conjunction of fire arises the production of red, &c., in the atom; fourthly, from conjunction with a soul possessing merit arises an action[184] in the atom for the production of a substance; fifthly, by that action is produced a separation of that atom from its former place; sixthly, there is produced thereby the destruction of its conjunction with that former place; seventhly, is produced the conjunction with another atom; eighthly, from these two atoms arises the compound of two atoms; ninthly, from the qualities, &c., of the causes (*i.e.*, the atoms) are produced colour, &c., the qualities of the effect (*i.e.*, the*dvyaṇuka*). Such is the order of the series of nine moments. The other two series,[185] that of the ten and that of the eleven moments, are omitted for fear of prolixity. Such is the mode of production, if we hold (with the Vaiśeshikas) that the baking process takes place in the atoms of the jar.[186] The Naiyáyikas, however, maintain that the baking process takes place in the jar.

"Disjunction produced by disjunction" is twofold,—that produced by the disjunction of the intimate [or material] causes only, and that produced by the disjunction of the intimate cause and the non-cause [*i.e.*, the place]. We will first describe the former kind.

It is a fixed rule that when the action of breaking arises in the [material] cause which is inseparably connected with the effect [*i.e.*, in one of the two halves of the pot], and produces a disjunction from the other half, there is not produced at that time a disjunction from the place or point of space occupied by the pot; and, again, when there is a disjunction from that point of space occupied by the pot, the disjunction from the other half is not contemporary with it, but has already taken place. For just as we never see smoke without its cause, fire, so we never see that effect of the breaking in the pot which we call the disjunction from the point of space,[187] without there having previously been the origination of that disjunction of the halves which stops the conjunction whereby the pot was brought into being. Therefore the action of breaking in the parts produces the disjunction of one part from another, but not the disjunction from the point of space; next, this disjunction of one part from another produces the destruction of that conjunction which had brought the pot into existence; and thence arises the destruction of the pot, according to the principle, *cessante causâ cessat effectus*. The pot being thus destroyed, that disjunction, which resides in both the halves (which are the material or intimate causes of the pot) during the time that is marked by the destruction of the pot or perhaps having reference only to one independent half, initiates, in the case of that half where the breaking began, a disjunction from the point of space which had been connected with the pot; but not in the case of the other half, as there is no cause to produce it.[188]

But the second kind is as follows:—As action which arises in the hand, and causes a disjunction from that with which it was in contact, initiates a disjunction[189] from the points of space in which the original conjunction took place; and this is "the disjunction of the intimate cause and the non-cause." When the action in the hand produces an effect in relation to any points of space, it initiates also in the same direction a disjunction of the intimate effect and the non-effect; thus the disjunction of the body [the intimate effect] and the points of space arises from the disjunction of the hand and the points of space [the hand being an intimate or material cause of the body, but the points of space being not a cause]. This second disjunction is not produced by the action of the body, because the body is supposed to be at the time inactive; nor is it produced by the action of the hand, because it is impossible that an action residing in some other place [as the hand] should produce the effect of disjunction [in the body]. Therefore we conclude by exhaustion that we must accept the view—that it is the disjunction of the intimate cause and the non-cause[190] which causes the second disjunction of the body and the points of space.

But an opponent may here object that "what you formerly stated (p. 147) as to existence being denied of darkness, &c., is surely unreasonable; for, in fact, there are no less than four different opinions maintained on this point,—thus (*a.*) the Bháṭṭa Mímáṃsakas and the Vedántins hold that darkness is a substance; (*b.*) Śrídhara Áchárya[191] holds that the colour of dark blue is imposed [and thus darkness will be a quality]; (*c.*) some of the Prábhákara Mímáṃsakas hold that it is the absence of the cognition of light; (*d.*) the Naiyáyikas, &c., hold that it is the absence of light." In reply, we assert that as for the first alleged opinion (*a.*) it is quite out of the question, as it is consistent with neither of the two possible alternatives; for if darkness is a substance, it must either be one of the nine well-known substances, earth, &c.,[192] or some different one. But it cannot be any one of the nine, since, under whichever one you would place it, all the qualities of that substance should certainly be found in it; nor can you, on the other hand, assert that it is some substance different from these nine, since, being in itself destitute of qualities, it cannot properly be a substance at all [the very definition of substance being "that which is the substratum of qualities"], and therefore, of course, it cannot be a different substance from the nine. But you may ask, "How can you say that darkness is destitute of qualities, when it is perceived as possessed of the dark blue of the tamála blossom?" We reply, that this is merely an error, as when men say that the [colourless] sky is blue. But enough of this onslaught on ancient sages.[193] (*b.*) Hence it follows that darkness cannot have its colour imposed upon it, since you cannot have an imposition of colour without supposing some substratum to receive it;[194] and again, we cannot conceive the eye as capable of imposing a colour when deprived of the concurrent cause, the external light. Nor can we accept that it is an impression independent of the eye [*i.e.*, produced by the internal sense, mind], because the concurrence of the eye is not a superfluous but an indispensable condition to its being produced. Nor can you maintain that "absence or non-existence (*abháva*[195]) is incapable of being expressed by affirmative tense affixes [and, therefore, as we *do* use such phrases as *tenebræ oriuntur*, darkness cannot be a mere non-existence"]; because your assertion is too broad, as it would include such cases of non-existence as a mundane collapse, destruction, inattention,[196] &c. [and yet we all know that men do speak of any of these things as past, present, or future, and yet all are cases of *abháva*]. (*c.*) Hence darkness cannot be the absence of the cognition of light, since, by the well-known rule that that organ which perceives a certain object can also perceive its absence, it would follow that darkness would be perceived by the mind [since it is the mind which perceives cognitions].[197] Hence we conclude that the fourth or remaining opinion must be the true one, viz., that darkness is only the absence of light. And it need not be objected that it is very difficult to account for the attribution to non-existence of the qualities of existence, for we all see that the quality happiness *is*attributed to the absence of pain, and the idea of separation is connected with the absence of conjunction. And you need not assert that "this absence of light must be the object of a cognition produced by the eye in dependence on light, since it is the absence of an object possessing colour,[198] as we see in the case of a jar's absence," because by the very rule on which you rely, viz., that that on which the eye depends to perceive an object, it must also depend on to perceive that object's absence, it follows that as there is no dependence of the eye on light to perceive light, it need not depend thereon to perceive this light's absence. Nor need our opponent retort that "the cognition of darkness [as the absence of light] necessitates the cognition of the place where the absence resides [and *this* will require light]," as such an assertion is quite untenable, for we cannot admit that in order to have a conception of absence it is necessary to have a conception of the place where the absence resides, else we could not have the perception of the cessation of sound, as is implied in such an expression as "the tumult has ceased."[199] Hence, having all these difficulties in his mind, the venerable Kaṇáda uttered his aphorism [as an *ipse dixit* to settle the question]: "*Dravya-guṇa-karma-nish-patti-vaidharmyád abhávas tamas*" (*Vaiś. Sút.* v. 2, 19), "Darkness is really non-existence, since it is dissimilar to the production of substances, qualities, or actions." The same thing has been also established by the argument that darkness is perceived by the eye[200] [without light, whereas all substances, if perceptible at all, require the presence of light as well as of the eye to be visible].

Non-existence (*abháva*) is considered to be the seventh category, as established by negative proofs. It may be concisely defined as that which, itself not having intimate relation, is *not* intimate relation;[201] and this is twofold, "relative non-existence"[202] and "reciprocal non-existence."

The former is again divided into "antecedent," "emergent," and "absolute." "Antecedent" is that non-existence which, though without any beginning, is not everlasting; "emergent" is that which, though having a beginning, is everlasting; "absolute" is that non-existence which abides in its own counter-entity;[203] "reciprocal non-existence" is that which, being different from "absolute," has yet no defined limit [*i.e.*, no *terminus ad quem* nor *terminus a quo*, as "antecedent" and "emergent" have].

If you raise the objection that "'reciprocal non-existence' is really the same as 'absolute non-existence,'" we reply that this is indeed to lose one's way in the king's highroad; for "reciprocal non-existence" is that negation whose opposite is held to be identity, as "a jar is not cloth;" but "absolute non-existence" is that negation whose opposite is connection, as "there is no colour in the air."[204] Nor need you here raise the objection that "*abháva* can never be a means of producing any good to man," for we maintain that it is his *summum bonum*, in the form of final beatitude, which is only another term for the absolute abolition of all pain [and therefore comes under the category of *abháva*].

—E. B. C.

CHAPTER XI.

THE AKSHAPÁDA (OR NYÁYA) DARŚANA.

The principle that final bliss, *i.e.*, the absolute abolition of pain, arises from the knowledge of the truth [though in a certain sense universally accepted], is established in a special sense as a particular tenet[205] of the Nyáya school, as is declared by the author of the aphorisms in the words "proof, that which is to be proved, &c.,—from knowledge of the truth as to these things there is the attainment of final bliss." This is the first aphorism of the Nyáya Śástra. Now the Nyáya Śástra consists of five books, and each book contains two "daily portions." In the first daily portion of the first book the venerable Gotama discusses the definitions of nine categories, beginning with "proof," and in the second those of the remaining seven, beginning with "discussion" (*váda*). In the first daily portion of the second book he examines "doubt," discusses the four kinds of "proof," and refutes the suggested objections to their being instruments of right knowledge; and in the second he shows that "presumption," &c., are really included in the four kinds of "proof" already given [and therefore need not be added by the Mímáṃsakas as separate ones]. In the first daily portion of the third book he examines the soul, the body, the senses, and their objects; in the second, "understanding" (*buddhi*), and "mind" (*manas*). In the first daily portion of the fourth book he examines "volition" (*pravṛitti*), the "faults," "transmigration," "fruit" [of actions], "pain," and "final liberation;" in the second he investigates the truth[206] as to the causes of the "faults," and also "wholes" and "parts." In the first daily portion of the fifth book he discusses the various kinds of futility (*játi*), and in the second the various kinds of "occasion for rebuke" (*nigrahasthána*, or "unfitness to be argued with").

In accordance with the principle that "to know the thing to be measured you must first know the measure," "proof" (*pramáṇa*) is first enunciated, and as this must be done by defining it, we have first a definition of "proof." "Proof" is that which is always accompanied by right knowledge, and is at the same time not disjoined from the proper instruments [as the eye, &c.], and from the site of knowledge [*i.e.*, the soul];[207] and this definition thus includes the peculiar tenet of the Nyáya School that God is a source of right knowledge,[208] as the author of the aphorisms has expressly declared (ii. 68), "and the fact of the Veda's being a cause of right knowledge, like spells and the medical science, follows from the fact that the fit one who gave the Veda was a source of right knowledge." And thus too hath the universally renowned teacher Udayana, who saw to the farthest shore of the ocean of logic, declared in the fourth chapter of the Kusumáñjali:

"Right knowledge is accurate comprehension, and right knowing is the possession thereof; authoritativeness is, according to Gotama's school, the being separated from all absence thereof.

"He in whose intuitive unerring perception, inseparably united to Him and dependent on no foreign inlets, the succession of all the various existing objects is contained,—all the chaff of our suspicion being swept away by the removal of all possible faults as caused by the slightest want of observation in Him,—He, Śiva, is my authority; what have I to do with others, darkened as their authority must ever be with rising doubts?"

"Proof" is fourfold, as being divided into perception, inference, analogy, and testimony. The "thing to be proved" [or the "object of right notion"] is of twelve kinds, viz., soul, body, the senses, their objects, understanding, mind, volition, faults, transmigrations, fruit, pain, and final liberation. "Doubt" is a knowledge whose nature is uncertainty; and this is threefold, as being caused by the object's possessing only qualities which are common to other things also, and therefore not distinctive,—or by its possessing only irrelevant qualities of its own, which do not help us in determining the particular point in question,[209]—or by conflicting testimony. The thing which one proposes to one's self before proceeding to act, is "a motive" (*prayojana*); this is twofold, *i.e.*, visible and invisible. "An example" is a fact brought forward as a ground for establishing a general principle, and it may be either affirmative or negative.[210] A "tenet" (*siddhánta*) is something which is accepted as being authoritatively settled as true; it is of four kinds, as being "common to all the schools," "peculiar to one school," "a pregnant assumption" [leading, if conceded, to a further conclusion], and "an implied dogma" (i. 26-31). The "member" (of a demonstration) is a part of the sentence containing an inference for the sake of another; and these are five, the proposition, the reason, the example, the application, and the conclusion (i. 32-38). "Confutation" (*tarka*, i. 39) is the showing that the admission of a false minor necessitates the admission of a false major[211] (cf. Sút. i. 39, and iv. 3); and this is of eleven kinds, as *vyágháta*, *átmáśraya*, *itaretaráśraya*, &c.

"Ascertainment" (*nirṇaya*, i. 40) is right knowledge or a perception of the real state of the case. It is of four kinds as produced by perception, inference, analogy, or testimony. "Discussion" (*váda*) is a particular kind of conversation, having as its end the ascertainment of truth (i. 41). "Wrangling" (*jalpa*) is the talk of a man only wishing for victory, who is ready to employ arguments for either side of the question (i. 42). "Cavilling" (*vitaṇḍá*) is the talk of a man who does not attempt to establish his own side of the question (i. 43). "Dialogue" (*kathá*) is the taking of two opposite sides by two disputants. A "fallacy" is an inconclusive reason which is supposed to prove something, and this may be of five kinds, the "erratic," the "contradictory," the "uncertain," the "unproved," and the "precluded" or "mistimed" (Sút. i. 44-49). "Unfairness" (*chhala*) is the bringing forward a contrary argument by using a term wilfully in an ambiguous sense; this is of three kinds, as there may be fraud in respect of a term, the meaning, or a metaphorical phrase (i. 50-54). "Futility" (*játi*) is a self-destructive argument (i. 58). This is of twenty-four kinds (as described in the fifth book of the Nyáya aphorisms) (1-38). "Occasion for rebuke" is where the disputant loses his cause [by stupidity], and this is of twenty-two kinds (as described in the fifth book of the aphorisms, 44-67). We do not insert here all the minute subdivisions through fear of being too prolix,—they are fully explained in the aphorisms.

But here an objector may say, "If these sixteen topics, proof, &c., are all thus fully discussed, how is it that it has received the name of the Nyáya Śástra, [as reasoning, *i.e.*, *Nyáya*, or logic, properly forms only a small part of the topics which it treats of?]" We allow the force of the objection; still as names are proverbially said to be given for some special reason, we maintain that the name Nyáya was rightly applied to Gotama's system, since "reasoning," or inference for the sake of another, is justly held to be a predominant feature from its usefulness in all kinds of knowledge, and from its being a necessary means for every kind of pursuit. So it has been said by Sarvajña, "This is the pre-eminent science of Nyáya from its establishing our doctrines against opponents, and from its producing action;"[212] and by Pakshila Swámin, "This is the science of reasoning (*ánvíkshikí*) divided into the different categories, 'proof,' &c.; the lamp of all sciences, the means for aiding all actions, the ultimate appeal of all religious duties, well proved in the declarations of science."[213]

But here an objector may say, "When you declare that final liberation arises from the knowledge of the truth, do you mean that liberation ensues immediately upon this knowledge being attained?" We reply, "No," for it is said in the second Nyáya aphorism, "Pain, birth, activity, faults, false notions,—on the successive annihilation of these in turn, there is the annihilation of the one next before it," by means of this knowledge of the truth. Now false notions are the thinking the body, &c., which are not the soul, to be the soul; "faults" are a desire for those things which seem agreeable to the soul, and a dislike to those things which seem disagreeable to it,[214] though in reality nothing is either agreeable or disagreeable to the soul. And through the mutual reaction of these different "faults" the stupid man desires and the desiring man is stupid; the stupid man is angry, and the angry man is stupid. Moreover the man, impelled by these faults, does those things which are forbidden: thus by the body he does injury, theft, &c.; by the voice, falsehood, &c.; by the mind, malevolence, &c.; and this same sinful "activity" produces demerit. Or, again, he may do laudable actions by his body, as alms, saving others, &c., truthful speaking, upright counsel, &c., by his voice, and guilelessness, &c., by his mind; and this same right activity produces merit. But both are forms of activity, and each leads to a similar laudable or blamable birth or bodily manifestation; and while this birth lasts there arises the impression of "pain," which we are conscious of as of something that jars against us. Now this series, beginning with "false notions" and ending with "pain," is continually going on, and is what we mean by the words "mundane existence," which rolls on ceaselessly, like a waterwheel. And whenever some pre-eminent man, by the force of his previous good deeds, obtains through the teaching of a great teacher the knowledge that all this present life is only a scene of pain and bound up with pain, he recognises that it is all to be avoided, and desires to abolish the ignorance, &c., which are the causes that produced it.[215] Then he learns that the one means to abolish it is the knowledge of the truth; and as he meditates on the objects of right knowledge divided into the four sciences,[216] there arises in his mind the knowledge of the truth, or, in other words, a right view of things as they are; and from this knowledge of the truth false notions disappear. When false notions disappear, the "faults" pass away; with them ceases "activity;" and with it ceases "birth;" and with the cessation of "birth" comes the entire abolition of "pain," and this absolute abolition is final bliss. Its absoluteness consists in this, that nothing similar to that which is thus abolished can ever revive, as is expressly said in the second aphorism of the Nyáya Sútras: "Pain, birth, activity, faults, false notions,—since, on the successive annihilation of these in turn, there is the annihilation of the one next before it, there is [on the annihilation of the last of them] final beatitude."

"But is not your definition of the *summum bonum*, liberation, *i.e.*, 'the absolute abolition of pain,' after all as much beyond our reach as treacle on the elbow is to the tongue;[217] why then is this continually put forth as if it were established beyond all dispute?" We reply that as all those who maintain liberation in any form do include therein the absolute abolition of pain, our definition, as being thus a tenet accepted in all the schools, may well be called the royal highway[218] of philosophy. No one, in fact, maintains that pain is possible without the individual's activity. Thus even the Mádhyamika's opinion that "liberation consists in the abolition of soul," does not controvert our point, so far at any rate as that it is the abolition of pain. But if you proceed to argue that the soul, as being the cause of pain, is to be abolished just like the body, &c., we reply that this does not hold, since it fails under either alternative. For do you mean by "the soul," (*a.*) the continued succession of cognitions, or (*b.*) something different therefrom? (*a.*) If the former, we make no objection, [since we Naiyáyikas allow that cognition is evanescent,[219] and we do desire to abolish cognition as a cause of *pravṛitti* or action[220]], for who would oppose a view which makes for his own side? (*b.*) But if the latter, then, since it must be eternal,[221] its abolition is impossible; and, again, a second objection would be that no one would try to gain your supposed "*summum bonum*;" for surely no sensible person would strive to annihilate the soul, which is always the dearest of all, on the principle that "everything else is dear for the soul's pleasure;" and, again, everybody uses such a phrase as "liberated," [and this very term refutes the idea of annihilation or abolition].

"But why not say with those Bauddhas who hold the doctrine of pure intelligence [*i.e.*, the Yogácháras and the Sautrántikas[222]], that 'the *summum bonum*' is the rising of pure intelligence consequent on the cessation of the conscious subject?" To this view we object that there is an absence of means; and also it cannot be established that the locus [or subject] of the two states is the same. For the former, if it is replied that the well-known fourfold set of Bauddha contemplations[223] are to be accepted as the cause, we answer that, as [according to the Bauddha tenet of the momentary existence of all things] there cannot be one abiding subject of these contemplations, they will necessarily exercise a languid power like studies pursued at irregular intervals, and be thus ineffectual to produce any distinct recognition of the real nature of things.

And for the latter, since the continued series of cognitions when accompanied by the natural obstacles[224] is said to be "bound," and when freed from those obstacles is said to be "liberated," you cannot establish an identity of the subject in the two states so as to be able to say that the very same being which *was* bound *is* now liberated.

Nor do we find the path of the Jainas, viz., that "Liberation is the releasing from all 'obstructions,'" a path entirely free from bars to impede the wayfarer. Pray, will our Jaina friend kindly inform us what he means by "obstruction"?[225] If he answers "merit, demerit, and error," we readily grant what he says. But if he maintains that "the body is the true obstruction, and hence Liberation is the continual upspringing of the soul consequent on the body's annihilation, as of a parrot released from its cage," then we must inquire whether this said soul possesses form or not. If it possesses form, then has it parts or not? If it has no parts, then, since the well-known definition of an atom will apply here as "that which has form without parts," it will follow that the attributes of the soul are, like those of an atom, imperceptible to the senses.[226] If you say that it has parts, then the general maxim that "whatever has parts is non-eternal," would necessitate that the soul is non-eternal; and if this were conceded, then two grand difficulties [against the Providential course of the world] would burst in unopposed, viz., that what the soul has done would, at its cessation, perish with it [and thus fail of producing the proper fruit], while it would have reaped during life the effects of what it had not done [as the good and evil which happened to it would not be the consequences of its actions in a former birth]. If, on the other hand, the Jaina maintains that the soul does not possess form at all, then how can he talk of the soul's "upspringing," since all such actions as motion necessarily involve an agent possessing form?[227]

Again, if we take the Chárváka's view "that the only bondage is dependence on another, and therefore independence is the true liberation,"—if by "independence" he means the cessation of pain, we have no need to controvert it. But if he means autocratic power, then no sensible man can concede it, as the very idea of earthly power involves the idea of a capability of being increased and of being equalled.[228]

Again, the Sánkhya opinion, which first lays down that nature and soul are utterly distinct, and then holds that "liberation is the soul's remaining as it is in itself after nature [on being known] has withdrawn,"—even this opinion accepts our tenet of the abolition of pain; but there is left a difficulty as to whether this cognition of the distinction between nature and soul resides in the soul or in nature. It is not consistent to say that it resides in the soul, since the soul is held to be unchangeable, and this would seem to involve that previously it had been hampered by ignorance; nor can we say that it resides in nature, since nature is always held to be unintelligent. Moreover, is nature spontaneously active or inactive? If the former, then it follows that there can be no liberation at all, since the spontaneous actions of things cannot be set aside; and if the latter, the course of mundane existence would at once cease to go on.

Again, we have the same recognition of our "abolition of pain" in the doctrine of Bhaṭṭa Sarvajña and his followers, that "Liberation is the manifestation of an eternal happiness incapable of being increased;" but here we have the difficulty that an eternal happiness does not come within the range of definite proof. If you allege Śruti as the proof, we reply that Śruti has no place when the thing itself is precluded by a valid non-perception;[229] or if you allow its authority, then you will have to concede the existence of such things as floating stones.[230]

"But if you give up the view that 'liberation is the manifestation of happiness,' and then accept such a view as that which holds it to be only the cessation of pain, does not your conduct resemble that of the dyspeptic patient who refused sweet milk and preferred sour rice-gruel?"

Your satire, however, falls powerless, as fitter for some speech in a play [rather than for a grave philosophical argument]. The truth is that all happiness must be included under the category of pain, since, like honey mixed with poison, it is always accompanied by pain, either as admitting of increase,[231] or as being an object of perception, or as being exposed to many hostile influences, or as involving an irksome necessity of seeking all kinds of instruments for its production. Nor may you retort on us that we have fulfilled the proverb of "seeking one thing and dropping another in the search," since we have abolished happiness as being ever tainted by some incidental pain, and, at the same time, our own favourite alternative is one which no one can consider desirable. For the truth is that any attempt to establish happiness as the *summum bonum*, since it is inevitably accompanied by various causes of pain, is only like the man who would try to grasp a red-hot ball of iron under the delusion that it was gold. In the case of objects of enjoyment got together by rightful means, we may find many firefly-like pleasures; but then how many are the rainy days to drown them? And in the case of those got together by wrong means, the mind cannot even conceive the future issue which will be brought about. Let our intelligent readers consider all this, and not attempt to disguise their own conscious experience. Therefore it is that we hold it as indisputable that for him, pre-eminent among his fellows, who, through the favour of the Supreme Being, has, by the regular method of listening to the revealedŚruti, &c., attained unto the knowledge of the real nature of the soul, for him the absolute abolition of pain is the true Liberation.

But it may be objected, "Is there any proof at all for the existence of a Supreme Being, *i.e.*, perception, inference, or Śruti? Certainly perception cannot apply here, since the Deity, as devoid of form, &c., must be beyond the senses. Nor can inference hold, since there is no universal proposition or true middle term which can apply.[232] Nor can Śruti, since neither of the resulting alternatives can be sustained; for is it supposed to reveal, as being itself eternal, or as non-eternal? Under the former view an established tenet of our school would be contradicted [viz., that the Veda is non-eternal]; under the latter, we should be only arguing in a circle.[233] As for comparison and any other proof which might be adduced [as that sometimes called presumption, &c.], they need not be thought of for a moment, as their object matter is definitely limited, and cannot apply to the present case.[234] Therefore the Supreme Being seems to be as unreal as a hare's horn." But all this elaborate disputation need excite no flurry in the breast of the intelligent, as it can be at once met by the old argument, "The mountain, seas, &c., must have had a maker from their possessing the nature of effects just like a jar." (*a.*) Nor can our middle term [possessing the nature of effects] be rejected as unproved (*asiddha*), since it can be established beyond a doubt by the fact of the subject's possessing parts. "But what are we to understand by this 'possessing parts'? Is it 'existing in contact with parts,' or 'in intimate relation with parts'? It cannot be the first, since this would equally apply to such eternal things as ether,[235] &c.; nor can it be the second, since this would prove too much, as applying to such cases as the [eternal] species, thread, which abides in intimate relation with the individual threads. It therefore fails as a middle term for your argument." We reply, that it holds if we explain the "possessing parts" as "belonging to the class of those substances which exist in intimate relation."[236] Or we may adopt another view and maintain that it is easy to infer the "possessing the nature of effects" from the consideration of their possessing intermediate magnitude.[237]

(*b.*) Nor can our middle term be rejected as "contradictory" (*viruddha*),[238] since there is no such acknowledged universal proposition connected with it as would establish the opposite major term to that in our syllogism [*i.e.*, that they must have had no maker]. (*c.*) Nor is our middle term too general (*anaikánta*), since it is never found in opposite instances [such as the lake, which is the *vipaksha* in the argument, "The mountain has fire because it has smoke"]. (*d.*) Nor again is it precluded (*bádhita* or *kálátyayopadishṭa*), for there is no superior evidence to exercise such a precluding power. (*e.*) Nor is it counter-balanced (*sat-pratipakshita*), for there does not appear to be any such equally valid antagonist.

If you bring forward as an antagonistic syllogism, "The mountains,& c., cannot have had a maker, from the fact that they were not produced by a body, just as is the case with the eternal ether,"—this pretended inference will no more stand examination than the young fawn can stand the attack of the full-grown lion; for the additional words "by a body" are useless, since "from the fact that they were not produced" would be a sufficient middle term by itself [and the argument thus involves the fallacy called *vyápyatvásiddhi*].[239] Nor can you retort, "Well, let this then be our middle term;" for you cannot establish it as a real fact. Nor again is it possible to raise the smallest shadow of a fear lest our middle term should be liable to limitation by any suggested condition (*upádhi*),[240] [such as "the being produced by a corporeal agent," to limit our old reason "from having the nature of effects"], because we have on our side a valid line of argument to establish our view, viz., "If the mountains,& c., had no maker, then they would not be effects" [but all do acknowledge that they have the nature of effects], for in this world that is not an effect which can attain its proper nature independently of any series of concurrent causes. And this series inevitably involves the idea of some sort of maker; and I mean by "being a maker" the being possessed of that combination of volition, desire to act, and knowledge of the proper means, which sets in motion all other causes, but is itself set in motion by none. And hence we hold that if the necessity of a maker were overthrown, the necessity of the action of all the other causes would be simultaneously overthrown, since these are dependent thereon; and this would lead to the monstrous doctrine that effects could be produced without any cause at all. There is a rule laid down by Śaṅkara-kiṅkara which applies directly to the present case—

> "When a middle term is accompanied by a sound argument to establish its validity,
>
> "Then you cannot attempt to supply a limiting condition on account of the [supposed] non-invariable concomitance of the major term."

If you maintain that there are many sound counter-arguments, such as "If the Supreme Being were a maker, He would be possessed of a body,"& c., we reply, that all such reasoning is equally inconsistent, whether we allow that Supreme Being's existence to be established or not.[241]

As has been said by Udayana Áchárya [in the Kusumáñjali, iii. 5]—

> "If Śruti, &c., have any authority, your negative argument fails from being precluded; if they are fallacious, our old objection of a 'baseless inference' returns stronger than ever."

Nor need we fear the possibility of any other contradiction to our argument, since it would be overthrown by either alternative of God's being known or unknown.[242]

"Well, let all this be granted; but the activity of God in creating the world, what end did it have in view? His own advantage or some other being's? If it was for the former end, was it in order to attain something desired, or to avoid something not desired? It could not be the first, because this would be quite incongruous in a being who possesses every possible desire gratified; and for the same reason too it could not be the second. If it was for the latter end [the advantage of another] it would be equally incongruous; for who would call that being "wise" who busied himself in acting for another? If you replied that His activity was justified by compassion, any one would at once retort that this feeling of compassion should have rather induced Him to create all living beings happy, and not checkered with misery, since this militates against His compassion; for we define compassion as the disinterested wish to avoid causing another pain. Hence we conclude that it is not befitting for God to create the world." This has been said by Bhaṭṭáchárya—

> "Not even a fool acts without some object in view;
> "Suppose that God did not create the world, what end would be left undone by Him?"—

We reply, O thou crest-jewel of the atheistic school, be pleased for a moment to close thy envy-dimmed eyes, and to consider the following suggestions. His action in creation is indeed solely caused by compassion; but the idea of a creation which shall consist only of happiness is inconsistent with the nature of things, since there cannot but arise eventual differences from the different results which will ripen from the good or evil actions of the beings who are to be created. Nor need you object that this would interfere with God's own independence [as He would thus seem to depend on others' actions], since there is the well-known saying, "One's own body does not hinder one;" nay rather it helps to carry out one's aims;[243] and for this there is authority in such passages of the Veda as that (in theŚvetáśvatara Upanishad, iii. 2), "There is one Rudra only; he admits[244] not of a second," &c. "But then how will you remedy your deadly sickness of reasoning in a circle? [for you have to prove the Veda by the authority of God, and then again you have to prove God's existence by the Veda"]. We reply, that we defy you to point out any reasoning in a circle in our argument. Do you suspect this "reciprocal dependence of each," which you call "reasoning in a circle," in regard to their being produced or in regard to their being known?[245] It cannot be the former, for though the production of the Veda is dependent on God, still as God Himself is eternal, there is no possibility of *His* being produced; nor can it be in regard to their being known, for even if our knowledge of God were dependent on the Veda, the Veda might be learned from some other source; nor, again, can it be in regard to the knowledge of the non-eternity of the Veda, for the non-eternity of the Veda is easily perceived by any *yogin*endowed with the transcendent faculties (*tívra*,[246] &c.)

Therefore, when God has been rendered propitious by the performance of duties which produce His favour, the desired end, Liberation, is obtained; thus everything is clear.

—E. B. C.

CHAPTER XII.

THE JAIMINI-DARŚANA.

An objector may here ask, "Are you not continually repeating that merit (*dharma*) comes from the practice of duty (*dharma*), but how is duty to be defined or proved?" Listen attentively to my answer. A reply to this question has been given in the older[247] Mímáṃsá by the holy sage Jaimini. Now the Mímáṃsá consists of twelve books.[248] In the first book is discussed the authoritativeness of those collections of words which are severally meant by the terms injunction (*vidhi*), "explanatory passage" (*arthaváda*), hymn (*mantra*), tradition (*smṛiti*), and "name." In the second, certain subsidiary discussions [as *e.g.*, on *apúrva*] relating to the difference of various rites, refutation of (erroneously alleged) proofs, and difference of performance [as in "constant" and "voluntary" offerings]. In the third, *Śruti*, "sign" or "sense of the passage" (*liṅga*), "context" (*vákya*), &c., and their respective weight when in apparent opposition to one another, the ceremonies called *pratipatti-karmáṇi*, things mentioned incidentally (*anárabhyádhíta*), things accessory to several main objects, as *prayájas*, &c., and the duties of the sacrificer. In the fourth, the influence on other rites of the principal and subordinate rites, the fruit caused by the *juhú* being made of the *butea frondosa*, &c., and the dice-playing, &c., which form subordinate parts of the *rájasúya* sacrifice. In the fifth, the relative order of different passages of *Śruti*, &c., the order of different parts of a sacrifice [as the seventeen animals at the *vájapeya*], the multiplication and non-multiplication of rites, and the respective force of the words of *Śruti*, order of mention, &c., in determining the order of performance. In the sixth, the persons qualified to offer sacrifices, their obligations, the substitutes for enjoined materials, supplies for lost or injured offerings, expiatory rites, the *sattra* offerings, things proper to be given, and the different sacrificial fires. In the seventh, transference of the ceremonies of one sacrifice to another by direct command in the Vaidic text, and then as inferred by "name" or "sign." In the eighth, transference by virtue of the clearly expressed or obscurely expressed "sign," or by the predominant "sign," and cases where no transference takes place. In the ninth, the beginning of the discussion on the adaptation of hymns when quoted in a new connection (*úha*), the adaptation of *sámans* and *mantras*, and collateral questions connected therewith. In the tenth, the discussion of occasions where the non-performance of the primary rite involves the "preclusion" and non-performance of the dependent rites, and of occasions where rites are precluded because other rites produce their special result, discussions connected with the *graha* offerings, certain *sámans*, and various other things, and a discussion on the different kinds of negation. In the eleventh, the incidental mention and subsequently the fuller discussion of *tantra*[249] [where several acts are combined into one], and *ávápa* [or the performing an act more than once]. In the twelfth, a discussion on *prasaṅga* [where the rite is performed for one chief purpose, but with an incidental further reference],*tantra*, cumulation of concurrent rites (*samuchchaya*) and option.

Now the first topic which introduces the discussions of the Púrva-Mímáṃsá arises from the aphorism, "Now therefore a desire to know duty [is to be entertained by thee"]. Now the learned describe a "topic" as consisting of five members, and these are (*a.*) the subject, (*b.*) the doubt, (*c.*) the *primâ facie* argument, (*d.*) the demonstrated conclusion, and (*e.*) the connection (*saṅgati*). The topic is discussed according to the doctrines held by the great teachers of the system. Thus the "subject" to be discussed is the sentence, "The Veda is to be read." Now the "doubt" which arises is whether the study of Jaimini's *śástra* concerning duty, beginning with the aphorism, "Duty is a thing which is to be recognised by an instigatory passage," and ending with "and from seeing it in the-*anváhárya*," is to be commenced or not. The *primâ facie* argument is that it is not to be commenced, whether the injunction to read the Veda be held to have a visible and present or an invisible and future fruit. (*a.*) If you say that this injunction must have a visible fruit, and this can be no other[250] than the knowledge of the meaning of what is read, we must next ask you whether this said reading is enjoined as something which otherwise would not have been thought of, or whether as something which otherwise would have been optional, as we see in the rule for shelling rice.[251] It cannot be the former, for the reading of the Veda is a means of knowing the sense thereof from its very nature as reading, just as in the parallel instance of reading the Mahábhárata; and we see by this argument that it would present itself as an obvious means quite independently of the injunction. Well, then, let it be the latter alternative; just as the baked flour cake called *puroḍása* is made only of rice prepared by being unhusked in a mortar, when, but for the injunction, it might have been unhusked by the finger-nails. There, however, the new moon and full moon sacrifices only produce their unseen effect, which is the principal *apúrva*, by means of the various minor effects or subordinate *apúrvas*, produced by the various subordinate parts of the whole ceremony; and consequently the minor *apúrva* of the unhusking is the reason there for the restricting injunction. But in the case which we are discussing, there is no such reason for any such restriction, as the rites can be equally well performed by gaining the knowledge of the Veda's meaning by reading a written book, or by studying under an authorised teacher. Hence we conclude that there is no injunction to study the Púrva Mímáṃsá as a means of knowing the sense of the Veda. (*b.*) "What, then, becomes of the Vedic injunction, 'The Veda is to be read'?" Well, you must be content with the fact that the injunction will have heaven as its [future] fruit, although it merely enjoins the making oneself master of the literal words of the Vedic text [without any care to understand the meaning which they may convey], since heaven, though not expressly mentioned, is to be assumed as the fruit, according to the analogy of the Viśvajit offering. Just as Jaimini, in his aphorism (iv. 3, 15), "Let that fruit be heaven, since it equally applies to all," establishes that those who are not expressly mentioned are still qualified to offer the Viśvajit sacrifice, and infers by argument that its characteristic fruit is heaven, so let us assume it to be in the present case also. As it has been said—

"Since the visible fruit would be equally obtained without the injunction, this cannot be its sole object; we must rather suppose heaven to be the fruit from the injunction's significance, after the analogy of the Viśvajit, &c."

Thus, too, we shall keep the Smṛiti rule from being violated: "Having read the Veda, let him bathe." For this rule clearly implies that no long interval is to take place between reading the Veda and the student's return to his home; while, according to your opinion, after he had read the Veda, he would still have to remain in his preceptor's house to read the Mímáṃsá discussions, and thus the idea of no interval between would be contradicted. Therefore for these three reasons, (*a.*) that the study of Mímáṃsá is not enjoined, (*b.*) that heaven can be obtained by the simple reading of the text, and (*c.*) that the rule for the student's return to his home is thus fulfilled, we maintain that the study of the Mímáṃsá discussions on duty is not to be commenced.

The "authoritative conclusion" (*siddhánta*), however, is as follows:—

We grant that it cannot be a case of *vidhi*, for it might have been adopted on other grounds; but not even Indra with his thunderbolt could make us lose our hold of the other alternative that it is a case of *niyama*. In the sentence, "The Veda is to be read," the affix *tavya* expresses an enforcing power in the word,[252] which is to be rendered visible by a corresponding action in man, bringing a certain effect into existence; and this enforcing power seeks some corresponding end which is connected with the man's creative effort. Now it cannot be the act itself of reading, as suggested by the whole word *adhyetavya*, which it thus seeks as an end; for this act of reading, thus expressed by the word, could never be regarded as an end, since it is a laborious operation of the voice and mind, consisting in the articulate utterance of the portion read. Nor could the portion read, as suggested by the whole sentence, be regarded as the end. For the mass of words called "Veda," which is what we really mean by the words "portion read," being eternal and omnipresent, could never fulfil the conditions of the four "fruits of action," production, &c.[253] Therefore the only true end which remains to us is the knowledge of the meaning, as obtained by carrying out the sense of the words of the injunction. According to the old rule, "He has the right who has the want, the power, and the wit," those who are aiming to understand certain things, as the new and full moon sacrifices, use their daily reading to learn the truth about them. And the injunction for reading, since it virtually excludes the reading of written books, &c. [from the well-known technical sense of the word "read" when used in this connection], conveys the idea that the reading the Veda enjoined has a consecrated character [as taught by a duly authorised teacher]. Therefore, as the principal *apúrva*, produced by the great new and full moon sacrifices, necessitates and establishes the subordinate *apúrvas* produced by the inferior sacrificial acts, as unhusking the rice, &c., so the mass of *apúrva*produced by all the sacrifices necessitates and establishes a previous*apúrva* produced by the restricting injunction (*niyama*), which prescribes reading the Veda as the means to know how to perform these sacrifices. If you hesitate to concede that a *niyama* could have this future influence called *apúrva*, the same doubt might equally invalidate the efficacy of a *vidhi* [as the two stand on the same level as to their enjoining power]. Nor is the supposition a valid one that heaven is the fruit, according to the analogy of the *Viśvajit*offering, since, if there is a present and visible fruit in the form of a knowledge of the meaning of the sacred text, it is improper to suppose any other future and unseen fruit. Thus it has been said—

> "Where a seen fruit is obtained, you must not suppose an unseen one; but if a *vidhi* has the restricting meaning of a *niyama*, it does not thereby become meaningless."

But an objector may say, "Although a man who reads the simple text of the Veda may not attain to a knowledge of its meaning, still, as he who reads the Veda with its *aṅgas*, grammar, &c., may attain to this knowledge, the study of Mímáṃsá will be useless." But this is not true: for even though he may attain to a simple knowledge of the literal meaning, all deeper investigation must depend on this kind of discussion. For instance, when it is said, "He offers anointed gravel," neither grammar nor *nigama*[254] nor *nirukta* will determine the true meaning that it is to be anointed with ghee and not with oil, &c.; it is only by a Mímáṃsá discussion that the true meaning is unravelled from the rest of the passage, "Verily, ghee is brightness."[255] It is therefore established that the study of

Mímáṃsá is enjoined. Nor need it be supposed that this contradicts the passage of Smṛiti, "Having read the Veda, let him bathe," which implies that he should now leave his teacher's house, and prohibits any further delay; as the words do not necessarily imply that the return to the paternal roof is to follow immediately on his having read the Veda, but only that it is to follow it at some time, and that both actions are to be done by the same person, just as we see in the common phrase, "Having bathed, he eats." Therefore from the purport of the injunction we conclude that the study of the Púrva Mímáṃsá Śástra, consisting of a thousand "topics,"[256] is to be commenced. This topic is connected with the main subject of the Śástra as being a subsidiary digression, as it is said, "They call that a subsidiary digression which helps to establish the main subject."[257]

I now proceed to give a sketch of the discussion of the same "topic" in accordance with the teaching of the Guru Prabhákara.

In the Smṛiti rule,[258] "Let him admit as a pupil the Brahman lad when eight years old (by investing him with the sacred cord), let him instruct him," the object of the direction appears to be the pupil's instruction. Now a direction must have reference to somebody to be directed; and if you ask who is here to be directed, I reply, "He who desires to be a teacher," since, by Páṇini's rule (i. 3, 36), the root *ní* is used in the *átmanepada* when honour, &c., are implied, *i.e.*, here the duty which a teacher performs to his pupils. He who is to be directed as to admitting a pupil is the same person who is to be directed as to teaching him, since both are the object of one and the same command. Hence the inspired sage Manu has said (ii. 140), "The Bráhman who girds his pupil with the sacrificial cord and then instructs him in the Veda, with its subsidiary *aṅgas* and mystic doctrines, they call a spiritual teacher (*áchárya*)." Now the teaching which is the function of the teacher cannot be fulfilled without the learning which is the function of the pupil, and therefore the very injunction to teach implies and establishes a corresponding obligation to learn, since the influencer's efforts fail without those of one to be influenced. If you object that this view does not make reading the Veda the object of definite injunction, I reply, What matters it to us if it is not? For even if there is no reason for us to admit a separate injunction for reading the Veda, it will still remain perpetually enjoined as a duty, because the passage which mentions it is a perpetual *anuváda*or "supplementary repetition."[259] Therefore the former *primâ facie* argument and its answer, which were given before under the idea that there was a definite injunction to read the Veda, must now be discussed in another way to suit this new view.

Now the *primâ facie* argument was that the study of Mímáṃsá, not being authoritatively enjoined, is not to be commenced; the "conclusion" was that it is to be commenced as being thus authoritatively enjoined.

Now the upholders of the former or *primâ facie* view argue as follows:—"We put to the advocates of the conclusion the following dilemma: Does the injunction to teach imply that the pupil is to understand the meaning of what is read, or does it only refer to the bare reading? It cannot be the former, for obviously the act of teaching cannot depend for its fulfilment on the pupil's understanding what is taught [as this will depend on his ability as a recipient]; and the latter will not help you, as, if the bare reading is sufficient, the Mímáṃsá discussions in question will have no subject or use. For their proper subject is a point in the Veda, which is doubted about from having been only looked at in a rough and impromptu way; now if there is no need of understanding the meaning at all, why should we talk of doubts and still more of any hope of ascertaining the true meaning by means of laborious discussion? And therefore in accordance with the well-known principle, 'That which is a thing of use and not a matter of doubt is an object of attainment to an intelligent man, as, for instance, a jar which is in broad light and in contact with the external and internal senses,' as there is in the present case no such thing as a subject to exercise it upon, or a useful end to be attained by it, we maintain that the study of Mímáṃsá is not to be commenced."

We grant, in reply, that the injunction to teach does not imply a corresponding necessity that the student must understand the meaning; still when a man has read the Veda with its subsidiary *aṅgas*, and has comprehended the general connection of the words with their respective meanings, this will imply an understanding of the meaning of the Veda, just as it would in any ordinary human compositions. "But may we not say that, just as in the case of the mother who said to her son, 'Eat poison,' the meaning literally expressed by the words was not what she wished to convey, since she really intended to forbid his eating anything at all in such and such a house; so if the literal meaning of the Veda does not express its real purport, the old objection will recur with full force that the study of Mímáṃsá will have neither subject nor end [as there will be no use in understanding the literal meaning, since, as in the mother's case, it may only lead astray, and so common sense must be the ultimate judge"]. We reply, that your supposed illustration and the case in question are not really parallel. In the supposed illustration the primary meaning of the words would be obviously precluded, because a direction to eat poison would be inconceivable in the mouth of an authoritative and trustworthy speaker like a mother, and you would know at once that this could not be what she wished to say; but in the case of the Veda, which is underived from any personal author, why should not the literal meaning be the one actually intended? And it is just the doubts that arise, as they occasionally will do, in reference to this intended meaning, which will be the proper "subject" of Mímáṃsá discussion; and the settlement of these doubts will be its proper "end." Therefore, whenever the true meaning of the Veda is not obtained[260] by that reading which is virtually prescribed by the authoritative injunction to a Brahman to teach, it will be a proper subject for systematic discussion; and hence we hold that the study of Mímáṃsá *is* enjoined, and should be commenced.

"Well,[261] be it so" [say the followers of the Nyáya], "but how can the Vedas be said to be underived from any personal author, when there is no evidence to establish this? Would you maintain that they have no personal author because, although there is an unbroken line of tradition, there is no remembrance of any author, just as is the case with the soul"?[262] This argument is weak, because the alleged characteristics [unbroken tradition, &c.] are not proved; for those who hold the human origin of the Vedas maintain that the line of tradition was interrupted at the time of the dissolution of the universe. And, again, what is meant by this assertion that the author is not remembered? Is it (1.) that no author is believed, or (2.) that no author is remembered? The first alternative cannot be accepted, since we hold that God is proved to have been the author. Nor can the second, because it cannot stand the test of the following dilemma, viz., is it meant (*a.*) that no author of the Veda is remembered by some one person, or (*b.*) by any person whatever? The former supposition breaks down, as it would prove too much, since it would apply to such an isolated stanza as "He who is religious and has overcome pride and anger," &c.[263] And the latter supposition is inadmissible, since it would be impossible for any person who was not omniscient to know that no author of the Veda was recollected by any person whatever. Moreover, there is actual proof that the Veda had a personal author, for we argue as follows:—The sentences of the Veda must have originated from a personal author, since they have the character of sentences like those of Kálidása and other writers. And, again, the sentences of the Veda have been composed by a competent person, since, while they possess authority, they have, at the same time, the character of sentences, like those of Manu and other sages.

But [ask the Mímáṃsakas] may it not be assumed that "all study of the Veda was preceded by an earlier study of it by the pupil's preceptor, since the study of the Veda must always have had one common character which was the same in former times as now;" and therefore this uninterrupted succession has force to prove the eternity of the Veda? This reasoning, however [the Naiyáyikas answer], cannot rise to the height of proof, for it has no more validity than such obviously illusory reasoning, as "All study of the Mahábhárata was preceded by an earlier study of it by the pupil's preceptor, since it is the study of the Mahábhárata, which must have been the same in former times as now." But [the Mímáṃsakas will ask whether there is not a difference between these two cases, since] the Smṛiti declares that [Vishṇu incarnate as] Vyása was the author of the Mahábhárata, in accordance with the line, "Who else than the lotus-eyed Vishṇu could be the maker of the Mahábhárata?" [while nothing of this sort is recorded in any Smṛiti in regard to the Veda]. This argument, however, is pithless, since those words of the Purushasúkta (Rig V., x. 90), "From him sprang the Ṛich and Sáman verses; from him sprang the Metres; from him the Yajus arose;" prove that the Veda had a maker.

Further [proceed the Naiyáyikas] we hold that sound is non-eternal[264] because it has genus, and is also perceptible to the external organs of beings such as ourselves, just as a jar is.[265] "But," you may object, "is not this argument refuted by the proof arising from the fact that we recognise the letter *g* (for example) as the same we have heard before?" This objection, however, is extremely weak, for the recognition in question is powerless to refute our argument, since it has reference only to identity of *species*, as in the case of a man whose hair has been cut and has grown again, or of a jasmine which has blossomed afresh. "But [asks the Mímáṃsaka] how can the Veda have been uttered by the incorporeal Parameśvara, who has no palate or other organs of speech, and therefore cannot have pronounced the letters?" "This objection [answers the Naiyáyika] is not happy, because, though Parameśvara is by nature incorporeal, he can yet assume a body in sport, in order to show kindness to his worshippers. Consequently the arguments in favour of the doctrine that the Veda had no personal author are inconclusive."

I shall now [says the Mímáṃsaka] clear up the whole question. What is meant by this *paurusheyatva* ["derivation from a personal author"] which it is sought to prove? Is it (1.) mere procession (*utpannatva*) from a person, like the procession of the Veda from persons such as ourselves, when we daily utter it? or (2.) is it the arrangement—with a view to its manifestation—of knowledge acquired by other modes of proof, as in the case of treatises composed by persons like ourselves? If the first meaning be intended, there will be no dispute between us.[266] If the second sense be meant, I ask whether it is established (*a.*) by inference,[267] or (*b.*) by supernatural testimony? (*a.*) The former alternative cannot be correct, because your argument would equally apply to the sentences in dramas such as the Málatímádhava [which, of course, being a work of fiction, has no authoritative character]. If you qualify your argument by inserting the saving clause, "while they possess authority,"[268] [as supra, p. 188, line 21], even this explanation will fail to satisfy a philosopher.

For the sentences of the Veda are universally defined to be sentences which prove things that are not provable by other evidence. But if you could establish that these Vedic sentences only prove what is provable by other evidence, this definition would be at once contradicted, just as if a man were to say that his mother was a barren woman. And even if we granted that Parameśvara might assume a body in sport, in order to show kindness to his worshippers, it would not at all follow that he would perceive things beyond the reach of the senses, from the want of any means of apprehending objects removed from him in place, in time, and in nature.[269] Nor is it to be assumed that his eyes and other senses alone would have the power of producing such knowledge, for we can only draw upon our imagination in accordance with our past experience. This has been declared by the Guru [Prabhákara] when he refutes the supposition of an omniscient author—

> "Wherever we do find the power of an organ intensified,[270] it is done without its going beyond its own proper objects; thus it may appear in the power of seeing the very distant or the very minute, but not in the ear's becoming cognisant of form."

Hence (*b.*) we also maintain that your position cannot be established by any supposed supernatural testimony [as that quoted above from the Rig-Veda, "from him sprang the Ṛich and Sáman verses"]. For the rule of Páṇini (iv. 3, 101) will still remain inviolate, that the grammatical affixes with which such names as Káṭhaka, Kálápa, and Taittiríya are formed, impart to those derivatives the sense of "uttered by" Kaṭha, Kalápin, &c., though we maintain that these names have reference [not to those parts of the Veda as first composed by these sages, but] to the fact that these sages instituted certain schools of traditional study. And in the same way we hold [in reference to this verse from the Rig-Veda] that it only refers to the institution of certain schools of traditional study of these Vedas.

Nor will any supposed inference establish the non-eternity of sound, because [as we said before] it is opposed to the evidence of our consciousness, [since we certainly recognise the letter now heard as the one heard before]. Nor is it reasonable to reply that, although the letters are not the same, they seem to be so on account of their identity of species. For here we ask our opponents a question—Is this idea that "the apparent sameness arises from identity of species" put forward from a wish to preclude entirely any idea of the letters being the same, or only [from an imagined fear of error] because experience shows that the recognition will sometimes be erroneous [as in the cases of the hair and jasmine mentioned above]? (*a.*) If it arises from the latter reason, we Mímáṃsakas, who hold that the Veda is its own evidence, have said in reference to this timid imagination—

> "He who foolishly imagines that something as yet unknown to him will come hereafter to stop his present conclusion, will go to utter ruin in every transaction of life, his mind a mass of doubts."

(*b.*) "But [the Naiyáyikas will ask] does not this recognition of *g*and other letters [as the same which we heard before] refer to the species which exists the same in each, and not to the several individual letters, since, in fact, we perceive that they are different as uttered by different persons, otherwise we could not make such distinctions as we do when we say 'Somaśarman is reading'?" This objection, however, has as little brilliancy as its predecessors, for as there is no proof of any distinction between the individual *g*'s, there is no proof that we ought to assume any such thing as a species*g*; and we maintain that, just as to the man who does not understand [the Naiyáyika doctrine of] the species *g*, the one species [in the Naiyáyika view] will by the influence of distinction of place, magnitude, form, and individual sounds, appear as if it were variously modified as itself distinct in place, as small, as great, as long, as short; so to the man who does not understand our [Mímáṃsaka doctrine of] one individual *g*, the one *g* (in our view) will by the diversity of "manifesters,"[271] appear to him associated with their respective peculiarities; and as contrary characters are in this way ascribed [to the letter *g*], there is a fallacious appearance of distinction [between different *g*'s]. But does this ascription of contrary characters, which is thus regarded as creating a difference [between the *g*'s], result (1.) from the nature of the thing, or (2.) from our imagination? There is no proof of the former alternative; for, if it were true, as an inherent difference would have to be admitted between different *g*'s, we should have to say, "Chaitra has uttered ten *g's*," and not "Chaitra has uttered the same *g* ten times." On the latter supposition, there is no proof of any inherent distinction between *g*'s, for inherent oneness is not destroyed by a difference of external disguises. Thus we must not conceive, from the apparent distinction caused by such external disguises as jars, &c., that there is any inherent distinction, as of parts, in the one indivisible ether. The current use of the rejected phrase [*i.e.*, "different" as applied to the *g*'s] is really caused by the *noise*, which in each case is different. This has been said by the great teacher—

> "The object which the Naiyáyikas seek by supposing a species is, in fact, gained from the letter itself; and the object which they aim at by supposing an individuality in letters, is attained from audible noises;[272] so that the assumption of species is useless."

And again—

> "Since in regard to sounds such an irresistible instinct of recognition is always awake within us, it precludes by its superior evidence all the inferences to prove sound's non-eternity."

This at once refutes the argument given in the [Naiyáyika] treatise by Vágíśwara, entitled *Mána-manohara*, "sound is non-eternal from the fact of its being a special quality belonging to an organ of sense[273] (*sc.* the ear), just as colour is to the eye."

We can also refute it in the following ways: (*a.*) If we follow the [Sáṅkhya and Vedánta] view that sound is a substance, it is evidently overthrown[274] [as in that case sound cannot be a quality]; (*b.*) if we take it as referring to the *noise*, not the *sound*, we have no dispute, as it only establishes what we ourselves allow; and (*c.*) the inference is overthrown by the "limiting condition" [*upádhi*] of*aśrávaṇatva*, or "the not causing audition."[275] So Udayana tries at great length to establish that, although ether, the site of sound, is imperceptible, the non-existence of that which abides in this site is perceptible; and he then brings forward as an evidence for the non-eternity of sound, that sense perception which causes the use of such common expressions as "The tumult is stopped," "The sound has arisen."[276] But he is sufficiently answered[277] by our old reply [in p. 193], that the fallacious appearance of distinction arises from contrary characters being erroneously ascribed, just as, in the story, the demon Tála went away [as well as Betála] when the offering of blood was given to the latter.[278] And as for the objection raised by the author of the *Nyáyabhúshaṇa*,[279] that, if sound were eternal, the conclusion must follow that it would be either always perceptible or always imperceptible, this also is obviated by our allowing that we only perceive that sound which is manifested by our articulate noise.[280] And as for the (Naiyáyika) argument against the existence[281] of such a constant relation as this which is supposed between the manifested "sound" and the manifesting "noise," since they both come simultaneously in contact with the sense of hearing, this is invalid, as it will indisputably apply with equal force in the case of the soul.[282]

Therefore as the Veda is thus proved to have not originated from any personal author, and as the minutest germ of suspicion against it is thus absolutely destroyed, we hold it as satisfactorily demonstrated that it has a self-established authority in all matters relating to duty.

"Well"[283] [say our opponents], "let this question rest; but how about another well-known controversy? It is said—

"'The Sáṅkhyas hold that both authoritativeness and non-authoritativeness are self-proved; the followers of the Nyáya hold that both are proved by something else [as inference, &c.]; the Buddhists hold that the latter is self-proved and the former proved by something else; the teachers of the Veda maintain that authoritativeness is self-proved and non-authoritativeness proved by something else.' Now we ask, amidst all this discussion, how do the Mímáṃsakas accept as established their tenet that the authoritativeness of duty is self-proved? And what is the meaning of this so-called self-proved authoritativeness? Is it (*a.*) that authoritativeness springs from itself? or (*b.*) that it springs from the right knowledge in which it resides? or (*c.*) that it springs from the instrumental causes [as the eye, &c.] which produced the right knowledge in which it resides? or (*d.*) that it resides in a particular knowledge produced by the instrumental causes which produced the right knowledge?[284] or (*e.*) that it resides in a particular knowledge produced by the instrumental causes *only* which produced the right knowledge?

"(*a.*) It cannot be the *first*, because wherever the relation of cause and effect is found there must be a difference, and therefore these two cannot reside in the same subject [*i.e.*, authoritativeness cannot cause itself]. (*b.*) It cannot be the *second*, because if knowledge, which is a quality, were the cause of authoritativeness, it would have to be a substance, as being an intimate cause.[285] (*c.*) It cannot be the *third*, because 'authoritativeness' cannot properly be 'produced' at all,[286] whether we call it a general characteristic (*upádhi*) or a species (*játi*);[287] for if we call it an *upádhi*, it is defined as the absolute non-existence of any contradiction to a certain kind of knowledge which does not possess the nature of recollection[288] and this cannot be produced, for we all allow that absolute non-existence is eternal; and still less can we speak of its being produced, if we regard it as a species. (*d.*) Nor can it be the *fourth*, for wrong knowledge [as well as right knowledge] is a particular kind of knowledge, and the instrumental causes which produce the general are included in those which produce the particular,[289] just as the general idea 'seed,' as applied to 'tree,' is included in the particular seed of any special tree, as,*e.g.*, the Dalbergia Sisu; otherwise we might suppose that the particular had no instrumental cause at all. Your definition would therefore extend too far [and include erroneous as well as true knowledge]; for non-authoritativeness, which Vedantists and most Mímáṃsakas allow to be produced by something external, must also be considered as residing in a particular knowledge [*i.e.*, a wrong knowledge] produced [in part] by the instrumental causes which produced the right knowledge. (*e.*) As for your *fifth* view, we ask whether by being produced by the instrumental causes *only* which produced right knowledge, you mean to include or exclude the absence of a 'defect'? It cannot be the former alternative; because the followers of the Nyáya who hold that authoritativeness is proved by something external [as inference, &c.], would at once grant that authoritativeness is produced by the instrumental causes of knowledge combined with the absence of a 'defect.' Neither can it be the latter alternative; for, inasmuch as it is certain that the absence of a 'defect' is found combined with the various instrumental causes, this absence of a 'defect' is fixed as by adamantine glue to be a cause of right knowledge, since right knowledge will always accompany its presence, and be absent if it is absent,[290] and it will at the same time be not an unimportant condition.[291] If you object that non-existence (or absence) cannot be a cause, we reply by asking you whether non-existence can be an effect or not? If it cannot, then we should have to allow that cloth is eternal, as its "emergent non-existence" or destruction would be impossible. If it can be an effect, then why should it not be a cause also? So this rope binds you at both ends. This has also been said by Udayana [in his Kusumáñjali, i. 10]—

> "'As existence, so too non-existence is held to be a cause as well as an effect.'

"The argument, in my opinion, runs as follows:—Right knowledge depends on some cause[292] other than the common causes of knowledge, from the very fact that, while it is an effect, it is also knowledge, just as wrong knowledge does.[293] Authoritativeness is known through something external to itself [*e.g.*, inference], because doubt arises in regard to it in an unfamiliar case, as we also see in non-authoritativeness.

"Therefore, as we can prove that authoritativeness is both produced and recognised by means of something external, the Mímáṃsá tenet that 'authoritativeness is self-proved' is like a gourd overripe and rotten."

This long harangue of our opponent, however, is but a vain attempt to strike the sky with his fist; for (*a.*) we mean by our phrase "self-proved" that while right knowledge is produced by the instrumental causes of knowledge, it is not produced by any other cause (as "defect," &c.) The following is our argument as drawn out in full:—Right knowledge is not produced by any other instrumental causes than those of knowledge, while, at the same time, it is produced by these, because it is not the site of wrongness of knowledge,—just like a jar.[294] Nor can Udayana's[295] argument be brought forward as establishing the dependence of authoritativeness on something external, for it is swallowed up by the dragon of the equally potent contradictory argument. "Right knowledge is not produced by any cause which is other than the causes of knowledge and is also other than 'defect,'[296] from the very fact of its being knowledge—

like wrong knowledge." Again, since right knowledge can arise from the causes of knowledge *per se*, it would be a needless complexity to suppose that anything else is a cause, whether you call it a *guṇa* or the absence of a "defect" (*dosha*).[297]

"But surely if the presence of a defect is the cause of wrong knowledge, it is difficult to deny that its absence must be a cause of right knowledge?" We meet this, however, by maintaining that the absence of defect is only an indirect and remote cause, as it only acts negatively by preventing wrong knowledge. As it has been said—

> "Therefore we reasonably conclude from the presence of*guṇas* the absence of 'defects,'[298] from their absence the non-existence of the two kinds of non-authoritativeness,[299] and from this the general conclusion."[300]

(*b.*) We maintain that the recognition of right knowledge is produced by the same causes only which make us perceive the first knowledge[301] [*sc.* the eye, mind, &c.] Nor can you object that this view is precluded, because it would imply that there could be no such thing as doubt; for we answer that doubt arises in cases where, although all the causes which produce knowledge are present, there is also the simultaneous presence of some opposing cause, as a "defect,"& c.

As for your argument [O Naiyáyika! given *supra*, in p. 198, lines 17-24], I ask, Is your own argument an authoritative proof by itself or not? If it is, it proves too much [for it would properly apply to itself and lead us to infer its own dependence on external proof, whereas you hold it to be independent of such]; and if it is not, we should have a case of *regressus in infinitum*, for it will want some other proof to confirm its authoritativeness, and this too in its turn will want some fresh proof, and so on for ever.

As for the argument urged by Udayana[302] in the Kusumáñjali, when he tries to establish that immediate and vehement action does not depend on the agent's certainty as to the authoritativeness of the speech which sets him acting: "Action depends on wish, its vehemence on that of the wish,[303] wish on the knowledge that the thing wished for is a means to attain some wished-for end, and this is only ascertained by an inference based on some 'sign' which proves that the thing is closely connected with the wished-for end, and this inference depends on the things being in direct contact with the agent's senses; but throughout the whole series of antecedent steps the Mímáṃsá idea of the perception of authoritativeness is never once found as a cause of action." All this appears to us simple bluster, like that of the thief who ostentatiously throws open all his limbs before me, when I had actually found the gold under his armpit. It is only the knowledge that the thing is a means to attain the desired end, and this knowledge recognised as authoritative and right knowledge, which causes the definite volition to arise at all; and in this we can distinctly trace the influence of that very perception of authoritativeness [whose existence he so vehemently pretended to deny]. If unhesitating action ever arose in any case from doubt, then, as it might always arise so in every given case, all ascertainment of authoritativeness would be useless; and as the very existence of what is unascertained is rendered uncertain, poor authoritativeness would have to be considered as dead and buried! But enough of this prolix controversy; since it has been said—

> "Therefore the authoritativeness of a cognition, which (authoritativeness) presented itself as representing a real fact, may be overthrown by the perception of a 'defect,' which perception is produced by some sign that proves the discrepancy between the cognition and the fact."[304]

Now with regard to the Veda, which is the self-proved and authoritative criterion in regard to duty, [we have the following divergency between the two great Mímáṃsá schools]:—The Veda is composed of three portions, respectively called "hymns" (*mantra*), "explanatory passages" (*arthaváda*), and "injunctions" (*vidhi*); and by "injunction" we mean such sentences as "Let him who desires heaven sacrifice with the jyotishṭoma." Here *ta*, the affix of the third person singular, denotes an enjoining power, which is "coloured" [or rendered definite] by the meaning of the root, according to the opinion of the followers of Bhaṭṭa Kumárila, who maintain that words signify[305] something definite by themselves [apart from the sentence]. The followers of Guru Prabhákara, on the contrary, hold that the whole sentence is a command relating to the sacrifice, as they maintain that words only signify an action or something to be done.[306] Thus all has been made plain.

—E. B. C.

CHAPTER XIII.

THE PÁṆINI-DARŚANA.[307]

If any one asks, "Where are we to learn how to separate a root and an affix so as to be able to say, 'This part is the original root and this is an affix,'" may we not reply that to those who have drunk the waters of Patañjali this question produces no confusion, since it is notorious that the rules of grammar have reference to this very point of the separation of the original roots and affixes? Thus the very first sentence of the venerable Patañjali, the author of the "Great Commentary," is "*atha śabdánuśásanam*," "Now comes the exposition of words." The particle *atha* ("now") is used here as implying a new topic or a commencement; and by the phrase, "exposition of words," is meant the system of grammar put forth by Páṇini. Now a doubt might here arise as to whether this phrase implies that the exposition of words is to be the main topic or not; and it is to obviate any such doubt that he employed the particle *atha*, since this particle implies that what follows is to be treated as the main topic to the exclusion of everything else.

The word "exposition" (*anuśásana*), as here used, implies that thereby Vaidic words, such as those in the line *śaṃ no devír abhishṭaye*,[308] & c., and secular words as ancillary to these, as the common words for "cow," "horse," "man," "elephant," "bird," &c., are made the subject of the exposition, *i.e.*, are deduced from their original roots and properly formed, or, in other words, are explained as divided into root and affix. We must consider that the compound in this phrase represents a genitive of the object [*śabdánuśásanam* standing for *śabdasyánuśásanam*], and as there is a rule of Páṇini (*karmaṇi cha*, ii. 2, 14), which prohibits composition in such a construction, we are forced to concede that the phrase *śabdánuśásanam* does not come before us as a duly authorised compound.

Here, however, arises a discussion [as to the true application of the alleged rule of Páṇini], for we hold that, by ii. 3, 66, wherever an object and an agent are both expressed in one and the same sentence in connection with a word ending with a *kṛit* affix, there the object alone can be put in the genitive and not the agent;[309] this limitation arising from our taking *ubhayaprápti* in the sútra as a*bahuvríhi* compound.[310] Thus we must say, "Wonderful is the milking of cows by an unpractised cowherd." We may, however, remark in passing that some authors do maintain that the agent may in such cases be put in the genitive (as well as the object); hence we find it stated in the Káśiká Commentary: "Some authors maintain that there should be an option in such cases without any distinction, and thus they would equally allow such a construction as 'the exposition of words *of* the teacher' or '*by* the teacher.'" Inasmuch, however, as the words of the phrase in question really mean that the "exposition" intended relates to *words* and not to *things*, and since this can be at once understood without any mention of the agent, *i.e.*, the teacher, any such mention would be plainly superfluous; and therefore as the object and the agent are *not* both expressed in one and the same sentence, this is not an instance of the genitive of the object (coming under ii. 3, 66, and ii. 2, 14), but rather an instance of quite another rule, viz., ii. 3, 65, which directs that an agent or an object, in connection with a word ending with a kṛit affix, is to be put in the genitive [which in this instance is expressed by the *tatpurusha*-compound]; and the compound in question will be strictly analogous to such recognised forms as *idhma-pravraśchana, paláśa-śátana*,& c.[311] Or we might argue that the genitive case implied in this *shashṭhítatpurusha* is one of the class called "residual," in accordance with Páṇini's rule (ii. 3, 50), "Let the genitive be used in the residuum," [*i.e.*, in the other constructions not provided for by special rules];[312] and in this way we might defend the phrase against the opponent's attack. "But," it might be replied, "your alleged 'residual genitive' could be assumed everywhere, and we should thus find all the prohibitions of composition in constructions with a genitive case rendered utterly nugatory." This we readily grant, and hence Bhartṛihari in his *Vákyapadíya* has shown that these rules are mainly useful where the question relates to the *accent*.[313] To this effect are the words of the great doctor Vardhamána—

> "In secular utterances men may proceed as they will,
> "But in Vaidic paths let minute accuracy of speech be employed.
> "Thus have they explained the meaning of Páṇini's sútras, since
> "He himself uses such phrases as *janikartuḥ* and *tatprayojakaḥ*."[314]

Hence it follows that the full meaning of the sentence in question (of the *Mahábháshya*) is that "it is to be understood that the rules of grammar which may be taken as a synonym for 'the exposition concerning words' are now commenced."

"Well, then, for the sake of directly understanding this intended meaning, it would have been better to have said 'now comes grammar,' as the words 'now comes the exposition of words' involve a useless excess of letters." This objection cannot, however, be allowed, since the employment of such a word as *śabdánuśásanam*, the sense of which can be so readily inferred from its etymology, proves that the author intends to imply an end which shall establish that grammar is a subordinate study (*aṅga*) to the Veda.[315] Otherwise, if there were no such end set forth, there would be no consequent application of the readers to the study of grammar. Nor may you say that this application will be sufficiently enforced by the injunction for study, "the Veda with its six subordinate parts must be read as a duty without any (special) end,"[316] because, even though there be such an injunction, it will not follow that students will apply to this study, if no end is mentioned which will establish that it is an *aṅga* of the Veda. Thus in old times the students, after reading the Veda, used to be in haste to say—

> "Are not Vaidic words established by the Veda and secular by common life,
> "And therefore grammar is useless?"

Therefore it was only when they understood it to be an *aṅga* of the Veda that they applied themselves to its study. So in the same way the students of the present day would not be likely to apply themselves to it either. It is to obviate this danger that it becomes necessary to set forth some end which shall, at the same time, establish that grammar is an *aṅga* of the Veda. If, when the end is explained, they should still not apply themselves, then, being destitute of all knowledge of the true formation of secular words, they would become involved in sin in the course of sacrificial acts, and would consequently lose their religious merit. Hence the followers of sacrifice read, "One who keeps up a sacrificial fire, on using an incorrect word, should offer an expiatory offering to Saraswatí." Now it is to declare this end which establishes that it is an *aṅga* of the Veda that he uses the words *atha śabdánuśásanam* and not *atha vyákaraṇam*. Now the rules of grammar must have an end, and a thing's end is determined by men's pursuit of it with a view thereto. Just as in a sacrifice undertaken with a view to heaven, heaven is the end; in the same way the end of the exposition of words is instruction concerning words, *i.e.*, propriety of speech. "But," an objector may say, "will not the desired end be still unattained for want of the true means to it? Nor can it be said that reading the Veda word by word is the true means; for this cannot be a means for the understanding of words, since their number is infinite, as divided into proper and improper words.[317] Thus there is a tradition that Bṛihaspati for a thousand divine years taught to Indra the study of words as used in their individual forms when the Veda is read word by word,[318] and still he came not to the end. Here the teacher was Bṛihaspati, the pupil was Indra, and the time of study a thousand years of the gods; and yet the termination was not reached,—how much less, then, in our day, let a man live ever so long? Learning is rendered efficient by four appropriate means,—reading, understanding, practising, and handing it on to others; but in the proposed way life would only suffice for the bare time of reading; therefore the reading word by word is not a means for the knowledge of words, and consequently, as we said at first, the desired end is not established." We reply, however, that it was never conceded that the knowledge of words was to be attained by this reading word by word. And again, since general and special rules apply at once to many examples, when these are divided into the artificial parts called roots, &c. (just as one cloud rains over many spots of ground), in this way we can easily comprehend an exposition of many words. Thus, for instance, by the general rule (iii. 2, 1), *karmaṇi*, the affix *aṇ* is enjoined after a root when the object is in composition with it; and by this rule we learn many words, as *kumbhakára*, "a potter," *káṇḍaláva*, "a cutter of stems," &c. But the supplementary special rule (iii. 2, 3), *áto 'nupasarge kaḥ*, directing that the affix *ka* is to be used after a root that ends in long *á* when there is no *upasarga*, shows how impracticable this reading word by word would be [since it would never teach us how to distinguish an *upasarga*]. "But since there are other *aṅgas*, why do you single out grammar as the one object of honour?" We reply, that among the six *aṅgas* the principal one is grammar, and labour devoted to what is the principal is sure to bear fruit. Thus it has been said—

> "Nigh unto Brahman himself, the highest of all religious austerities,
> "The wise have called grammar the first *aṅga* of the Veda."

Hence we conclude that the exposition of words is the direct end of the rules of grammar, but its indirect end is the preservation, &c., of the Veda. Hence it has been said by the worshipful author of the great Commentary [quoting a Várttika], "the end (or motive) is preservation, inference, scripture, facility, and assurance."[319] Moreover prosperity arises from the employment of a correct word; thus Kátyáyana has said, "There is prosperity in the employment of a word according to the *śástra*; it is equal to the words of the Veda itself." Others also have said that "a single word thoroughly understood and rightly used becomes in Swarga the desire-milking cow." Thus (they say)—

> "They proceed to heaven, with every desired happiness, in well-yoked chariots of harnessed speech;
> "But those who use such false forms as *achíkramata* must trudge thither on foot."[320]

Nor need you ask "how can an irrational word possess such power?" since we have revelation declaring that it is like to the great god. For the Śruti says, "Four are its horns, three its feet, two its heads, and seven its hands,—roars loudly the threefold-bound bull, the great god enters mortals" (Rig-Veda, iv. 58, 3). The great commentator thus explains it:—The "four horns" are the four kinds of words—nouns, verbs, prepositions, and particles; its "three feet" mean the three times, past, present, and future, expressed by the tense-affixes, *laṭ*, &c.; the "two heads," the eternal and temporary (or produced) words, distinguished as the "manifested" and the "manifester;" its "seven hands" are the seven case affixes, including the conjugational terminations; "threefold bound," as enclosed in the three organs—the chest, the throat, and the head. The metaphor "bull" (*vṛishabha*) is applied from its pouring forth (*varshaṇa*), *i.e.*, from its giving fruit when used with knowledge. "Loudly roars,"*i.e.*, utters sound, for the root *ru* means "sound;" here by the word "sound" developed speech (or language)[321] is implied; "the great god enters mortals,"—the "great god," *i.e.*, speech,—enters mortals, *i.e.*, men endowed with the attribute of mortality. Thus is declared the likeness [of speech][322] to the supreme Brahman.

The eternal word, called *sphoṭa*, without parts, and the cause of the world, is verily Brahman; thus it has been declared by Bhartṛihari in the part of his book called the Brahmakáṇḍa—

> "Brahman, without beginning or end, the indestructible essence of speech,
> "Which is developed in the form of things, and whence springs the creation of the world."

"But since there is a well-known twofold division of words into nouns and verbs, how comes this fourfold division?" We reply, because this, too, is well known. Thus it has been said in the Prakírṇaka—

> "Some make a twofold division of words, some a fourfold or a fivefold,
> "Drawing them up from the sentences as root, affix, and the like."

Helárája interprets the fivefold division as including *karmapravachaníyas*.[323] But the fourfold division, mentioned by the great commentator, is proper, since *karmapravachaníyas* distinguish a connection produced by a particular kind of verb, and thus, as marking out a particular kind of connection and so marking out a particular kind of verb, they are really included in compounded prepositions (*upasargas*).[324]

"But," say some, "why do you talk so much of an eternal sound called *sphoṭa*? This we do not concede, since there is no proof that there is such a thing." We reply that our own perception is the proof. Thus there is one word "cow," since all men have the cognition of a word distinct from the various letters composing it. You cannot say, in the absence of any manifest contradiction, that this perception of the word is a false perception.

Hence you must concede that there is such a thing as *sphoṭa*, as otherwise you cannot account for the cognition of the meaning of the word. For the answer that its cognition arises from the letters cannot bear examination, since it breaks down before either horn of the following dilemma:—Are the letters supposed to produce this cognition of the meaning in their united or their individual capacity? Not the first, for the letters singly exist only for a moment, and therefore cannot form a united whole at all; and not the second, since the single letters have no power to produce the cognition of the meaning [which the word is to convey]. There is no conceivable alternative other than their single or united capacity; and therefore it follows (say the wise in these matters) that, as the letters cannot cause the cognition of the meaning, there must be a *sphoṭa* by means of which arises the knowledge of the meaning; and this *sphoṭa* is an eternal sound, distinct from the letters and revealed by them, which causes the cognition of the meaning. "It is disclosed (*sphuṭyate*) or revealed by the letters," hence it is called *sphoṭa*, as revealed by the letters; or "from it is disclosed the meaning," hence it is called*sphoṭa* as causing the knowledge of the meaning,—these are the two etymologies to explain the meaning of the word. And thus it hath been said by the worshipful Patañjali in the great Commentary, "Now what is the word '*cow*' *gauḥ*? It is that word by which, when pronounced, there is produced the simultaneous cognition of dewlap, tail, hump, hoofs, and horns." This is expounded by Kaiyaṭa in the passage commencing, "Grammarians maintain that it is the word, as distinct from the letters, which expresses the meaning, since, if the letters expressed it, there would be no use in pronouncing the second and following ones [as the first would have already conveyed all we wished]," and ending, "The *Vákyapadíya* has established at length that it is the *sphoṭa* which, distinct from the letters and revealed by the sound, expresses the meaning."[325]

Here, however, an objector may urge, "But should we not rather say that the *sphoṭa* has no power to convey the meaning, as it fails under either of the following alternatives, for is it supposed to convey the meaning when itself manifested or unmanifested? Not the latter, because it would then follow that we should find the effect of conveying the meaning always produced, since, as *sphoṭa* is supposed to be eternal, and there would thus be an ever-present cause independent of all subsidiary aids, the effect could not possibly fail to appear. Therefore, to avoid this fault, we must allow the other alternative, viz., that *sphoṭa* conveys the meaning when it is itself manifested. Well, then, do the manifesting letters exercise this manifesting power separately or combined? Whichever alternative you adopt, the very same faults which you alleged against the hypothesis of the letters expressing the meaning, will have to be met in your hypothesis that they have this power to manifest *sphoṭa*." This has been said by Bhaṭṭa in his Mímáṃsá-śloka-várttika—

> "The grammarian who holds that *sphoṭa* is manifested by the letters as they are severally apprehended, though itself one and indivisible, does not thereby escape from a single difficulty."

The truth is, that, as Páṇini (i. 4, 14) and Gotama (Sút. ii. 123) both lay it down that letters only then form a word when they have an affix at the end, it is the letters which convey the word's meaning through the apprehension of the conventional association of ideas which they help.[326] If you object that as there are the same letters in *rasa* as in *sara*, in *nava* as in *vana*, in *díná* as in *nadí*, in *mára* as in *ráma*, in *rája* as in *jára*, &c., these several pairs of words would not convey a different meaning, we reply that the difference in the order of the letters will produce a difference in the meaning. This has been said by Tautátita—

> "As are the letters in number and kind, whose power is perceived in conveying any given meaning of a word, so will be the meaning which they convey."

Therefore, as there is a well-known rule that when the same fault attaches to both sides of an argument it cannot be urged against one alone, we maintain that the hypothesis of the existence of a separate thing called *sphoṭa* is unnecessary, as we have proved that it is the letters which express the word's meaning [your arguments against our view having been shown to be irrelevant].

All this long oration is really only like a drowning man's catching at a straw;[327] for either of the alternatives is impossible, whether you hold that it is the single letters or their aggregation which conveys the meaning of the word. It cannot be the former, because a collection of separate letters, without any one pervading cause,[328] could never produce the idea of a word any more than a collection of separate flowers would form a garland without a string. Nor can it be the latter, because the letters, being separately pronounced and done with, cannot combine into an aggregate. For we use the term "aggregate" where a number of objects are perceived to be united together in one place; thus we apply it to a Grislea tomentosa, an Acacia catechu, a Butea frondosa, &c., or to an elephant, a man, a horse, &c., seen together in one place; but these letters are not perceived thus united together, as they are severally produced and pass away; and even on the hypothesis of their having a "manifesting" power, they can have no power to form an aggregate, as they can only manifest a meaning successively and not simultaneously. Nor can you imagine an artificial aggregate in the letters, because this would involve a "mutual dependence" (or reasoning in a circle); for, on the one hand, the letters would only become a word when their power to convey one meaning had been established; and, on the other hand, their power to convey one meaning would only follow when the fact of their being a word was settled. Therefore, since it is impossible that letters should express the meaning, we must accept the hypothesis of*sphoṭa*. "But even on your own hypothesis that there is a certain thing called *sphoṭa* which expresses the meaning, the same untenable alternative will recur which we discussed before; and therefore it will only be a case of the proverb that 'the dawn finds the smuggler with the revenue-officer's house close by.'"[329] This, however, is only the inflation of the world of fancy from the wide difference between the two cases. For the first letter, in its manifesting power, reveals the invisible *sphoṭa*, and each successive letter makes this*sphoṭa* more and more manifest, just as the Veda, after one reading, is not retained, but is made sure by repetition; or as the real nature of a jewel is not clearly seen at the first glance, but is definitely manifested at the final examination. This is in accordance with the authoritative saying (of the teacher): "The seed is implanted by the sounds, and, when the idea is ripened by the successive repetition, the word is finally ascertained simultaneously with the last uttered letter." Therefore, since Bhartṛihari has shown in his first book that the *letters* of a word [being many and successive] cannot manifest the meaning of the word, as is implied by the very phrase, "We gain such and such a meaning from such and such a *word*," we are forced to assume the existence[330] of an indivisible *sphoṭa* as a distinct category, which has the power to manifest the word's meaning. All this has been established in the discussion (in the Mahábháshya) on "genus" (*játi*), which aims at proving that the meaning of all words is ultimately that *summum genus*, *i.e.*, that existence whose characteristic is perfect knowledge of the supreme reality[331] (Brahman).

"But if all words mean only that supreme existence, then all words will be synonyms, having all the same meaning; and your grand logical ingenuity would produce an astonishing result in demonstrating the uselessness of human language as laboriously using several words to no purpose at the same time!" Thus it has been said—

> "The employment of synonymous terms at the same time is to be condemned; for they only express their meaning in turn and not by combination."
>
> "Therefore this opinion of yours is really hardly worth the trouble of refuting."

All this is only the ruminating of empty ether; for just as the colourless crystal is affected by different objects which colour it as blue, red, yellow, &c., so, since the *summum genus*, Brahman, is variously cognised through its connection with different things, as severally identified with each, we thus account for the use of the various conventional words which arise from the different species,[332] as cow, &c., these being "existence" (the *summum genus*) as found in the individual cow, &c. To this purport we have the following authoritative testimony—

"Just as crystal, that colourless substance, when severally joined with blue, red, or yellow objects, is seen as possessing that colour."

And so it has been said by Hari, "Existence [pure and simple] being divided, when found in cows, &c., by reason of its connection with different subjects, is called this or that species, and on it all words depend. This they call the meaning of the stem and of the root. This is existence, this the great soul; and it is this which the affixed *tva*, *tal*, &c., express" (Páṇini v. 1, 119).

"Existence" is that great *summum genus* which is found in cows, horses, &c., differentiated by the various subjects in which it resides; and the inferior species, "cow," "horse," &c., are not really different from it; for the species "cow" and "horse" (*gotva* and *aśvatva*) are not really new subjects, but each is "existence" as residing in the subject "cow" and "horse." Therefore all words, as expressing definite meanings, ultimately rest on that one *summum genus* existence, which is differentiated by the various subjects, cows, &c., in which it resides; and hence "existence" is the meaning of the stem-word (*prátipadika*). A "root" is sometimes defined as that which expresses *bháva*;[333] now, as *bháva* is "existence," the meaning of a root is really existence.[334] Others say that a root should be defined as that which expresses "action" (*kriyá*); but here again the meaning of a root will really be "existence," since this "action" will be a genus, as it is declared to reside in many subjects, in accordance with the common definition of a genus, in the line—

> "Others say that action (*kriyá*) is a genus, residing in many individuals."

So, too, if we accept Páṇini's definition (v. 1, 119), "Let the affixes *tva* and *tal* come after a word [denoting anything], when we speak of the nature (*bháva*) thereof," it is clear from the very fact that abstract terms ending in *tva* or *tá* [as *aśvatva* and *aśvatá*] are used in the sense of *bháva*, that they do express "existence." "This is pure existence" from its being free from all coming into being or ceasing to be; it is eternal, since, as all phenomena are developments thereof, it is devoid of any limit in space, time, or substance: this existence is called "the great soul." Such is the meaning of Hari's two *kárikás* quoted above. So, too, it is laid down in the discussion on *sambandha* [in Hari's verses] that the ultimate meaning of all words is that something whose characteristic is perfect knowledge of the real meaning of the word Substance.

"The true Reality is ascertained by its illusory forms; the true substance is declared by words through illusory disguises; as the object, 'Devadatta's house,' is apprehended by a transitory cause of discrimination,[335] but by the word 'house' itself, the pure idea [without owners] is expressed."[336]

So, too, the author of the Mahábháshya, when explaining the Várttika,[337] "a word, its meaning, and its connection being fixed," in the passage beginning "substance is eternal," has shown that the meaning of all words is Brahman, expressed by the word "substance" and determined by various unreal[338] conditions [as "the nature of horse," &c.]

According to the opinion of Vájapyáyana, who maintains that all words mean a genus, words like "cow," &c.,[339] denote a genus which resides by intimate relation in different substances; and when this genus is apprehended, through its connection with it we apprehend the particular substance in which it resides. Words like "white," &c., denote a genus which similarly resides in qualities; through the connection with genus we apprehend the quality, and through the connection with the quality we apprehend the individual substance. So in the case of words expressing particular names, in consequence of the recognition that "this is the same person from his first coming into existence to his final destruction, in spite of the difference produced by the various states of childhood, youth, adolescence, &c.," we must accept a fixed genus as Devadatta-hood,[340] &c. [as directly denoted by them]. So, too, in words expressing "action" a genus is denoted; this is the root-meaning, as in *paṭhati*, "he reads," &c., since we find here a meaning common to all who read.

In the doctrine of Vyáḍi, who maintained that words meant individual things [and not classes or genera], the individual thing is put forward as that which is primarily denoted, while the genus is implied [as a characteristic mark]; and he thus avoids the alleged faults of "indefiniteness," and "wandering away from its proper subject."[341]

Both views are allowed by the great teacher Páṇini; since in i. 2, 58, he accepts the theory that a word means the genus, where he says that "when the singular is used to express the class the plural may be optionally used" [as in the sentence, "A Bráhman is to be honoured," which may equally run, "Bráhmans are to be honoured"]; while in i. 2, 64, he accepts the theory that a word means the individual thing, where he says, "In any individual case there is but one retained of things similar in form" [*i.e.*, the dual means Ráma and Ráma, and the plural means Ráma, and Ráma and Ráma; but we retain only one, adding a dual or plural affix]. Grammar, in fact, being adapted to all assemblies, can accept both theories without being compromised. Therefore both theories are in a sense true;[342] but the real fact is that all words ultimately mean the Supreme Brahman.

As it has been said—

> "Therefore under the divisions of the meanings of words, one true universal meaning, identical with the one existent, shines out in many forms as the thing denoted."

Hari also, in his chapter discussing *sambandha*, thus describes the nature of this true meaning—

> "That meaning in which the subject, the object, and the perception [which unites them] are insusceptible of doubt,[343] *that* only is called the truth by those who know the end of the three Vedas."

So too in his description of substance, he says—

"*That* which remains as the Real during the presence of modification, as the gold remains under the form of the earring,—*that* wherein change comes and goes, *that* they call the Supreme Nature."

The essential unity of the word and its meaning is maintained in order to preserve inviolate the non-duality of all things which is a cardinal doctrine of our philosophy.

"This [Supreme Nature] is the thing denoted by all words, and it is identical with the word; but the relation of the two, while they are thus ultimately identical, varies as does the relation of the two souls."[344]

The meaning of this Káriká is that Brahman is the one object denoted by all words; and this one object has various differences imposed upon it according to each particular form; but the conventional variety of the differences produced by these illusory conditions is only the result of ignorance. Non-duality is the true state; but through the power of "concealment"[345] [exercised by illusion] at the time of the conventional use of words a manifold expansion takes place, just as is the case during sleep. Thus those skilled in Vedánta lore tell us—

> "As all the extended world of dreams is only the development of illusion in me, so all this extended waking world is a development of illusion likewise."

When the unchangeable Supreme Brahman is thus known as the existent joy-thought and identical with the individual soul, and when primeval ignorance is abolished, final bliss is accomplished, which is best defined as the abiding in identity with this Brahman, according to the text, "He who is well versed in the Word-Brahman attains to the Supreme Brahman."[346] And thus we establish the fact that the "exposition of words" is the means to final bliss.

Thus it has been said—

> "They call it the door of emancipation, the medicine of the diseases of speech, the purifier of all sciences, the science of sciences."[347]

And so again—

> "This is the first foot-round of the stages of the ladder of final bliss, this is the straight royal road of the travellers to emancipation."

Therefore our final conclusion is that the Śástra of grammar should be studied as being the means for attaining the chief end of man.

—E. B. C.

CHAPTER XIV.

THE SÁṄKHYA-DARŚANA.

"But how can we accept the doctrine of illusory emanation [thus held by the grammarians, following the guidance of the *púrva* and *uttara* Mímáṃsá schools], when the system of development propounded by the Sáṅkhyas is still alive to oppose it?" Such is their loud vaunt. Now the Śástra of this school may be concisely said to maintain four several kinds of existences, viz., that which is evolvent[348] only, that which is evolute only, that which is both evolute and evolvent, and that which is neither. (*a.*) Of these the first is that which is only evolvent, called the root-evolvent or the primary; it is not itself the evolute of anything else. It evolves, hence it is called the evolvent (*prakṛiti*) since it denotes in itself the equilibrium of the three qualities, goodness, activity, and darkness. This is expressed [in the Sáṅkhya Káriká], "the root-evolvent is no evolute." It is called the root-evolvent, as being both root and evolvent; it is the root of all the various effects, as the so-called "great one,"& c., but of it, as the primary, there is no root, as otherwise we should have a *regressus ad infinitum*. Nor can you reply that such a *regressus ad infinitum* is no objection, if, like the continued series of seed and shoot, it can be proved by the evidence of our senses,[349]—because here there is no evidence to establish the hypothesis. (*b.*) The "evolutes and evolvents" are the great one, egoism, and the subtile elements,—thus the Sáṅkhya Káriká (§ 3), "the seven, the great one, &c., are evolute-evolvents." The seven are the seven principles, called the great one, &c. Among these the great principle, called also the intellect,[350] &c., is itself the evolute of nature and the evolvent of egoism; in the same manner the principle egoism, called also "self-consciousness" (*abhimána*), is the evolute of the great one, intellect; but this same principle, as affected by the quality of darkness, is the evolvent of the five rudiments called subtile elements; and, as affected by the quality of goodness, it is the evolvent of the eleven organs, viz., the five organs of perception, the eye, ear, nose, tongue, and skin; the five organs of action, the voice, hands, feet, anus, and generative organ; and the mind, partaking of the character of both; nor can you object that in our arrangement the third quality, activity, is idle, as it acts as a cause by producing action in the others. This has been thus declared by Íśvara Kṛishṇa in his Kárikás[351] (§ 24-27), "Self-consciousness is egoism. Thence proceeds a twofold creation, the elevenfold set and the five elemental rudiments. From modified[352] egoism originates the class of eleven imbued with goodness; from egoism as the source of the elements originate the rudimentary elements, and these are affected by darkness; but it is only from egoism as affected by activity that the one and the other rise. The intellectual organs are the eyes, the ears, the nose, the tongue, and the skin; those of action are the voice, feet, hands, anus, and organ of generation. In this set is mind, which has the character of each; it determines, and it is an organ (like the other ten) from having a common property with them."[353] All this has been explained at length by the teacher Váchaspati Miśra in the Sáṅkhya-tattva-kaumudí.

(*c.*) The "evolute only" means the five gross elements, ether, &c., and the eleven organs, as said in the Káriká, "The evolute consists of sixteen;" that is, the set of sixteen is evolute only, and not evolvent. Although it may be said that earth, &c., are the evolvents of such productions as cows, jars, &c., yet these are not a different "principle" (*tattva*) from earth, &c., and therefore earth, &c., are not what we term "evolvents;" as the accepted idea of an evolvent is that which is the material cause of a separate principle; and in cows, jars, &c., there is the absence of being any such first principle, in consequence of their being all alike gross [*i.e.*, possessed of dimensions] and perceptible to the senses. The five gross elements, ether, &c., are respectively produced from sound, touch, form, taste, and smell, each subtile element being accompanied by all those which precede it, and thus the gross elements will have respectively one, two, three, four, and five qualities.[354] The creation of the organs has been previously described. This is thus propounded in the Sáṅkhya Káriká (§ 22)—

"From nature springs the great one, from this egoism, from this the set of sixteen, and from five among the sixteen proceed the five gross elements."

(*d.*) The soul is neither,—as is said in the Káriká, "The soul is neither evolvent nor evolute." That is, the soul, being absolute, eternal, and subject to no development, is itself neither the evolvent nor the evolute of aught beside. Three kinds of proof are accepted as establishing these twenty-five principles; and thus the Káriká (§ 4).

"Perception, inference, and the testimony of worthy persons are acknowledged to be the threefold proof, for they comprise every mode of demonstration. It is from proof that there results belief of that which is to be proven."

Here a fourfold discussion arises as to the true nature of cause and effect. The Saugatas[355] maintain that the existent is produced from the non-existent; the Naiyáyikas, &c., that the (as yet) non-existent is produced from the existent; the Vedántins, that all effects are an illusory emanation from the existent and not themselves really existent; while the Sáṅkhyas hold that the existent is produced from the existent.

(*a.*) Now the first opinion is clearly untenable, since that which is itself non-existent and unsubstantial can never be a cause any more than the hare's horn; and, again, the real and unreal can never be identical.

(*b.*) Nor can the non-existent be produced from the existent; since it is impossible that that which, previous to the operation of the originating cause, was as non-existent as a hare's horn should ever be produced, *i.e.*, become connected with existence; for not even the cleverest man living can make blue yellow.[356] If you say, "But are not existence and non-existence attributes of the same jar?" this is incorrect, since we cannot use such an expression as "its quality" in regard to a non-existent subject, for it would certainly imply that the subject itself did exist. Hence we conclude that the effect is existent even previously to the operation of the cause, which only produces the manifestation of this already existent thing, just like the manifestation of the oil in sesame seed by pressing, or of the milk in cows by milking. Again, there is no example whatever to prove the production of a thing previously non-existent.

Moreover, the cause must produce its effect as being either connected with it or not connected; in the former alternative the effect's existence is settled by the rule that connection can only be between two existent things; in the latter, any and every effect might arise from any and every cause, as there is nothing to determine the action of an unconnected thing. This has been thus put by the Sáṅkhya teacher:—"From the supposed non-existence of the effect, it can have no connection with causes which always accompany existence; and to him who holds the production of a non-connected thing there arises an utter want of determinateness." If you rejoin that "the cause, though not connected with its effect, can yet produce it, where it has a capacity of so doing, and this capacity of producing is to be inferred from seeing the effect actually produced," still this cannot be allowed, since in such a case as "there is a capacity for producing oil in sesame seeds," you cannot determine, while the oil is non-existent, that there is this capacity in the sesame seeds, whichever alternative you may accept as to their being connected or not with the oil [since our before-mentioned dilemma will equally apply here].

From our tenet that the cause and effect are identical, it follows that the effect does not exist distinct from the cause; thus the cloth is not something distinct from the threads, as it abides in the latter [as its material cause]; but where this identity is not found, there we do not find the relation of cause and effect; thus a horse and a cow are distinct from each other [for one is not produced from the other, and therefore their qualities are not the same]; but the cloth is an acknowledged effect, and therefore not anything different from its cause.[357] If you object that, if this were true, the separate threads ought to fulfil the office of clothing, we reply, that the office of clothing is fulfilled by the threads manifesting the nature of cloth when they are placed in a particular arrangement. As the limbs of a tortoise when they retire within its shell are concealed, and, when they come forth, are revealed, so the particular effects, as cloth, &c., of a cause, as threads, &c., when they come forth and are revealed, are said to be produced; and when they retire and are concealed, they are said to be destroyed; but there is no such thing as the production of the non-existent or the destruction of the existent. As has been said in the Bhagavad Gítá (ii. 16)—

> "There is no existence for the non-existent, nor non-existence for the existent."

And, in fact, it is by inference from its effects that we establish the existence of the great evolvent, Nature (*prakṛiti*). This has been said [in the Káriká, § 9]—

> "Effect exists, for what exists not can by no operation of cause be brought into existence; materials, too, are selected which are fit for the purpose; everything is not by every means possible; what is capable does that to which it is competent; and like is produced from like."[358]

Nor can we say [with the Vedántin] that the world is an illusory emanation from the one existent Brahman, because we have no contradictory evidence to preclude by its superior validity the *primâ facie* belief that the external world is real [as we have in the case of mistaking a rope for a snake, where a closer inspection will discover the error]; and again, where the subject and the attributed nature are so dissimilar as the pure intelligent Brahman and the unintelligent creation, we can no more allow the supposed attribution to be possible than in the case of gold and silver [which no one mistakes for each other]. Hence we conclude that an effect which is composed of happiness, misery, and stupidity, must imply a cause similarly composed; and our argument is as follows:—The subject of the argument, viz., the external world, must have a material cause composed of happiness, misery, and stupidity, because it is itself endued therewith; whatever is endued with certain attributes must have a cause endued with the same,—thus a ring has gold for its material cause, because it has the attributes of gold; our subject is a similar case, therefore we may draw a similar conclusion. What we call "being composed of happiness" in the external world is the quality of goodness; the "being composed of misery" is the quality of activity;[359] the "being composed of stupidity" is the quality of darkness; hence we establish our cause composed of the three qualities (*i.e.*, *prakṛiti*, Nature). And we see that individual objects are found by experience to have these three qualities; thus Maitra's happiness is found in his wife Satyavatí, because the quality of "goodness" in her is manifested towards him; but she is the misery of her fellow-wives, because the quality of "activity" is manifested towards them; while she causes indifference to Chaitra who does not possess her, because towards him the quality of "darkness" is manifested. So, too, in other cases also; thus a jar, when obtained, causes us pleasure; when seized by others it causes us pain; but it is viewed with indifference by one who has no interest in it. Now this being regarded with no interest is what we mean by "stupidity," since the word *moha* is derived from the root *muh*, "to be confused," since no direct action of the mind arises towards those objects to which it is indifferent. Therefore we hold that all things, being composed of pleasure, pain, and stupidity, must have as their cause Nature, which consists of the three qualities. And so it is declared in the Śvetáśvatara Upanishad (iv. 5)—

> "The one unborn, for his enjoyment, approaches the one unborn (Nature) which is red, white, and black, and produces a manifold and similar offspring; the other unborn abandons her when once she has been enjoyed."

Here the words "red," "white," and "black," express the qualities "activity," "goodness," and "darkness," from their severally possessing the same attributes of colouring, manifesting, and concealing.

Here, however, it may be objected, "But will not your unintelligent Nature, without the superintendence of something intelligent, fail to produce these effects, intellect, &c.? therefore there must be some intelligent superintendent; and hence we must assume an all-seeing, supreme Lord." We reply that this does not follow, since even unintelligent Nature will act under the force of an impulse; and experience shows us that an unintelligent thing, without any intelligent superintendent, does act for the good of the soul, just as the unintelligent milk acts for the growth of the calf, or just as the unintelligent rain acts for the welfare of living creatures; and so unintelligent Nature will act for the liberation of the soul. As it has been said in the Káriká (§ 57)—

> "As the unintelligent milk acts for the nourishment of the calf, so Nature acts for the liberation of soul."

But as for the doctrine of "a Supreme Being who acts from compassion," which has been proclaimed by beat of drum by the advocates of his existence, this has well-nigh passed away out of hearing, since the hypothesis fails to meet either of the two alternatives. For does he act thus *before* or *after* creation? If you say "before," we reply that as pain cannot arise in the absence of bodies, &c., there will be no need, as long as there is no creation, for his desire to free living beings from pain [which is the main characteristic of compassion]; and if you adopt the second alternative, you will be reasoning in a circle, as on the one hand you will hold that God created the world through compassion [as this is His motive in acting at all], and on the other hand[360] that He compassionated after He had created. Therefore we hold that the development of unintelligent Nature [even without any intelligent superintendent]—in the order of the series intellect, self-consciousness, &c.,—is caused by the union of Nature and Soul, and the moving impulse is the good of Soul. Just as there takes place a movement in the iron in the proximity of the unmoved magnet, so there takes place a movement in Nature in the proximity of the unmoved Soul; and this union of Nature and Soul is caused by mutual dependence, like the union of the lame man and the blind man. Nature, as the thing to be experienced, depends on Soul the experiencer; and Soul looks to final bliss, as it seeks to throw off the three kinds of pain, which, though really apart from it, have fallen upon it by its coming under the shadow of intellect through not recognising its own distinction therefrom.[361] This final bliss [or absolute isolation] is produced by the discrimination of Nature and Soul, nor is this end possible without it; therefore Soul depends on Nature for its final bliss. Just as a lame man and a blind man,[362] travelling along with a caravan, by some accident having become separated from their companions, wandered slowly about in great dismay, till by good luck they met each other, and then the lame man mounted on the blind man's back, and the blind man, following the path indicated by the lame man, reached his desired goal, as did the lame man also, mounted on the other's shoulders; so, too, creation is effected by Nature and the soul, which are likewise mutually dependent. This has been said in the Káriká (§ 21)—

> "For the soul's contemplation of Nature and for its final separation the union of both takes place, as of the lame man and the blind man. By that union a creation is formed."

"Well, I grant that Nature's activity may take place for the good of the soul, but how do you account for its ceasing to act?" I reply, that as a wilful woman whose faults have once been seen by her husband does not return to him, or as an actress, having performed her part, retires from the stage, so too does Nature desist. Thus it is said in the Káriká (§ 59)—

> "As an actress, having exhibited herself to the spectators, desists from the dance, so does Nature desist, having manifested herself to Soul."

For this end has the doctrine of those who follow Kapila, the founder of the atheistic Sáṅkhya School, been propounded.

CHAPTER XV.

THE PATANJALI-DARSÁNA.

We now set forth the doctrine of that school which professes the opinions of such Munis as Patañjali and others, who originated the system of the Theistic Sáṅkhya philosophy. This school follows the so-called Yoga Śástra promulgated by Patañjali, and consisting of four chapters, which also bears the name of the "Sáṅkhya Pravachana," or detailed explanation of the Sáṅkhya.[363] In the first chapter thereof the venerable Patañjali, having in the opening aphorism, "Now is the exposition of Concentration" (*yoga*), avowed his commencement of the Yoga Śástra, proceeds in the second aphorism to give a definition of his subject, "Concentration is the hindering of the modifications of the thinking principle," and then he expounds at length the nature of Meditation (*samádhi*). In the second chapter, in the series of aphorisms commencing, "The practical part of Concentration is mortification, muttering, and resignation to the Supreme," he expounds the practical part of *yoga* proper to him whose mind is not yet thoroughly abstracted (iii. 9), viz., the five external subservients or means, "forbearance," and the rest. In the third chapter, in the series commencing "Attention is the fastening [of the mind] on some spot," he expounds the three internal subservients—attention, contemplation, and meditation, collectively called by the name "subjugation" (*saṃyama*), and also the various superhuman powers which are their subordinate fruit. In the fourth chapter, in the series commencing, "Perfections spring from birth, plants, spells, mortification, and meditation," he expounds the highest end, Emancipation, together with a detailed account of the five so-called "perfections" (*siddhis*). This school accepts the old twenty-five principles [of the Sáṅkhya], "Nature," &c.; only adding the Supreme Being as the twenty-sixth—a Soul untouched by affliction, action, fruit, or stock of desert, who of His own will assumed a body in order to create, and originated all secular or Vaidic traditions,[364] and is gracious towards those living beings who are burned in the charcoal of mundane existence.

"But how can such an essence as soul, undefiled as the [glossy] leaf of a lotus, be said to be burned, that we should need to accept any Supreme Being as gracious to it?" To this we reply, that the quality Goodness develops itself as the understanding, and it is this which is, as it were, burned by the quality Activity; and the soul, by the influence of Darkness, blindly identifying itself with this suffering quality, is also said itself to suffer. Thus the teachers have declared—

> "It is Goodness which suffers under the form of the understanding and the substances belonging to Activity which torment,[365]
> And it is through the modification of Darkness, as wrongly identifying, that the Soul is spoken of as suffering."

It has been also said by Patañjali,[366] "The power of the enjoyer, which is itself incapable of development or of transference, in an object which is developed and transferred experiences the modifications thereof."

Now the "power of the enjoyer" is the power of intelligence, and this is the soul; and in an object which is "developed" and "transferred," or reflected,—*i.e.*, in the thinking principle or the understanding,—it experiences the modifications thereof, *i.e.*, the power of intelligence, being reflected in the understanding, receives itself the shadow of the understanding, and imitates the modifications of it. Thus the soul, though in itself pure, sees according to the idea produced by the understanding; and, while thus seeing at second-hand, though really it is different from the understanding, it appears identical therewith. It is while the soul is thus suffering, that, by the practice of the eight subservient means, forbearance, religious observance, &c., earnestly, uninterruptedly, and for a long period, and by continued resignation to the Supreme Being, at length there is produced an unclouded recognition of the distinction between the quality Goodness and the Soul; and the five "afflictions," ignorance, &c., are radically destroyed, and the various "stocks of desert," fortunate or unfortunate, are utterly abolished, and, the undefiled soul abiding emancipated, perfect Emancipation is accomplished.

The words of the first aphorism, "Now is the exposition of concentration," establish the four preliminaries which lead to the intelligent reader's carrying the doctrine into practice, viz., the object-matter, the end proposed, the connection [between the treatise and the object], and the person properly qualified to study it. The word "now" (*atha*) is accepted as having here an inceptive meaning, [as intimating that a distinct topic is now commenced]. "But," it may be objected, "there are several possible significations of this word *atha*; why, then, should you show an unwarranted partiality for this particular 'inceptive' meaning? The great Canon for nouns and their gender [the Amara Kosha Dictionary] gives many such meanings. '*Atha* is used in the sense of an auspicious particle,—after,—now (inceptive),—what? (interrogatively),—and all (comprehensively).' Now we willingly surrender such senses as interrogation or comprehensiveness; but since there are four senses certainly suitable, *i.e.*, 'after,' 'an auspicious particle,' 'reference to a previous topic,' and 'the inceptive now,' there is no reason for singling out the *last*." This objection, however, will not stand, for it cannot bear the following alternative. If you maintain the sense of "after," then do you hold that it implies following after anything whatever, or only after some definite cause as comprehended under the general definition of causation,[367] *i.e.*, "previous existence [relatively to the effect]"? It cannot be the former, for, in accordance with the proverb that "No one stands for a single moment inactive," everybody must always do everything after previously doing something else; and since this is at once understood without any direct mention at all, there could be no use in employing the particle*atha* to convey this meaning. Nor can it be the latter alternative; because, although we fully grant that the practice of concentration does in point of fact follow after previous tranquillity, &c., yet these are rather the necessary preliminaries to the work of exposition, and consequently cannot have that avowed predominance [which the presumed *cause* should have]. "But why should we not hold that the word *atha* implies that this very exposition is avowedly the predominant object, and does follow after previous tranquillity of mind, &c.?" We reply, that the aphorism uses the term "exposition" (*anuśásana*), and this word, etymologically analysed, implies that by which the *yoga* is explained, accompanied with definitions, divisions, and detailed means and results; and there is no rule that such an exposition must follow previous tranquillity of mind, &c., the rule rather being that, as far as the teacher is concerned, it must follow a profound knowledge of the truth and a desire to impart it to others; for it is rather the student's desire to know and his derived knowledge, which should have quiet of mind, &c., as their precursors, in accordance with the words of Śruti: "Therefore having become tranquil, self-subdued, loftily indifferent, patient, full of faith and intent, let him see the soul in the soul."[368] Nor can the word*atha* imply the necessary precedence, in the teacher, of a profound knowledge of the truth and a desire to impart it to others; because, even granting that both these are present, they need not to be mentioned thus prominently, as they are powerless in themselves to produce the necessary intelligence and effort in the student. Still [however we may settle these points] the question arises, Is the exposition of the *yoga* ascertained to be a cause of final beatitude or not? If it is, then it is still a desirable object, even if certain presupposed conditions should be absent; and if it is not, then it must be undesirable, whatever conditions may be present.[369] But it is clear that the exposition in question *is* such a cause, since we have such a passage of the Śruti as that [in the Kaṭha Upanishad, ii. 12]: "By the acquirement of *yoga* or intense concentration on the Supreme Soul, the wise man having meditated leaves behind joy and sorrow;" and again, such a passage of the Smṛiti as that [in the Bhagavad Gítá, ii. 53]: "The intellect unwavering in contemplation will then attain *yoga*." Hence we conclude that it is untenable to interpret *atha* as implying that the exposition must follow "after" a previous inquiry on the part of the student, or "after" a previous course of ascetic training and use of elixirs, &c. [to render the body strong].

But in the case of the Vedánta Sútras, which open with the aphorism, "Now, therefore, there is the wish to know Brahman," Śaṅkara Ácharya has declared that the inceptive meaning of *atha* must be left out of the question, as the wish to know Brahman is not to be undertaken [at will]; and therefore it must be there interpreted to mean "after,"*i.e.*, that this desire must follow a previous course of tranquillity, &c., as laid down by the well-known rule which enjoins the practice of tranquillity, self-control, indifference, endurance, contemplation, and faith, the object being to communicate the teaching to a proper student as distinguished by the possession of the four so-called "means."[370]

"Well, then, let us grant that *atha* cannot mean 'after;' but why should it not be simply an auspicious particle?" But this it cannot be, from the absence of any connection between the context and such auspicious meaning. Auspiciousness implies the obtaining of an unimpeached and desired good, and what is desired is so desired as being the attainment of pleasure or the avoidance of pain; but this auspiciousness cannot belong to the exposition of *yoga*, since it is in itself neither pleasure nor the cessation of pain.[371] Therefore it cannot be at all established that the meaning of the aphorism is that "the exposition of the *yoga* is auspicious;" for auspiciousness cannot be either the primary meaning of *atha* or its secondary meaning by metonymy, since it is its very sound which is in itself auspicious [without any reference to the meaning], like that of a drum. "But why not say that just as an implied meaning may enter into the direct meaning of a sentence, so an effect [like this of auspiciousness] may also be included, since both are equally unexpressed so far as the actual words are concerned?"[372] We reply, that in the meaning of a sentence the connection must be between the meaning of one word and that of another; otherwise we should be guilty of breaking the seal which the rule of the grammarians has set, that "verbal expectancy[373] can be fulfilled by *words* alone."

"But ought not a prayer for an auspicious commencement to be put at the beginning of a Śástra, in order to lay the hosts of obstacles that would hinder the completion of the work which the author desires to begin, and also to observe the immemorial practice of the good, since it has been said by the wise, 'Those śástras become widely famous which have auspicious commencements, auspicious middles, and auspicious endings, and their students have long lives and are invincible in disputation'?[374] Now the word *atha* implies 'auspiciousness,' since there is a Smṛiti which says,

"'The word *Om* and the word *atha*,—these two in the ancient time,

"'Cleaving the throat of Brahman, came forth; therefore they are both auspicious.'

"Therefore let the word *atha* stand here as signifying 'auspiciousness,' like the word '*vṛiddhi*' used by Páṇini in his opening sútra '*vṛiddhir ád aich*.'"'[375] This view, however, is untenable; since the very word *atha*, when heard, has an auspicious influence, even though it be employed to convey some other special signification, just as the hearing the sound of lutes, flutes, &c. [is auspicious for one starting on a journey]. If you still object, "How can the particle *atha* have any other effect, if it is specially used here to produce the idea that the meaning of the sentence is that a new topic is commenced?" we reply that it certainly *can* have such other additional effect, just as we see that jars of water brought for some other purpose are auspicious omens at the commencement of a journey.[376] Nor does this contradict the smṛiti, since the smṛiti will still hold good, as the words "they are both auspicious" mean only that they produce an auspicious effect.

Nor can the particle *atha* have here the meaning of "reference to a previous topic," since the previously mentioned faults will all equally apply here, as this meaning really involves that of "after" [which we have already discussed and rejected]. And again, in such discussions as this, as to whether this particular *atha* means "the inceptive now" or "after," if another topic had been previously suggested, then "reference thereto" would be a possible meaning; but in the present case [where no other topic has been previously suggested] it is not a possible meaning. Therefore, by exhaustion, the commentator finally adopts, for the *atha* of the sútra, the remaining meaning of "the inceptive now." So, when it is said [in the Táṇḍya Bráhmaṇa, xvi. 8, 1; xvi. 10, 1], "Now this is the Jyotis," "Now this is the Viśvajyotis,"[377] the particle *atha* is accepted as signifying the commencement of the description of a particular sacrifice, just as the *atha* in the commencement of the Mahábháshya, "now comes the exposition of words," signifies the commencement of the Institutes of Grammar. This has been declared by Vyása in his Commentary on the Yoga Aphorisms, "the *atha* in this opening aphorism indicates a commencement;" and Váchaspati has similarly explained it in his gloss; therefore it may be considered as settled that the *atha* here indicates a commencement and also signifies auspiciousness. Therefore, accepting the view that this*atha* implies a commencement, let the student be left in peace to strive after a successful understanding of the śástra through the attainment of the *yoga*, which is its proposed subject, by means of the teacher's explanation of its entire purport. But here some one may say, "Does not the smṛiti of Yájñavalkya say, 'Hiraṇyagarbha is the promulgator of the Yoga, and no other ancient sage?' how then is Patañjali the teacher thereof?" We reply that it was for this reason that the venerable Patañjali,[378] that ocean of compassion, considering how difficult it was to grasp all the different forms of Yoga scattered up and down in the Puráṇas, &c., and wishing to collect together their essence, commenced his *anuśásana,*—the preposition *anu* implying that it was a teaching which followed a primary revelation and was not itself the immediate origin of the system.

Since this *atha* in the aphorism signifies "commencement," the full meaning of the sentence comes out as follows: "be it known that the institute for the exposition of the *yoga* is now commenced." In this institute the "object-matter," as being that which is produced by it, is *yoga* [or the "concentration of the mind"], with its means and its fruit; the producing this is its inferior "end;" supreme absorption (*kaivalya*) is the highest "end" of the *yoga* when it is produced. The "connection" between the institute and *yoga* is that of the producer and the thing to be produced; the "connection" between *yoga*and supreme absorption is that of the means and the end; and this is well known from Śruti and Smṛiti, as I have before shown. And it is established by the general context that those who aim at liberation are the duly qualified persons to hear this institute. Nor need any one be alarmed lest a similar course should be adopted with the opening aphorism of the Vedánta sútras, "Now, therefore, there is a wish to know Brahman;" and lest here, too, we should seek to establish by the general context that all persons who aim at liberation are duly qualified students of the Vedánta. For the word*atha,* as there used, signifies "succession" [or "after"]; and it is a settled point that the doctrine can only be transmitted through a regular channel to duly qualified students, and consequently the question cannot arise as to whether any other meaning is suggested by the context. Hence it has been said, "When Śruti comes [as the determining authority] 'the subject-matter' and the rest have no place."[379] The full meaning of this is as follows: Where a thing is not apprehended from the Veda itself, there the "subject-matter" and the rest can establish the true meaning, not otherwise; but wherever we can attain the meaning by a direct text, there the other modes of interpretation are irrelevant. For when a thing is declared by a text of the Veda which makes its meaning obvious at once, the "subject-matter" and the rest either establish a contrary conclusion or one not contrary. Now, in the former case, the authority which would establish this contrary conclusion is [by the very nature of "*śruti*"] already precluded from having any force; and in the latter it is useless. This is all declared in Jaimini's aphorism [iii. 3, 14]; "A definite text, a 'sign,' the 'sentence,' the 'subject-matter,' the 'relative position,' or 'the title,'—when any of these come into collision, the later in order is the weaker because its meaning is more remote"[380] [and therefore less obvious]. It has been thus summed up—

"A text always precludes the rest; the 'title' is always precluded by any of the preceding modes;

"But whether any intervening one is precluded, or itself precludes, depends on circumstances."

Therefore [after all this long discussion] it may be now considered as settled that, since it has an "object," as well as the other preliminaries, the study of the Śástra, which teaches the Yoga, is to be commenced like that of the Vedánta, which discusses the nature of Brahman. "But," it may be objected, "it is the Yoga which was said to be the object-matter, since it is this which is to be produced, not the Śástra." We grant that the Yoga is the principal object, as that which is to be produced; but since it is produced by the Śástra, especially directed thereto, this Śástra is the means for its production, and, as a general rule, the agent's activity is directly concerned with the means rather than with the end. Just as the operations of Devadatta the woodcutter, *i.e.*, his lifting his arm up and down, &c., relate rather to the instrument, *i.e.*, the axe, than to the object, *i.e.*, the tree, so here the speaker, Patañjali, in his immediate action of speaking, means the Yoga-Śástra as his primary object, while he intends the Yoga itself in his ultimate action of "denotation." In consequence of this distinction, the real meaning is that the commencing the Yogaśástra is that which primarily claims our attention; while the "yoga," or the restraint of the modifications of the mind, is what is to be expounded in this Sáśtra. "But as we read in the lists of roots that the root *yuj* is used in the sense of 'joining,' should not the word *yoga*, its derivative, mean 'conjunction,' and not 'restraint'? And indeed this has been said by Yájñavalkya:[381]—

'The conjunction of the individual and the supreme souls is called *yoga*.'"

This, however, is untenable, since there is no possibility of any such action,[382] &c., in either as would produce this conjunction of the two souls. [Nor, again, is such an explanation needed in order to remove the opposition of other philosophical schools]; for the notion of the conjunction of two eternal things is opposed to the doctrines of the Vaiśeshika and Nyáya schools [and therefore they would still oppose our theory]. And even if we accepted the explanation in accordance with the Mímáṃsá [or Vedánta], our Yogaśástra would be rendered nugatory by this concession [and the very ground cut from under our feet]; because the identity of the individual and supreme souls being in that school something already accomplished, it could not be regarded as something to be produced by our Śástra. And lastly, as it is notorious that roots are used in many different senses, the root *yuj* may very well be used here in the sense of "contemplation."[383] Thus it has been said—

> "Particles, prepositions, and roots—these three are all held to be of manifold meaning; instances found in reading are their evidence."

Therefore some authors expressly give *yuj* in this sense, and insert in their lists "*yuj* in the sense of *samádhi*." Nor does this contradict Yájñavalkya's declaration, as the word *yoga*, used by him, may bear this meaning; and he has himself said—

> "*Samádhi* is the state of identity of the individual and supreme souls; this abiding absolutely in Brahman is the *samádhi* of the individual soul."

It has been also said by the venerable Vyása [in his Commentary on the Yoga-sútras, i. 1], "*Yoga is samádhi.*"

An objection however, may be here raised that "the term *samádhi* is used by Patañjali [in ii. 29] in the sense of one of the eight ancillary parts[384] of the eightfold concentration (or *yoga*); and the whole cannot be thus itself a part as well as a whole, since the principal and the ancillary must be completely different from each other, as all their attendant circumstances must be different, just as we see in the *darśapúrṇamása* sacrifices and their ancillary rites the *prayájas*, and therefore *samádhi* cannot be the meaning of *yoga*." We however reply that this objection is incorrect; for although the term *samádhi* is used for etymological reasons[385] to express the ancillary part which is really defined [in iii. 3] as "the contemplation which assumes the form of the object, and is apparently devoid of any nature of its own;" still the further use of this term to describe the principal state is justified by the author's wish to declare the ultimate oneness of the two states [as the inferior ultimately merges into the superior]. Nor can you hold that etymology alone can decide where a word can be used; because if so, as the word*go*, "a bull," is derived by all grammarians from the root *gam*, "to go," we ought never to use the phrase "a standing bull" [as the two words would be contradictory], and the man Devadatta, when going, would properly be called *go*, "a bull;" and, moreover, the Sútra, i. 2, distinctly gives us a definite justification for employing the word in this sense when it declares that "concentration (*yoga*) is the suppression of the modifications of the thinking principle." [The second or principal sense of *samádhi* will therefore be quite distinct from the first or inferior.]

"But surely if *yoga* is held to be the suppression of the modifications of the thinking principle, then as these modifications abide in the soul as themselves partaking of the nature of knowledge, their suppression, or in other words their 'destruction,' would also abide in the soul, since it is a principle in logic that the antecedent non-existence and destruction abide in the same subject as the counter-entity to these negations;[386] and consequently in accordance with the maxim, 'This newly produced character will affect the subject in which it resides,' the absolute independence of the soul itself would be destroyed." This, however, we do not allow; because we maintain that these various modifications which are to be hindered,[387] such as "right notion," "misconception," "fancy," "sleep," and "memory" (i. 6), are attributes of the internal organ (*chitta*), since the power of pure intelligence, which is unchangeable, cannot become the site of this discriminative perception. Nor can you object that this unchangeable nature of the intelligent soul[388] has not been proved, since there is an argument to establish it; for the intelligent soul must be unchangeable from the fact that it always knows, while that which is not always knowing is not unchangeable, as the internal organ, &c. And so again, if this soul were susceptible of change, then, as this change would be occasional, we could not predicate its always knowing these modifications. But the true view is, that while the intelligent soul always remains as the presiding witness, there is another essentially pure substance[389] which abides always the same; and as it is this which is affected by any given object, so it is this perceptible substance which is reflected as a shadow on the soul, and so produces an impression;[390] and thus Soul itself is preserved in its own proper independence, and it is maintained to be the always knowing, and no suspicion of change alights upon it. That object by which the understanding becomes affected is known; that object by which it is not affected is not known; for the understanding is called "susceptible of change," because it resembles the iron, as it is susceptible of being affected or not by the influence or want of influence of the object which resembles the magnet,—this influence or want of influence producing respectively knowledge or the want of knowledge. "But inasmuch as the understanding and the senses which spring from egoism are all-pervading, are they not always connected with all objects, and thus would it not follow that there should be a knowledge everywhere and always of all things?" We reply that even although we grant that they are all-pervading, it is only where a given understanding has certain modifications in a given body, and certain objects are in a connection with that body, that the knowledge of these objects only, and none other, is produced to that understanding; and therefore, as this limitation is absolute, we hold that objects are just like magnets, and affect the understanding just as these do iron,—coming in contact with it through the channels of the senses. Therefore, the "modifications" belong to the understanding, not to the soul; and so says the Śruti, "Desire, volition, doubt, faith, want of faith, firmness, want of firmness,—all this is only the mind." Moreover, the sage Pañchaśikha declared the unchangeable nature of the intelligent soul, "The power that enjoys is unchangeable;" and so Patañjali also (iv. 18), "The modifications of the understanding are always known,—this arises from the unchangeableness of the Ruling Soul." The following is the argument drawn out formally to establish the changeableness of the understanding. The understanding is susceptible of change because its various objects are now known and now not known, just like the organ of hearing and the other organs of sense. Now, this change is notoriously threefold, *i.e.*, a change of "property," of "aspect,"[391] and of "condition." When the subject, the understanding, perceives the colour "blue," &c., there is a change of "property" just as when the substance "gold" becomes a bracelet, a diadem, or an armlet; there is a change of "aspect" when the property becomes present, past, or future; and there is a change of "condition" when there is a manifestation or non-manifestation[392] of the perception, as of blue, &c.; or, in the case of gold, the [relative] newness or oldness [at two different moments] would be its change of condition. These three kinds of change must be traced out by the reader for himself in different other cases. And thus we conclude that there is nothing inconsistent in our thesis that, since "right notion" and the other modifications are attributes of the understanding, their "suppression" will also have its site in the same organ.

[Our opponent now urges a fresh and long objection to what we have said above.] "But if we accept your definition that '*yoga* is the suppression of the modifications of the *chitta*,' this will apply also to 'sound sleep,' since there too we may find the suppression [or suspension] of the modifications found in *kshipta, vikshipta,múḍha*,[393] &c.; but this would be wrong, because it is impossible for the 'afflictions' to be abolished so long as those states called*kshipta*, &c., remain at all, and because they only hinder the attainment of the *summum bonum*. Let us examine this more closely. For the understanding is called *kshipta*, 'restless,' when it is restless [with an excess of the quality *rajas*], as being tossed about amidst various objects which engage it. It is called *múḍha*, 'blinded,' when it is possessed by the modification 'sleep' and is sunk in a sea of darkness [owing to an excess of the quality *tamas*]. It is called *vikshipta*, 'unrestless,' when it is different from the first state[394] [as filled with the quality *sattva*]." We must here, however, note a distinction; for, in accordance with the line of the Bhagavad Gítá (vi. 34), 'The mind, O Kṛishṇa, is fickle, turbulent, violent, and obstinate,' the mind, though naturally restless, may occasionally become fixed by the transient fixedness of its objects; but restlessness is innate to it, or it is produced in it by sickness,&

c., or other consequences of former actions; as it is said [in the Yoga Sútras, i. 30], 'Sickness, languor, doubt, carelessness, laziness, addiction to objects, erroneous perception, failure to attain some stage, and instability,—these distractions of the mind are called "obstacles".' Here 'sickness' means fever, &c., caused by the want of equilibrium between the three humours; 'languor' is the mind's want of activity; 'doubt' is a sort of notion which embraces two opposite alternatives; 'carelessness' is a negligence of using the means for producing meditation; 'laziness' is a want of exertion from heaviness of body, speech, or mind; 'addiction to objects' is an attachment to objects of sense; 'erroneous perception' is a mistaken notion of one thing for another; 'failure to attain some stage' is the failing for some reason or other to arrive at the state of abstract meditation; 'instability' is the mind's failure to continue there, even when the state of abstract meditation has been reached. Therefore we maintain that the suppression of the mind's modifications cannot be laid down as the definition of *yoga*.

We reply, that even although we allow that, so far as regards the three conditions of the mind called *kshipta, múḍha*, and *vikshipta*, which [as being connected with the three qualities] are all to be avoided as faulty states, the suppression of the modifications in these conditions is itself something to be avoided [and so cannot be called *yoga*], this does not apply to the other two conditions called *ekágra* and *niruddha*, which are to be pursued and attained; and therefore the suppression of the modifications in these two praiseworthy conditions is rightly to be considered as *yoga*. Now by *ekágra* we mean that state when the mind, entirely filled with the *sattva* quality, is devoted to the one object of meditation; and by *niruddha* we mean that state when all its developments are stopped, and only their latent impressions [or potentialities] remain.

Now this *samádhi*, "meditation" [in the highest sense], is twofold: "that in which there is distinct recognition" (*saṃprajñáta*), and "that in which distinct recognition is lost" (*asaṃprajñáta*) [Yoga S., i. 17, 18].[395] The former is defined as that meditation where the thought is intent on its own object, and all the "modifications," such as "right notion," &c., so far as they depend on external things, are suppressed, or, according to the etymology of the term, it is where the intellect[396] is thoroughly recognised (*samyak prajñáyate*) as distinct from Nature. It has a fourfold division, as *savitarka, savichára, sánanda*, and*sásmita*. Now this "meditation" is a kind of "pondering" (*bhávaná*), which is the taking into the mind again and again, to the exclusion of all other objects, that which is to be pondered. And that which is thus to be pondered is of two kinds, being either Íśwara or the twenty-five principles. And these principles also are of two kinds—senseless and not senseless. Twenty-four, including nature, intellect, egoism, &c., are senseless; that which is not senseless is Soul. Now among these objects which are to be pondered, when, having taken as the object the gross elements, as earth, &c., pondering is pursued in the form of an investigation as to which is antecedent and which consequent,[397] or in the form of a union of the word, its meaning, and the idea which is to be produced [cf. i. 42]; then the meditation is called "argumentative" (*savitarka*). When, having taken as its object something subtile, as the five subtile elements and the internal organ, pondering is pursued in relation to space, time, &c., then the meditation is called "deliberative" (*savichára*). When the mind, commingled with some "passion" and "darkness," is pondered, then the meditation is called "beatific" (*sánanda*), because "goodness" is then predominant, which consists in the manifestation of joy.[398] When pondering is pursued, having as its object the pure element of "goodness," unaffected by even a little of "passion" or "darkness," then that meditation is called "egoistical" (*sásmita*), because here personal existence[399] only remains, since the intellectual faculty becomes now predominant, and the quality of "goodness" has become quite subordinate [as a mere stepping-stone to higher things].

But the "meditation, where distinct recognition is lost," consists in the suppression of all "modifications" whatever.

"But" [it may be asked] "was not 'concentration' defined as the suppression of all the modifications? How, then, can the 'meditation where there is distinct recognition' be included in it at all, since we still find active in it that modification of the mind, with the quality of goodness predominant, which views the soul and the quality of goodness as distinct from each other?" This, however, is untenable, because we maintain that concentration is the suppression of the "modifications" of the thinking power, as especially stopping the operation of the "afflictions," the "actions," the "fructifications," and the "stock of deserts."[400]

The "afflictions" (*kleśa*) are well known as five, viz., ignorance, egoism, desire, aversion, and tenacity of mundane existence. But here a question is at once raised, In what sense is the word *avidyá*, "ignorance," used here? Is it to be considered as an *avyayibháva* compound, where the former portion is predominant, as in the word "above-board"?[401] or is it a *tatpurusha* [or *karmadháraya*] compound, where the latter portion is predominant, as in the word "town-clerk"? or is it a *bahuvríhi* compound, where both portions are dependent on something external to the compound, as "blue-eyed"? It cannot be the first; for if the former portion of the compound were predominant, then we should have the negation the emphatic part in*avidyá* (*i.e.*, it would be an instance of what is called the express negation, or *prasajya-pratishedha*);[402] and consequently, as *avidyá* would be thus emphatically a negation, it would be unable to produce positive results, as the "afflictions," &c., and the very form of the word should not be feminine, but neuter. It cannot be the second; for any knowledge, whatever thing's absence it may be characterised by (*a* + *vidyá*), opposes the "afflictions," &c., and cannot therefore be their source. Nor can it be the third; for then,—in accordance with the words of the author of the Vṛitti,[403] "there is a *bahuvríhi* compound which is formed with some word meaning 'existence' used after 'not,' with the optional elision of this subsequent word"[404]—we must explain this supposed *bahuvríhi*compound *avidyá* as follows: "That *buddhi* is to be characterised as*avidyá* (*sc.* an adjective), of which there is not a *vidyá* existing." But this explanation is untenable; for such an *avidyá*could not become the source of the "afflictions;"[405] and yet, on the other hand, it ought to be their source,[406] even though it were associated with the suppression of all the "modifications,"[407] and were also accompanied by that discriminative knowledge of the soul and the quality of goodness [which is found in the *sásmita* meditation].

Now it is said [in the Yoga Sútras, ii. 4], "Ignorance is the field [or place of origin, *i.e.*, source] of the others, whether they be dormant, extenuated, intercepted, or simple." They are said to be "dormant" when they are not manifested for want of something to wake them up; they are called "extenuated" when, through one's meditating on something that is opposed to them, they are rendered inert; they are called "intercepted" when they are overpowered by some other strong "affliction;" they are called "simple" when they produce their several effects in the direct vicinity of what co-operates with them. This has been expressed by Váchaspati Miśra, in his Gloss on Vyása's Commentary, in the following memorial stanza:—

> "The dormant 'afflictions' are found in those souls which are absorbed in the *tattvas* [*i.e.*, not embodied, but existing in an interval of mundane destruction]; the 'extenuated'[408] are found in *yogins*; but the 'intercepted' and the 'simple' in those who are in contact with worldly objects."

"No one proposes the fourth solution of the compound *avidyá* as a *dvandva* compound,[409] where both portions are equally predominant, because we cannot recognise here two equally independent subjects. Therefore under any one of these three admissible alternatives[410] the common notion of ignorance as being the cause of the 'afflictions' would be overthrown."

[We do not, however, concede this objector's view], because we may have recourse to the other kind of negation called *paryudása* [where the affirmative part is emphatic], and maintain that *avidyá* means a contradictory [or *wrong*] kind of knowledge, the reverse of *vidyá*; and so it has been accepted by ancient writers. Thus it has been said—

> "The particle implying 'negation' does not signify 'absence' [or 'non-existence'] when connected with a noun or a root; thus the words *abráhmaṇa* and *adharma* respectively signify, 'what is other than a Bráhman' and 'what is contrary to justice.'"

And again—

"We are to learn all the uses of words from the custom of the ancient writers; therefore a word must not be wrested from the use in which it has been already employed."

Váchaspati also says,[411] "The connection of words and their meanings depends on general consent for its certainty; and since we occasionally see that a *tatpurusha* negation, where the latter portion is properly predominant, may overpower the direct meaning of this latter portion by its contradiction of it, we conclude that even here too [in *avidyá*] the real meaning is something contrary to*vidyá*" [*i.e.*, the negative "non-knowledge" becomes ultimately the positive "ignorance"[412]]. It is with a view to this that it is said in the Yoga Aphorisms [ii. 5], "Ignorance is the notion that the non-eternal, the impure, pain, and the non-soul are (severally) eternal, pure, pleasure, and soul." *Viparyaya*, "misconception," is defined as "the imagining of a thing in what is not that thing,"[413] [*i.e.*, in its opposite]; as, for instance, the imagining the "eternal" in a "non-eternal" thing, *i.e.*, a jar, or the imagining the "pure" in the "impure" body,[414] when it has been declared by a proverbial couplett[415]—

> "The wise recognise the body as impure, from its original place [the womb],—from its primal seed,—from its composition [of humours, &c.],—from perspiration,—from death [as even a Bráhman's body defiles],—and from the fact that it has to be made pure by rites."

So,—in accordance with the principle enounced in the aphorism (ii. 15), "To the discriminating everything is simply pain, through the pain which arises in the ultimate issue of everything,[416] or through the anxiety to secure it [while it is enjoyed], or through the latent impressions which it leaves behind, and also from the mutual opposition of the influences of the three qualities" [in the form of pleasure, pain, and stupid indifference],—ignorance transfers the idea of "pleasure" to what is really "pain," as, *e.g.*, garlands, sandal-wood, women, &c.; and similarly it conceives the "non-soul,"*e.g.*, the body, &c., as the "soul." As it has been said—

"But ignorance is when living beings transfer the notion of 'soul' to the 'non-soul,' as the body, &c.;

"This causes bondage; but in the abolition thereof is liberation."

Thus this ignorance consists of four kinds.[417]

But [it may be objected] in these four special kinds of ignorance should there not be given some general definition applying to them all, as otherwise their special characteristics cannot be established? For thus it has been said by Bhaṭṭa Kumárila—

"'Without some general definition, a more special definition cannot be given by itself; therefore it must not be even mentioned here.'"

This, however, must not be urged here, as it is sufficiently met by the general definition of misconception, already adduced above, as "the imagining of a thing in its opposite."

"Egoism" (*asmitá*) is the notion that the two separate things, the soul and the quality of purity,[418] are one and the same, as is said (ii. 6), "Egoism is the identifying of the seer with the power of sight." "Desire" (*rága*) is a longing, in the shape of a thirst, for the means of enjoyment, preceded by the remembrance of enjoyment, on the part of one who has known joy. "Aversion" (*dvesha*) is the feeling of blame felt towards the means of pain, similarly preceded by the remembrance of pain, on the part of one who has known it. This is expressed in the two aphorisms, "Desire is what dwells on pleasure;" "Aversion is what dwells on pain" (ii. 7, 8).

Here a grammatical question may be raised, "Are we to consider this word *anuśayin* ('dwelling') as formed by the *kṛit* affix *ṇini* in the sense of 'what is habitual,' or the *taddhita* affix *ini* in the sense of *matup*? It cannot be the former, since the affix *ṇini* cannot be used after a root compounded with a preposition as *anuśí*; for, as the word *supi* has already occurred in the Sútra, iii. 2, 4, and has been exerting its influence in the following sútras, this word must have been introduced a second time in the Sútra, iii. 2, 78, *supy ajátau ṇinis táchchhílye*,[419] on purpose to exclude prepositions, as these have no case terminations; and even if we did strain a point to allow them, still it would follow by the Sútra, vii. 2, 115, *acho ñṇiti*,[420] that the radical vowel must be subject to *vṛiddhi*, and so the word must be *anuśáyin*, in accordance with the analogy of such words as *atiśáyin*, &c. Nor is the latter view tenable (*i.e.*, that it is the *taddhita* affix *ini*[421]), since*ini* is forbidden by the technical verse—

'These two affixes[422] are not used after a monosyllable nor a *kṛit* formation, nor a word meaning 'genus,' nor with a word in the locative case;'

and the word *anuśaya* is clearly a *kṛit* formation as it ends with the affix *ach*[423] [which brings it under this prohibition, and so renders it insusceptible of the affix *ini*]. Consequently, the word*anuśayin* in the Yoga aphorism is one the formation of which it is very hard to justify."[424] This cavil, however, is not to be admitted; since the rule is only to be understood as applying generally, not absolutely, as it does not refer to something of essential importance. Hence the author of the Vṛitti has said—

> "The word *iti*, as implying the idea of popular acceptation, is everywhere connected with the examples of this rule[425] [*i.e.*, it is not an absolute law]."

Therefore, sometimes the prohibited cases are found, as *káryin*, *káryika* [where the affixes are added after a *kṛit* formation], *taṇḍulin*, *taṇḍulika* [where they are added after a word meaning "genus"]. Hence the prohibition is only general, not absolute, after*kṛit* formations and words meaning "genus," and therefore the use of the affix *ini* is justified, although the word *anuśaya* is formed by a *kṛit* affix. This doubt therefore is settled.

The fifth "affliction," called "tenacity of mundane existence" (*abhiniveśa*), is what prevails in the case of all living beings, from the worm up to the philosopher, springing up daily, without any immediate cause, in the form of a dread, "May I not be separated from the body, things sensible, &c.," through the force of the impression left by the experience of the pain of the deaths which were suffered in previous lives, this is proved by universal experience, since every individual has the wish, "May I not cease to be," "May I be." This is declared in the aphorism, "Tenacity of mundane existence, flowing on through its own nature, is notorious even in the case of the philosopher" [ii. 9]. These five, "ignorance," &c., are well known as the "afflictions" (*kleśa*), since they afflict the soul, as bringing upon it various mundane troubles.

[We next describe the *karmáśaya* of ii. 12, the "stock of works" or "merits" in the mind.] "Works" (*karman*) consist of enjoined or forbidden actions, as the *jyotishṭoma* sacrifice, bráhmanicide, &c. "Stock" (*áśaya*) is the balance of the fruits of previous works, which lie stored up in the mind in the form of "mental deposits" of merit or demerit, until they ripen in the individual soul's own experience as "rank," "years," and "enjoyment" [ii. 13].

Now "concentration" [*yoga*] consists [by i. 2] in "the suppression of the modifications of the thinking principle," which stops the operation of the "afflictions," &c.; and this "suppression" is not considered to be merely the non-existence of the modifications [*i.e.*, a mere negation], because, if it were a mere negation, it could not produce positive impressions on the mind; but it is rather the site of this non-existence,[426]—a particular state of the thinking principle, called by the four names [which will be fully described hereafter], *madhumatí*, *madhupratíká*, *viśoká*, and *saṃskáraśeshatá*. The word *nirodha* thus corresponds to its etymological explanation as "that in which the modifications of the thinking principle, right notion, misconception, &c., are suppressed (*nirudhyante*). This suppression of the modifications is produced by "exercise" and "dispassion" [i. 12]. "Exercise is the repeated effort that the internal organ shall remain in its proper state" [i. 13]. This "remaining in its proper state" is a particular kind of development, whereby the thinking principle remains in its natural state, unaffected by those modifications which at different times assume the form of revealing, energising, and controlling.[427] "Exercise" is an effort directed to this, an endeavour again and again to reduce the internal organ to such a condition. The locative case,*sthitau*, in the aphorism is intended to express the object or aim, as in the well-known phrase, "He kills the elephant for its skin."[428] "Dispassion is the consciousness of having overcome desire in him who thirsts after neither the objects that are seen nor those that are heard of in revelation" [i. 15]. "Dispassion" is thus the reflection, "These objects are subject to me, not I to them," in one who feels no interest in the things of this world or the next, from perceiving the imperfections attached to them.

Now, in order to reduce the "afflictions" which hinder meditation and to attain meditation, the *yogin* must first direct his attention to practical concentration, and "exercise" and "dispassion" are of especial use in its attainment. This has been said by Kṛishṇa in the Bhagavad Gítá [vi. 3]—

> "Action is the means to the sage who wishes to rise to *yoga*;
> But to him who has risen to it, tranquillity is said to be the means."

Patañjali has thus defined the practical *yoga*: "Practical concentration is mortification, recitation of texts, and resignation to the Lord" [ii. 1]. Yájñavalkya has described "mortification"—

> "By the way prescribed in sacred rule, by the difficult chándráyaṇa fast, &c.,
> "Thus to dry up the body they call the highest of all mortifications."[429]

"Recitation of texts" is the repetition of the syllable Om, the *gáyatrí*, &c. Now these *mantras* are of two kinds, Vaidik and Tántrik. The Vaidik are also of two kinds, those chanted and those not chanted. Those chanted are the *sámans*; those not chanted are either in metre, *i.e.*, the *ṛichas*, or in prose, *i.e.*, the *yajúṃshi*, as has been said by Jaimini,[430] "Of these, that is a *ṛich* in which by the force of the sense there is a definite division into *pádas*[or portions of a verse]; the name *sáman* is applied to chanted portions; the word *yajus* is applied to the rest." Those *mantras* are called Tántrik which are set forth in sacred books that are directed to topics of voluntary devotion;[431] and these are again threefold, as female, male, and neuter; as it has been said—

"The *mantras* are of three kinds, as female, male, and neuter:
"The female are those which end in the wife of fire (*i.e.*, the exclamation *sváhá*); the neuter those which end in *namas*;
"The rest are male, and considered the best. They are all-powerful in mesmerising another's will, &c."

They are called "all-powerful" (*siddha*) because they counteract all defects in their performance, and produce their effect even when the ordinary consecrating ceremonies, as bathing, &c., have been omitted.

Now the peculiar "consecrating ceremonies" (*saṃskára*) are ten, and they have been thus described in the *Śáradá-tilaka*—

"There are said to be ten preliminary ceremonies which give to *mantras* efficacy:
"These mantras are thus made complete; they are thoroughly consecrated.
"The 'begetting,' the 'vivifying,' the 'smiting,' the 'awakening,'
"The 'sprinkling,' the 'purifying,' the 'fattening,'
"The 'satisfying,' the 'illumining,' the 'concealing,'—these are the ten consecrations of *mantras*.
"The 'begetting' (*janana*) is the extracting of the *mantra* from its vowels and consonants.
"The wise man should mutter the several letters of the *mantra*, each united to Om,
"According to the number of the letters. This they call the 'vivifying' (*jívana*).
"Having written the letters of the *mantra*, let him smite each with sandal-water,
"Uttering at each the mystic 'seed' of air.[432] This is called the 'smiting' (*táḍana*).
"Having written the letters of the *mantra*, let him strike them with oleander flowers,
"Each enumerated with a letter. This is called the 'awakening' (*bodhana*).
"Let the adept, according to the ritual prescribed in his own special *tantra*,
"Sprinkle the letters, according to their number, with leaves of the Ficus religiosa. This is the 'sprinkling' (*abhisheka*).
"Having meditated on the *mantra* in his mind, let him consume by the *jyotir-mantra*

"The threefold impurity of the *mantra.* This is the 'purification' (*vimalí-karaṇa*).

"The utterance of the *jyotir-mantra*, together with Om, and the *mantras* of Vyoman and Agni,

"And the sprinkling of every letter with water from a bunch of kuśa grass,

"With the mystical seed of water[433] duly muttered,—this is held to be the 'fattening' (*ápyáyana*).

"The satiating libation over the *mantra* with *mantra*-hallowed water is the 'satisfying' (*tarpaṇa*).

"The joining of the *mantra* with Om and the 'seeds' of Máyá[434] and Ramá[435] is called its 'illumining' (*dípana*).

"The non-publication of the *mantra* which is being muttered—this is its 'concealing' (*gopana*).

"These ten consecrating ceremonies are kept close in all *tantras*;

"And the adept who practises them according to the tradition obtains his desire;

"And *ruddha*, *kílita*, *vichhinna*, *supta*, *śapta*, and the rest,

"All these faults in the *mantra* rites are abolished by these excellent consecrations."

But enough of this venturing to make public the *tantra* mysteries connected with *mantras*, which has suddenly led us astray like an unexpected Bacchanalian dance.[436]

The third form of practical *yoga*, "resignation to the Lord" (*íś vara-praṇidhána*), is the consigning all one's works, whether mentioned or not, without regard to fruit, to the Supreme Lord, the Supremely Venerable. As it has been said—

"Whatever I do, good or bad, voluntary or involuntary,

"That is all made over to thee; I act as impelled by thee."

This self-resignation is also sometimes defined as "the surrender of the fruits of one's actions," and is thus a peculiar kind of faith, since most men act only with a selfish regard to the fruit. Thus it is sung in the Bhagavad Gítá [ii. 47]—

"Let thy sole concern be with action and never with the fruits;

"Be not attracted by the fruit of the action, nor be thou attached to inaction."

The harmfulness of aiming at the fruit of an action has been declared by the venerable Nílakaṇṭha-bhāratí—

"Even a penance accomplished by great effort, but vitiated by desire,

> "Produces only disgust in the Great Lord, like milk which has been licked by a dog."

Now this prescribed practice of mortification, recitation, and resignation is itself called *yoga*, because it is a means for producing *yoga*, this being an instance of the function of words called "superimponent pure Indication," as in the well-known example, "Butter is longevity." "Indication" is the establishing of another meaning of a word from the incompatibility of its principal meaning with the rest of the sentence, and from the connection of this new meaning with the former; it is twofold, as founded on notoriety or on a motive. This has been declared in the *Kávya-prakáśa* [ii. 9]—

> "When, in consequence of the incompatibility of the principal meaning of a word, and yet in connection with it, another meaning is indicated through notoriety or a motive, this is 'Indication,' the superadded function of the word."

Now the word "this" [*i.e.*, *tat* in the neuter, which the neuter *yat* in the extract would have naturally led us to expect instead of the feminine *sá*] would have signified some neuter word, like "implying," which is involved as a subordinate part of the verb "is indicated." But *sá* is used in the feminine [by attraction to agree with *lakshaṇá*], "this is indication," *i.e.*, the neuter "this" is put in the feminine through its dependence on the predicate. This has been explained by Kaiyaṭa, "Of those pronouns which imply the identity of the subject and the predicate, the former takes the gender of the former, the latter of the latter."[437] Now "expert (*kuśala*) in business" is an example of Indication from notoriety; for the word*kuśala*, which is significant in its parts by being analysed etymologically as *kuśaṃ* + *láti*, "one who gathers kuśa grass for the sacrifice," is here employed to mean "expert" through the relation of a similarity in character, as both are persons of discernment; and this does not need a motive any more than Denotation does, since each is the using a word in its recognised conventional sense in accordance with the immemorial tradition of the elders. Hence it has been said—

> "Some instances of 'indication' are known by notoriety from their immediate significance, just as is the case in 'denotation' [the primary power of a word]."

Therefore indication based on notoriety has no regard to any motive. Although a word, when it is employed, first establishes its principal meaning, and then by that meaning a second meaning is subsequently indicated, and so indication belongs properly to the principal meaning and not to the word; still, since it is superadded to the word which originally established the primary meaning, it is called [improperly by metonymy] a function of the word. It was with a view to this that the author of the Kávya-prakáśa used the expression, "This is 'Indication,' the superadded function of the word." But the indication based on a motive is of six kinds: 1. inclusive indication,[438] as "the lances enter" [where we really mean "men *with* the lances"]; 2. indicative indication, as "the benches shout" [where the spectators are meant *without* the benches]; 3. qualified[439] superimponent indication, as "the man of the Panjáb is an ox" [here the object is not swallowed up in the simile]; 4. qualified introsusceptive indication, as "that ox" [here the man is swallowed up in the simile]; 5. pure superimponent indication, as "*ghí* is life;" 6. pure introsusceptive indication, as "verily this is life." This has been all explained in the Kávya-prakáśa [ii. 10-12]. But enough of this churning of the depths of rhetorical discussions.

This *yoga* has been declared to have eight things ancillary to it (*aṅga*); these are the forbearances, religious observances, postures, suppression of the breath, restraint, attention, contemplation, and meditation [ii. 29]. Patañjali says, "Forbearance consists in not wishing to kill, veracity, not stealing, continence, not coveting" [ii. 30]. "Religious observances are purifications, contentment, mortification, recitation of texts, and resignation to the Lord" [ii. 32]; and these are described in the Vishṇu Puráṇa [vi. 7, 36-38]—

> "The sage who brings his mind into a fit state for attaining Brahman, practises, void of all desire,
>
> "Continence, abstinence from injury, truth, non-stealing, and non-coveting;
>
> "Self-controlled, he should practise recitation of texts, purification, contentment, and austerity,
>
> "And then he should make his mind intent on the Supreme Brahman.
>
> "These are respectively called the five 'forbearances' and the five 'religious observances;'
>
> "They bestow excellent rewards when done through desire of reward, and eternal liberation to those void of desire."

"A 'posture' is what is steady and pleasant" [ii. 46]; it is of ten kinds, as the *padma*, *bhadra*, *víra*, *svastika*, *daṇḍaka*, *sopáśraya*, *paryaṅka*, *krauñchanishadana*, *ushṭranishadana*,*samasaṃsthána*. Yájñavalkya has described each of them in the passage which commences—

> "Let him hold fast his two great toes with his two hands, but in reverse order,

"Having placed the soles of his feet, O chief of Bráhmans, on his thighs;

"This will be the *padma* posture, held in honour by all."

The descriptions of the others must be sought in that work.—When this steadiness of posture has been attained, "regulation of the breath" is practised, and this consists in "a cutting short of the motion of inspiration and expiration" [ii. 49]. Inspiration is the drawing in of the external air; expiration is the expelling of the air within the body; and "regulation of the breath" is the cessation of activity in both movements. "But [it may be objected] this cannot be accepted as a general definition of 'regulation of breath,' since it fails to apply to the special kinds, as *rechaka*, *púraka*, and *kumbhaka*." We reply that there is here no fault in the definition, since the "cutting short of the motion of inspiration and expiration" is found in all these special kinds. Thus *rechaka*, which is the expulsion of the air within the body, is only that regulation of the breath, which has been mentioned before as "expiration;" and *púraka*, which is the [regulated] retention of the external air within the body, is the "inspiration;" and *kumbhaka* is the internal suspension of breathing, when the vital air, called *práṇa*, remains motionless like water in a jar (*kumbha*). Thus the "cutting short of the motion of inspiration and expiration" applies to all, and consequently the objector's doubt is needless.

Now this air, beginning from sunrise, remains two *ghaṭikás* and a half[440] in each artery[441] (*náḍi*), like the revolving buckets on a waterwheel.[442] Thus in the course of a day and night there are produced 21,600 inspirations and expirations. Hence it has been said by those who know the secret of transmitting the *mantras*, concerning the transmission of the *ajapámantra*[443]—

"Six hundred to Gaṇeśa, six thousand to the self-existent Brahman,

"Six thousand to Vishṇu, six thousand to Śiva,

"One thousand to the Guru (Bṛihaspati), one thousand to the Supreme Soul,

"And one thousand to the soul: thus I make over the performed muttering."

So at the time of the passing of the air through the arteries, the elements, earth, &c., must be understood, according to their different colours, by those who wish to obtain the highest good. This has been thus explained by the wise—

"Let each artery convey the air two *ghaṭís* and a half from sunrise.

"There is a continual resemblance of the two arteries[444] to the buckets on a revolving waterwheel.

"Nine hundred inspirations and expirations of the air take place [in the hour],

"And all combined produce the total of twenty-one thousand six hundred in a day and night.

"The time that is spent in uttering thirty-six *guṇa*letters,[445]

"That time elapses while the air passes along in the interval between two arteries.

"There are five elements in each of the two conducting arteries,—

"They bear it along day and night; these are to be known by the self-restrained.

"Fire bears above, water below; air moves across;

"Earth in the half-hollow; ether moves everywhere.

"They bear along in order,—air, fire, water, earth, ether;

"This is to be known in its due order in the two conducting arteries.

"The *palas*[446] of earth are fifty, of water forty,

"Of fire thirty, of air twenty, of ether ten.

"This is the amount of time taken for the bearing; but the reason that the two arteries are so disturbed

"Is that earth has five properties,[447] water four,

"Fire has three, air two, and ether one.

"There are ten *palas* for each property; hence earth has fifty *palas*,

"And each, from water downwards, loses successively. Now the five properties of earth

"Are odour, savour, colour, tangibility, and audibleness; and these decrease one by one.

"The two elements, earth and water, produce their fruit by the influence of 'quiet,'

"But fire, air, and ether by the influence of 'brightness,' 'restlessness,' and 'immensity.'[448]

"The characteristic signs of earth, water, fire, air, and ether are now declared;—

"Of the first steadfastness of mind; through the coldness of the second arises desire;

"From the third anger and grief; from the fourth fickleness of mind;

"From the fifth the absence of any object, or mental impressions of latent merit.

"Let the devotee place his thumbs in his ears, and a middle finger in each nostril,

"And the little finger and the one next to it in the corners of his mouth, and the two remaining fingers in the corners of his eyes,

"Then there will arise in due order the knowledge of the earth and the other elements within him,

"The first four by yellow, white, dark red, and dark blue spots,[449]—the ether has no symbol."

When the element air is thus comprehended and its restraint is accomplished, the evil influence of works which concealed discriminating knowledge is destroyed [ii. 52]; hence it has been said—

> "There is no austerity superior to regulation of the breath."[450]

And again—

> "As the dross of metals, when they are melted, is consumed,
> "So the serpents of the senses are consumed by regulation of the breath."[451]

Now in this way, having his mind purified by the "forbearances" and the other things subservient to concentration, the devotee is to attain "self-mastery" (*saṃyama*)[452] and "restraint" (*pratyáhára*). "Restraint" is the accommodation of the senses, as the eye, &c., to the nature of the mind,[453] which is intent on the soul's unaltered nature, while they abandon all concernment with their own several objects, which might excite desire or anger or stupid indifference. This is expressed by the etymology of the word; the senses are drawn to it (*á* + *hṛi*), away from them (*pratípa*).

"But is it not the mind which is then intent upon the soul and not the senses, since these are only adapted for external objects, and therefore have no power for this supposed action? How, therefore, could they be accommodated to the nature of the mind?" What you say is quite true; and therefore the author of the aphorisms, having an eye to their want of power for this, introduced the words "as it were," to express "resemblance." "Restraint is, as it were, the accommodation of the senses to the nature of the mind in the absence of concernment with each one's own object" [ii. 54]. Their absence of concernment with their several objects for the sake of being accommodated to the nature of the mind is this "resemblance" which we mean. Since, when the mind is restrained, the eye, &c., are restrained, no fresh effort is to be expected from them, and they follow the mind as bees follow their king. This has been declared in the Vishṇu-puráṇa [vi. 7, 43, 44]—

> "Let the devotee, restraining his organs of sense, which ever tend to pursue external objects,
> "Himself intent on restraint, make them conformable to the mind;
> "By this is effected the entire subjugation of the unsteady senses;
> "If they are not controlled, the *yogin* will not accomplish his *yoga*."[454]

"Attention" (*dháraṇá*) is the fixing the mind, by withdrawing it from all other objects, on some place, whether connected with the internal self, as the circle of the navel, the lotus of the heart, the top of the *sushumṇá* artery, &c., or something external, as Prajápati, Vásava, Hiraṇyagarbha, &c. This is declared by the aphorism, "'Attention' is the fixing the mind on a place" [iii. 1]; and so, too, say the followers of the Puráṇas—

> "By regulation of breath having controlled the air, and by restraint the senses,
> "Let him next make the perfect asylum the dwelling-place of his mind."[455]

The continual flow of thought in this place, resting on the object to be contemplated, and avoiding all incongruous thoughts, is "contemplation" (*dhyána*); thus it is said, "A course of uniform thought there, is 'contemplation'" [iii. 2]. Others also have said—

> "A continued succession of thoughts, intent on objects of that kind and desiring no other,
> "This is 'contemplation,'—it is thus effected by the first six of the ancillary things."

We incidentally, in elucidating something else, discussed the remaining eighth ancillary thing, "meditation" (*samádhi*, see p. 243). By this practice of the ancillary means of *yoga*, pursued for a long time with uninterrupted earnestness, the "afflictions" which hinder meditation are abolished, and through "exercise" and "dispassion" the devotee attains to the perfections designated by the names Madhumatí and the rest.

"But why do you needlessly frighten us with unknown and monstrous words from the dialects of Karṇáṭa, Gauḍa,[456] and Láṭa?"[457] We do not want to frighten you, but rather to gratify you by explaining the meaning of these strange words; therefore let the reader who is so needlessly alarmed listen to us with attention.

i. The *Madhumatí* perfection,—this is the perfection of meditation, called "the knowledge which holds to the truth," consisting in the illumination of unsullied purity by means of the contemplation of "goodness," composed of the manifestation of joy, with every trace of "passion" or "darkness" abolished by "exercise," "dispassion," &c. Thus it is said in the aphorisms, "In that case there is the knowledge which holds to the truth" [i. 48]. It holds "to the truth," *i.e.*, to the real; it is never overshadowed by error. "In that case," *i.e.*, when firmly established, there arises this knowledge to the second yogin. For the *yogins* or devotees to the practice of *yoga* are well known to be of four kinds, viz.,—

i. The *práthamakalpika*, in whom the light has just entered[458] but, as it has been said, "he has not won the light which consists in the power of knowing another's thoughts, &c.;" 2. The *madhubhúmika*, who possesses the knowledge which holds to the truth; 3. The*prajñájyotis*, who has subdued the elements and the senses; 4. The *atikránta-bhávaníya*, who has attained the highest dispassion.

ii. The *Madhupratíká* perfections are swiftness like thought, &c. These are declared to be "swiftness like thought, the being without organs, and the conquest of nature" [iii. 49]. "Swiftness like thought" is the attainment by the body of exceeding swiftness of motion, like thought; "the being without bodily organs"[459] is the attainment by the senses, irrespective of the body, of powers directed to objects in any desired place or time; "the conquest of nature" is the power of controlling all the manifestations of nature. These perfections appear to the full in the third kind of yogin, from the subjugation by him of the five senses and their essential conditions.[460] These perfections are severally sweet, each one by itself, as even a particle of honey is sweet, and therefore the second state is called *Madhupratíká* [*i.e.*, that whose parts are sweet].

iii. The *Viśoká* perfection consists in the supremacy over all existences, &c. This is said in the aphorisms, "To him who possesses, to the exclusion of all other ideas, the discriminative knowledge of the quality of goodness and the soul, arises omniscience and the supremacy over all existences" [iii. 50]. The "supremacy over all existences" is the overcoming like a master all entities, as these are but the developments of the quality of "goodness" in the mind [the other qualities of "passion" and "darkness" being already abolished], and exist only in the form of energy and the objects to be energised upon.[461] The discriminative knowledge of them, as existing in the modes "subsided," "emerged," or "not to be named,"[462] is "omniscience." This is said in the aphorisms [i. 36], "Or a luminous immediate cognition, free from sorrow[463] [may produce steadiness of mind]."

iv. The *Saṃskáraśeshatá* state is also called *asaṃprajñáta*, *i.e.*, "that meditation in which distinct recognition of an object is lost;" it is that meditation "without a seed" [*i.e.*, without any object] which is able to stop the "afflictions" that produce fruits to be afterwards experienced in the shape of rank, length of life, and enjoyment; and this meditation belongs to him who, in the cessation of all modifications of the internal organ, has reached the highest "dispassion." "The other kind of meditation [*i.e.*, that in which distinct recognition of an object is lost] is preceded by that exercise of thought which produces the entire cessation of modifications; it has nothing left but the latent impressions" [of thought after the departure of all objects] [*i.e.*, *saṃskáraśesha*, i. 18]. Thus this foremost of men, being utterly passionless towards everything, finds that the seeds of the "afflictions," like burned rice-grains, are bereft of the power to germinate, and they are abolished together with the internal organ. When these are destroyed, there ensues, through the full maturity of his unclouded "discriminative knowledge," an absorption of all causes and effects into the primal *prakṛiti*; and the soul, which is the power of pure intelligence, abiding in its own real nature, and escaped from all connection with the phenomenal understanding (*buddhi*), or with existence, reaches "absolute isolation" (*kaivalya*). Final liberation is described by Patañjali as two perfections: "Absolute isolation is the repressive absorption[464] of the 'qualities' which have consummated the ends of the soul, *i.e.*, enjoyment and liberation, or the abiding of the power of intelligence in its own nature" [iv. 33]. Nor should any one object, "Why, however, should not the individual be born again even though this should have been attained?" for that is settled by the well-known principle that "with the cessation of the cause the effect ceases," and therefore this objection is utterly irrelevant, as admitting neither inquiry nor decision; for otherwise, if the effect could arise even in the absence of the cause, we should have blind men finding jewels, and such like absurdities; and the popular proverb for the impossible would become a possibility. And so, too, says the Śruti, "A blind man found a jewel; one without fingers seized it; one without a neck put it on; and a dumb man praised it."[465]

Thus we see that, like the authoritative treatises on medicine, the Yoga-śástra consists of four divisions; as those on medicine treat of disease, its cause, health, and medicine, so the Yoga-śástra also treats of phenomenal existence, its cause, liberation, and its cause. This existence of ours, full of pain, is what is to be escaped from; the connection of nature and the soul is the cause of our having to experience this existence; the absolute abolition of this connection is the escape; and right insight is the cause thereof.[466] The same fourfold division is to be similarly traced as the case may be in other Śástras also. Thus all has been made clear.

The system of Śaṅkara, which comes next in succession, and which is the crest-gem of all systems, has been explained by us elsewhere; it is therefore left untouched here.[467]

—E. B. C.

APPENDIX.

ON THE UPÁDHI.

[As the *upádhi* or "condition" is a peculiarity of Hindu logic which is little known in Europe, I have added the following translation of the sections in the Bháshá-parichchheda and the Siddhánta-muktávalí, which treat of it.]

cxxxvii. *That which always accompanies the major term (sádhya), but does not always accompany the middle (hetu), is called the Condition (upádhi); its examination is now set forth.*

Our author now proceeds to define the *upádhi* or condition,[468] which is used to stop our acquiescence in a universal proposition as laid down by another person;—"that which always accompanies," &c. The meaning of this is that the so-called condition, while it invariably accompanies that which is accepted as the major term, does not thus invariably accompany that which our opponent puts forward as his middle term. [Thus in the false argument, "The mountain has smoke because it has fire," we may advance "wet fuel," or rather "the being produced from wet fuel," as an *upádhi*, since "wet fuel" is necessarily found wherever smoke is, but not always where fire is, as *e.g.*, in a red-hot iron ball.]

"But," the opponent may suggest, "if this were true, would it not follow that (*a*) in the case of the too wide middle term in the argument, 'This [second] son of Mitrá's, whom I have not seen, must be dark because he is Mitrá's son,' we could not allege 'the being produced from feeding on vegetables'[469] as a 'condition,'—inasmuch as it does not invariably accompany a dark colour, since a dark colour does also reside in things like [unbaked] jars, &c., which have nothing to do with feeding on vegetables? (*b*) Again, in the argument, 'The air must be perceptible to sense[470] because it is the site of touch,' we could not allege the 'possessing proportionate form' as a 'condition;' because perceptibility [to the internal sense] is found in the soul, &c., and yet soul, &c., have no form [and therefore the 'possessing proportionate form' does not invariably accompany perceptibility]. (*c*) Again, in the argument,'Destruction is itself perishable, because it is produced,' we could not allege as a 'condition' the 'being included in some positive category of existence'[471] [destruction being a form of non-existence, called "emergent," *dvaṃśábháva*], inasmuch as perishability is found in antecedent non-existence, and this certainly cannot be said to be included in any positive category of existence."

We, however, deny this, and maintain that the true meaning of the definition is simply this,—that whatever fact or mark we take to determine definitely, in reference to the topic, the major term which our condition is invariably to accompany, that same fact or mark must be equally taken to determine the middle term which our said condition is not invariably to accompany. Thus (*a*) the "being produced from feeding on vegetables" invariably accompanies "a dark colour," as determined by the fact that it is Mitrá's son, whose dark colour is discussed [and this very fact is the alleged middle term of the argument; but the pretended contradictory instance of the dark jar is not in point, as this was not the topic discussed]. (*b*) Again, "possessing proportionate form" invariably accompanies perceptibility as determined by the fact that the thing perceived is an external object; while it does not invariably accompany the alleged middle term "the being the site of touch," which is equally to be determined by the fact that the thing perceived is to be an external object.[472] (*c*) Again, in the argument "destruction is perishable from its being produced," the "being included in some positive category of existence" invariably accompanies the major term "perishable," when determined by the attribute of being produced. [And this is the middle term advanced; and therefore the alleged contradictory instance, "antecedent non-existence," is not in point, since nobody pretends that this is produced at all.]

But it is to be observed that there is nothing of this kind in valid middle terms, *i.e.*, there is nothing *there* which invariably accompanies the major term when determined by a certain fact or mark, and does not so accompany the middle term when similarly determined. This is peculiar to the so-called condition. [Should the reader object that "in each of our previous examples there has been given a separate determining mark or attribute which was to be found in each of the cases included under each; how then, in the absence of some general rule, are we to find out what this determining mark is to be in any particular given case?" We reply that] in the case of any middle term which is too general, the required general rule consists in the constant presence of one or other of the following alternatives, viz., that the subjects thus to be included are either (i.) the acknowledged site of the major term, and also the site of the condition, or else (ii.) the acknowledged site of the too general middle term, but excluding the said condition; and it will be when the case is determined by the presence of one or other of these alternatives that the condition will be considered as "always accompanying the major term, and not always accompanying the middle term."[473]

cxxxviii. *All true Conditions reside in the same subjects with their major terms,*[474] *and, their subjects being thus common, the (erring) middle term will be equally too general in regard to the Condition and the major term.*[475]

cxxxix. *It is in order to prove faulty generality in a middle term that the Condition has to be employed.*

The meaning of this is that it is in consequence of the middle term being found too general in regard to the condition, that we infer that it is too general in regard to the major term; and hence the use of having a condition at all. (*a.*) Thus, where the condition invariably accompanies an unlimited[476] major term, we infer that the middle term is too general in regard to the major term, from the very fact that it is too general in regard to the condition; as, for example, in the instance "the mountain has smoke because it has fire," where we infer that the "fire" is too general in regard to "smoke," since it is too general in regard to "wet fuel;" for there is a rule that what is too general for that which invariably accompanies must also be too general for that which is invariably accompanied. (*b.*) But where we take some fact or mark to determine definitely the major term which the condition is invariably to accompany,—there it is from the middle term's being found too general in regard to the condition in cases possessing this fact, or mark that we infer that the middle term is equally too general in regard to the major term. Thus in the argument, "B is dark because he is Mitrá's son," the middle term "the fact of being Mitrá's son" is too general in regard to the *sádhya*, "dark colour," because it is too general in regard to the *upádhi*, "feeding on vegetables," as seen in the case of Mitrá's second son [Mitrá's parentage being the assumed fact or mark, and Mitrá herself not having fed on vegetables previous to his birth].

[But an objector might here interpose, "If your definition of a condition be correct, surely a pretended condition which fulfils your definition can always be found even in the case of a valid middle term. For instance, in the stock argument 'the mountain must have fire because it has smoke,' we may assume as our pretended condition 'the being always found elsewhere than in the mountain;' since this certainly does not always 'accompany the middle term,' inasmuch as it is not found in the mountain itself where the smoke is acknowledged to be; and yet it apparently does 'always accompany the major term,' since in every other known case of fire we certainly find it, and as for the present case you must remember that the presence of fire in this mountain is the very point in dispute." To this we reply] You never may take such a condition as "the being always found elsewhere than in the subject or minor term" (unless this can be proved by some direct sense-evidence which precludes all dispute); because, in the first place, you cannot produce any argument to convince your antagonist that this condition does invariably accompany the major term [since he naturally maintains that the present case is exactly one in point against you]; and, secondly, because it is self-contradictory [as the same nugatory condition may be equally employed to overthrow the contrary argument].

But if you can establish it by direct sense-evidence, then the "being always found elsewhere than in the subject" becomes a true condition, [and serves to render nugatory the false argument which a disputant tries to establish]. Thus in the illusory argument "the fire must be non-hot because it is artificial," we can have a valid condition in "the being always found elsewhere than in fire," since we can prove by sense-evidence that fire is hot,[477] [thus the *upádhi* here is a means of overthrowing the false argument].

Where the fact of its always accompanying the major term, &c., is disputed, there we have what is called a disputed condition.[478] But "the being found elsewhere than in the subject" can never be employed even as a disputed condition, in accordance with the traditional rules of logical controversy.[479]

NOTE ON THE YOGA.

There is an interesting description of the Yogins on the Mountain Raivataka in Mágha (iv. 55):—

"There the votaries of meditation, well skilled in benevolence (*maitrí*) and those other purifiers of the mind,—having successfully abolished the 'afflictions' and obtained the 'meditation possessed of a seed,' and having reached that knowledge which recognises the essential difference between the quality Goodness and the Soul,—desire yet further to repress even this ultimate meditation."

It is curious to notice that *maitrí*, which plays such a prominent part in Buddhism, is counted in the Yoga as only a preliminary condition from which the votary is to take, as it were, his first start towards his final goal. It is called a *parikarman* (=*prasádhaka*) in Vyása's Comm. i. 33 (cf. iii. 22), whence the term is borrowed by Mágha. Bhoja expressly says that this purifying process is an external one, and not an intimate portion of yoga itself; just as in arithmetic the operations of addition, &c., are valuable, not in themselves, but as aids in effecting the more important calculations which arise subsequently. The Yoga seems directly to allude to Buddhism in this marked depreciation of its cardinal virtue.

ENDNOTES.

[1] The most remarkable instance of this philosophical equanimity is that of Váchaspati Miśra, who wrote standard treatises on each of the six systems except the Vaiśeshika, adopting, of course, the peculiar point of view of each, and excluding for the time every alien tenet.

[2] An index of the names of authors and works quoted is given in Dr. Hall's Bibliographical Catalogue, pp. 162-164, and also in Professor Aufrecht's Bodleian Catalogue, p. 247.

[3] Śríharsha-charita, p. 204 (Calcutta ed.)

[4] Found in the Mahábh. iii. 17402, with some variations. I give them as I have heard them from Paṇḍit Rámanáráyaṇa Vidyáratna.

[5] Dr. A. C. Burnell, in his preface to his edition of the Vaṃśa-Bráhmaṇa, has solved the riddle of the relation of Mádhava and Sáyaṇa. Sáyaṇa is a pure Draviḍian name given to a child who is born after all the elder children have died. Mádhava elsewhere calls Sáyaṇa his "younger brother," as an allegorical description of his body, himself being the eternal soul. His use of the term Sáyaṇa-Mádhavaḥhere (not the dual) seems to prove that the two names represent the same person. The body seems meant by the Sáyaṇa of the third śloka. Máyaṇa was the father of Mádhava, and the true reading may be śríman-máyaṇa.

[6] "Śaṅkara, Bháskara, and other commentators name the Lokáyatikas, and these appear to be a branch of the Sect of Chárváka" (Colebrooke). Lokáyata may be etymologically analysed as "prevalent in the world" (*loka* and *áyata*). Laukáyatika occurs in Páṇini's ukthagaṇa.

[7] *Kiṇwa* is explained as "drug or seed used to produce fermentation in the manufacture of spirits from sugar, bassia, &c." Colebrooke quotes from Śaṅkara: "The faculty of thought results from a modification of the aggregate elements in like manner as sugar with a ferment and other ingredients becomes an inebriating liquor; and as betel, areca, lime, and extract of catechu chewed together have an exhilarating property not found in those substances severally."

[8] Of course Śaṅkara, in his commentary, gives a very different interpretation, applying it to the cessation of individual existence when the knowledge of the Supreme is once attained. Cf.Śabara's Comm. Jaimini Sút., i. i. 5.

[9] I take *kaṇa* as here equal to the Bengali *kunṛ*. Cf. Atharva-V., xi. 3, 5. *Aśváḥ kaṇá gávas taṇḍulá maśakás tusháḥ.*

[10] See Nyáya Sútras, ii. 57.

[11] *I.e.*, personality and fatness, &c.

[12] I read *dehe* for *dehaḥ*.

[13] Literally, "must be an attribute of the subject and have invariable concomitance (*vyápti*)."

[14] For the *sandigdha* and *niśchita upádhi* see Siddhánta Muktávali, p. 125. The former is accepted only by one party.

[15] Literally, the knowledge of the invariable concomitance (as of smoke by fire).

[16] The attributes of the class are not always found in every member,—thus idiots are men, though man is a rational animal; and again, this particular smoke might be a sign of a fire in some other place.

[17] See Sáhitya Darpaṇa (Ballantyne's trans. p. 16), and Siddhánta-M., p. 80.

[18] The properly logical, as distinguished from the rhetorical, argument.

[19] "*Upamána* or the knowledge of a similarity is the instrument in the production of an inference from similarity. This particular inference consists in the knowledge of the relation of a name to something so named." Ballantyne's Tarka Sangraha.

[20] The upádhi is the condition which must be supplied to restrict a too general middle term, as in the inference "the mountain has smoke because it has fire," if we add wet fuel as the condition of the fire, the middle term will be no longer too general. In the case of a true vyápti, there is, of course, no upádhi.

[21] 'Αντιστρέφει (Pr. Anal., ii. 25). We have here our A with distributed predicate.

[22] If we omitted the first clause, and only made the upádhi "that which constantly accompanies the major term and is constantly accompanied by it," then in the Naiyáyika argument "sound is non-eternal, because it has the nature of sound," "being produced" would serve as a Mímáṃsaka upádhi, to establish the *vyabhichára*fallacy, as it is reciprocal with "non-eternal;" but the omitted clause excludes it, as an upádhi must be consistent with *either*party's opinions, and, of course, the Naiyáyika maintains that "being produced" *always* accompanies the class of sound. Similarly, if we defined the upádhi as "not constantly accompanying the middle term and constantly accompanied by the major," we might have as an upádhi "the nature of a jar," as this

is never found with the middle term (the class or nature of sound only residing in sound, and that of a jar only in a jar), while, at the same time, wherever the class of jar is found there is also found non-eternity. Lastly, if we defined the upádhi as "not constantly accompanying the middle term, and constantly accompanying the major," we might have as a Mímáṃsaka upádhi "the not causing audition," *i.e.*, the not being apprehended by the organs of hearing; but this is excluded, as non-eternity is not always found where this is, ether being inaudible and yet eternal.

[23] This refers to an obscure śloka of Udayanácharya, "where a reciprocal and a non-reciprocal universal connection (*i.e.*, universal propositions which severally do and do not distribute their predicates) relate to the same argument (as *e.g.*, to prove the existence of smoke), there that non-reciprocating term of the second will be a fallacious middle, which is not invariably accompanied by the other reciprocal of the first." Thus "the mountain has smoke because it has fire" (here fire and smoke are non-reciprocating, as fire is not found invariably accompanied by smoke though smoke is by fire), or "because it has fire from wet fuel" (smoke and fire from wet fuel being reciprocal and always accompanying each other); the non-reciprocating term of the former (fire) will give a fallacious inference, because it is also, of course, not invariably accompanied by the special kind of fire, that produced from wet fuel. But this will not be the case where the non-reciprocating term *is* thus invariably accompanied by the other reciprocal, as "the mountain has fire because it has smoke;" here, though fire and smoke do not reciprocate, yet smoke will be a true middle, because it is invariably accompanied by heat, which is the reciprocal of fire. I wish to add here, once for all, that I own my explanation of this, as well as many another, difficulty in the Sarva-darśana-śaṅgraha to my old friend and teacher, Paṇḍit Maheśa Chandra Nyáyaratna, of the Calcutta Sanskrit College.

[24] Cf. Sextus Empiricus, P. Hyp. ii. In the chapter on the Buddhist system *infra*, we have an attempt to establish the authority of the universal proposition from the relation of cause and effect or genus and species.

[25] *Adṛishṭa*, *i.e.*, the merit and demerit in our actions which produce their effects in future births.

[26] This is an old Buddhist retort. See Burnouf, Introd., p. 209.

[27] Rig-Veda, x. 106. For the Aświamedha rites, see Wilson's Rig-Veda, Preface, vol. ii. p. xiii.

[28] Or this may mean "and all the various other things to be handled in the rites."

[29] This śloka is quoted in the "Benares Pandit," vol. i. p. 89, with a commentary, and the latter part of the second line is there read more correctly, *'darśanán na na darśanát.*

[30] Kusumánjali, iii. 7.

[31] The Bauddhas are thus divided into—

(1.) Mádhyamikas or Nihilists.
(2.) Yogácháras or Subjective Idealists.
(3.) Sautrántikas or Representationists.
(4.) Vaibháshikas or Presentationists.

[32] Cf. Ferrier's Lectures and Remains, vol. i. p. 119.

"Suppose yourself gazing on a gorgeous sunset. The whole western heavens are glowing with roseate hues, but you are aware that within half an hour all these glorious tints will have faded away into a dull ashen grey. You see them even now melting away before your eyes, although your eyes cannot place before you the conclusion which your reason draws. And what conclusion is that? That conclusion is that you never, even for the shortest time that can be named or conceived, see any abiding colour, any colour which truly *is*. Within the millionth part of a second the whole glory of the painted heavens has undergone an incalculable series of mutations. One shade is supplanted by another with a rapidity which sets all measurement at defiance, but because the process is one to which no measurement applies,... reason refuses to lay an arrestment on any period of the passing scene, or to declare that it is, because in the very act of being it is not; it has given place to something else. It is a series of fleeting colours, no one of which *is*, because each of them continually vanishes in another."

[33] Principium exclusi medii inter duo contradictoria.

[34] Query, Laṅkávatára?

[35] Cf. Ferrier's Institutes of Metaphysic, p. 213. "If every *completed* object of cognition must consist of object *plus*the subject, the object without the subject must be incomplete, that is, inchoate—that is, no possible object of knowledge at all. This is the distressing predicament to which matter is reduced by the tactics of speculation; and this predicament is described not unaptly by calling it a *flux*—or, as we have depicted it elsewhere, perhaps more philosophically, as a never-ending redemption of nonsense into sense, and a never-ending relapse of sense into nonsense."

[36] Cf. Burnouf, *Lotus*, p. 520.—Should we read*samudaya*?

[37] Cf. G. H. Lewes' History of Philosophy, vol. i. p. 85. "We not only see that the architect's plan determined the arrangement of materials in the house, but we see why it must have done so, because the materials have no spontaneous tendency to group themselves into houses; that not being a recognised property of bricks, mortar, wood, and glass. But what we know of organic materials is that theyhave this spontaneous tendency to arrange themselves in definite forms; precisely as we see chemical substances arranging themselves in definite forms without the intervention of any extra-chemical agency."

[38] These are not the usual four 'sublime truths;' cf. p. 30.

[39] Mádhava probably derived most of his knowledge of Buddhist doctrines from Brahmanical works; consequently some of his explanations (as, *e.g.*, that of *samudáya* or *samudaya*, &c.) seem to be at variance with those given in Buddhist works.

[40] *Vivasanas*, "without garments."

[41] "The Buddhists are also called *Muktakachchhas*, alluding to a peculiarity of dress, apparently a habit of wearing the hem of the lower garment untucked."—*Colebrooke.*

[42] In p. 26, line 3, read *Syád-vádinám.*

[43] I propose to read in p. 26, line 5, *infra*, *gráhyasya*for *agráhyasya.*

[44] As these terms necessarily relate to the perceiver.

[45] I correct the reading *tasyágrahaṇaṃ* to *tasyá grahaṇaṃ* (*tasyá* being *jaḍatáyáḥ*).

[46] *I.e.*, if you say that the *avayava* may be not seen though the *avayavin* is seen, then I may say that the post is the *avayavin*, and the unperceived three worlds its *avayava*!

[47] I read *arhatsvarúpam arhachchandra* in p. 27, line 3,*infra.*

[48] The following passage occurs in some part of Kumárila's writings in an argument against the Jainas. It is curious that in the Sáṅkara-digvijaya, chap. lv., it is mentioned that Kumárila had a little relenting towards the Jainas at the end of his life. He repented of having so cruelly persecuted them, and acknowledged that there was some truth in their teaching. *Jainagurumukhát kaśchid vidyáleśo játaḥ.*

[49] Kumárila tries to prove that no such being can exist, as his existence is not established by any one of the five recognised proofs,—the sixth, *abháva*, being negative, is, of course, not applicable. I understand the last śloka as showing the inapplicability of "presumption" or *arthá-patti.*

A Jaina would say, "If the Arhat were not omniscient, his words would not be true and authoritative, but we see that they are, therefore he is omniscient." He answers by retorting that the same argument might be used of Buddha by a Buddhist; and as the Jaina himself would disallow it in that case, it cannot be convincing in his own.

[50] In p. 29, line 2, read *tatsadbhávávedakasya* for *tatsadbhávádekasya.*

[51] In p. 29, line 9, for *nikhilárthajñanát notpatty*, I propose to read *nikhilárthajñánotpatty.*

[52] *Janya* is included in *Kárya* and equally disputed.

[53] Thus "I am possessed of a body" (*aham Śaríri*), "my hand," &c., are all sentences in which a predicate involving the notion of parts is applied to the soul "I."

[54] Reasoning in a circle. I suppose the &c. includes the *Anavasthádosha* or reasoning *ad infinitum*. He accepts the supposed fault, and holds that it is actually borne out in a case before everybody's eyes.

[55] In p. 31, line 5, *infra*, read *tattvárthe* for *tattvártham.*

[56] I read in p. 32, line 9, *Samyagdarśanádi* for *asamyagdarśanádi*; but the old text may mean "caused by the abolition of hindrances produced by the qualities, wrong intuition," &c.

[57] Cf. the five *yamas* in the *Yoga-sútras*, ii. 30. Hemachandra (*Abhidh* 81) calls them *yamas.*

[58] I read *kámánám* for *kámáṇám* in p. 33, line 7 (2 × 3 × 3 = 18).

[59] For *abháshaṇa*, see Hemach. 16.

[60] I propose in p. 33, line 17,*raśayanajñánaśraddhávachárаṇáni* for *rasáyaṇajñanaṃ śraddhánávaraṇáni*. For *avacháraṇa*, see *Suśruta*, vol. ii. p. 157,& c. If *anávaraṇa* be the true reading, I suppose it must mean "the absence of obstructions."

[61] This is a hard passage, but some light is thrown on it by the scholiast to Hemachandra, *Abhidh.* 79.

[62] Or this may mean "by the influence of *upaśamakshaya* or*kshayopaśama*, it appears characterised by one or the other."

[63] I read in p. 34, line 7, *kalushádyákáreṇa* for*kalushányákáreṇa*. The *upaśamakshaya* and *kshayopaśama* seem to correspond to the *aupaśamika* and *ksháyika* states about to be described.

[64] *Strychnos potatorum.*

[65] Just as in the Sánkhya philosophy, the soul is not really bound though it seems to itself to be so.

[66] A valid non-perception is when an object is not seen, and yet all the usual concurrent causes of vision are present, such as the eye, light, &c.

[67] I read in p. 35, line 5, *'stíti* for *sthiti.*

[68] Hence the term here used for "category"—*astikáya.*

[69] These (by Hemach. *Abhidh.* 21), possess only one sense—touch. In p. 35, line 10, I read *śaṅkhagaṇḍolakaprabhṛitayas trasáś chaturvidháḥ pṛithivyaptejo.*

[70] In p. 35, line 16, I read *tesháṃ ajívatvát* for *tesháṃjívatvát.* If we keep the old reading we must translate it, "because the former only are animate."

[71] In p. 35, line 3 from bottom, I read *sarvatrávasthite* for*sarvatrávasthiti.* In the preceding line I read *álokenávachchhinne* for *álokenávichchhinne.*

[72] Cf. Siddhánta-muktávali, p. 27. The *vishaya* is*upabhoga-sádhanam,* but it begins with the *dvyaṇuka.* This category takes up the forms of *sthávara* which were excluded from *jíva.*

[73] It is an interesting illustration how thoroughly Mádhava for the time throws himself into the Jaina system which he is analysing, when we see that he gives the Jaina terminology for this definition of *dravya,*—cf. *Vaiśesh. Sútra,* i. 1, 15. *Paryáya* is explained as *karman* in Hemach. *Anek. Paryáya,* in p. 36, line 11 (*infra,* p. 53, line 9), seems used in a different sense from that which it bears elsewhere. I have taken it doubtingly as in Hemach.*Abhidh.* 1503, *paryáyo 'nukramaḥ kramaḥ.*

[74] *Yoga* seems to be here the natural impulse of the soul to act.

[75] In line 18, read *ásravaṇakáraṇatvád.*

[76] The *jnána* is one, but it becomes apparently manifold by its connection with the senses and external objects.

[77] These are also called the eight *karmans* in Govindánanda's gloss, *Ved. Sút.,* ii. 2, 33.

[78] The Calcutta MS. reads *ádaraṇíyasya* for*ávaraṇíyasya,* in p. 37, last line. But *ávaraṇíya* may be used for*ávarana* (*Páṇ.* iii. 4, 68). Cf. *Yoga Sút.,* ii. 52, where Vyása's Comm. has *ávaraṇíya.*

[79] *Jálavat*? The printed text has *jalavat.*

[80] Umásvámi-?

[81] For the *ságaropama*, see Wilson's *Essays*, vol. i. p. 309. In p. 38, line 16, I read *ityádyuktakáláad úrdhvam api* for the obscure *ityádyuktaṃ káladurddhánavat*. I also read at the end of the line *prachyutiḥ sthitiḥ* for *prachyutisthitiḥ*.

[82] In p. 38, line 18, read *svakáryakaraṇe*.

[83] In p. 39, line 2 and line 5, for *írshyá* read *íryá*,—a bad misreading.

[84] In p. 39, line 6, I read *ápadyetá* for *ápadyatá*.

[85] In p. 39, line 9, for *seshaṇá* read *saishaṇá*.

[86] In p. 39, line 12, join *nirjantu* and *jagatítale*.

[87] Mádhava omits the remaining divisions of *saṃvara*. Wilson, *Essays*, vol. i. p. 311, gives them as *parishahá*, "endurance," as of a vow; *yatidharma*, "the ten duties of an ascetic, patience, gentleness," &c.; *bhávaná*, "conviction," such as that worldly existences are not eternal, &c.; *cháritra*, "virtuous observance."

[88] In p. 39, line 14, read *ásravasrotaso*.

[89] For *moha*, in line 16, read *moksha*.

[90] In p. 39, line 2 *infra*, I read *yathákála-* for *yathá kála-*.

[91] This passage is very difficult and not improbably corrupt, and my interpretation of it is only conjectural. The ordinary*nirjará* is when an action attains its end (like the lulling of a passion by the gratification), this lull is temporary. That *nirjará*is "ancillary" which is rendered by asceticism a means to the attainment of the highest good. The former is *akámá*, "desireless," because at the moment the desire is satisfied and so dormant; the latter is *sakámá*, because the ascetic conquers the lower desire under the overpowering influence of the higher desire for liberation.

[92] I read *nirodhe* for *nirodhah* in p. 40, line 6; cf. p. 37, line 13. The causes of bondage produce the assumption of bodies in which future actions are to be performed.

[93] Literally "absence of *sanga*."

[94] In p. 41, line 7, read *sapta-bhaṅgí-naya*, see Ved. S. Gloss., ii. 2, 23.

[95] I cannot understand the words at the end of the first line, *kim vṛitatadvidheḥ*, and therefore leave them untranslated.

[96] Thus Govindánanda applies it (*Ved. Sút.*, ii. 2, 33) to "may be it is one," "may be it is many," &c.

[97] 'Ακαταληψία This is Śriharsha's tenet in the *Khaṇḍana-khaṇḍa-khádya.*

[98] In p. 42, line 17, for *matenámiśritáni* read *matena miśritáni.*

[99] In p. 43, line 2, for *na yasya* read *nayasya.*

[100] This list is badly printed in the Calcutta edition. It is really identical with that given in Hemachandra's *Abhidhána-chintámaṇi*, 72, 73; but we must correct the readings to *antaráyás*, *rágadwesháv aviratiḥ smaraḥ*, and *háso* for *himsá*. The order of the eighteen*doshas* in the Calcutta edition is given by Hemachandra as 4, 5, 1, 2, 3, 10, 11, 12, 7, 9, 17, 16, 18, 8, 6, 15, 13, 14.

[101] In p. 43, line 13, for *vartini* read *vartiniḥ.*

[102] This seems corrupt,—a line is probably lost.

[103] In last line, for *saṃsrave* read *saṃvare.*

[104] Does this mean the knowledge of the world, the soul, the liberated and liberation? These are called *ananta.* See Weber's *Bhagavatí*, pp. 250, 261-266.

[105] *Sarajoharaṇáh* is explained by the *rajoharaṇadhárin*(= *vratin*) of Haláyudha, ii. 189.

[106] Cf. Wilson, *Essays*, i. 340. For *strím* read *strí.*

[107] Cf. "The argument in defence of the Maxim of Contradiction is that it is a postulate employed in all the particular statements as to matters of daily experience that a man understands and acts upon when heard from his neighbours; a postulate such that, if you deny it, no speech is either significant or trustworthy to inform and guide those who hear it. You may cite innumerable examples both of speech and action in the detail of life, which the Herakleitean must go through like other persons, and when, if he proceeded upon his own theory, he could neither give nor receive information by speech, nor ground any action upon the beliefs which he declares to co-exist in his own mind. Accordingly the Herakleitean Kratylus (so Aristotle says) renounced the use of affirmative speech, and simply pointed with his finger."—Grote's Aristotle, vol. ii. pp. 297, 298.

[108] Cf. the dictum of Herakleitus: Making worlds is Zeus's pastime; and that of Plato (Laws, Book vii. p. 803): Man is made to be the plaything of God.

[109] "Whose body nature is, and God the soul."—*Pope.*

[110] For further details respecting Rámánuja and his system, see Wilson's Works, vol. i. pp. 34-46; and Banerjea's Dialogues, ix. The *Tattva-muktávalí* was printed in the *Pandit* for September 1871; but the lines quoted in p. 73 are not found there.

[111] For a further account of Ánanda-tírtha or Madhva see Wilson, Works, vol. i. pp. 138-150. His Commentary on the Brahma-sútras has been printed in Calcutta.

[112] Colebrooke speaks of the *Paśupati-sástra* (*Maheśvara-siddhánta or Sivágama*), as the text-book of the Páśupata sect. The Ágamas are said to be twenty-eight (see their names in the Rev. T. Foulkes' "Catechism of the Śaiva Religion").

[113] "There must be three eternal entities, Deity, soul, matter;" "as the water is co-eternal with the sea and the salt with the water, so soul is co-eternal with the Deity, and *páśa* is eternally co-existent with soul" (J. A. O. S. iv. pp. 67, 85). In p. 58 we find the *advaita* of the Vedánta attacked. In p. 62 it is said that the soul is eternally entangled in matter, and God carries on his five operations (see *infra*) to disentangle it, bringing out all that is required for previous desert.

[114] These four feet are the four stages of religious life (see J. A. O. S. iv. pp. 135, 180), called in Tamil *sarithei*, *kirikei*, *yokam*, and *gnánam*. The first is the stage of practical piety and performance of the prescribed duties and rites; the second is that of the "confirmatory sacrament" and the five purifications involved in true *pújá*; the third is that of the eight observances of the yogin; the fourth is that of knowledge which prepares the soul for intimate union with God.

[115] Cf. Colebrooke, *Essays* (2d ed.), vol. i. p. 315.

[116] *Nyáyena* may here means "argument."

[117] *Scil.* if there were only one cause there would be only one invariable effect. The very existence of various effects proves that there must be other concurrent causes (as human actions) necessary. The argument seems to me to require here this unnatural stress to be laid on eva, but this is certainly not the original meaning of the passage; it occurs Mahábhárata, iii. 1144 (cf. Gauḍapáda, S. Kár. 61).

[118] In p. 82, line 3, *infra*, I read *Karaṇásambhaváchcha.*

[119] This may be the same with the Meykáṇḍa of the Tamil work in J. A. O. S. His poem was called the *Mṛigendra*(?).

[120] Should we read *távad anaśaríraḥ* in p. 83, line 2?

[121] I retain this word, see *infra.*

[122] "*Máyá* (or Prakṛiti) is the material, Śakti the instrumental, and Deity the efficient cause" (J. A. O. S. iv. p. 55).

[123] These are the five first names of the eleven mantras which are included in the five *kalás* (J. A. O. S. iv. pp. 238-243). The Śivalinga (the visible object of worship for the enlightened) is composed of mantras, and is to be regarded as the body of Śiva (see J. A. O. S. iv. p. 101). These five mantras are given in the inverse order in Taitt. Áraṇyaka, x. 43-47 (cf. *Nyáyá-málávist.* p. 3).

[124] These are the operations of the five manifestations ofŚiva (see J. A. O. S. iv. 8, 18) which in their descending order are*Sáthákkiyam* (*i.e.*, *Sadákshaya?*) or *Sadá-Śiva*, who is Śiva andŚakti combined, and the source of grace to all souls; *Ichchuran* or*Mayesuran*, the obscure; *Sutta-vittei* (*Śuddhavidyá*) which is properly the Hindu triad, *Rudra*, *Vishṇu*, and *Brahma*. They are respectively symbolised by the *náda*, *vindu*, *m*, *u*, and *a* of Om.

[125] In Wilson's Mackenzie Cat. i. p. 138, we find a Tántrik work, the *Narapati-jaya-charyá*, ascribed to Bhoja the king of Dhár.

[126] Ananta is a name of Śiva in the Atharva-śiras Upanishad (see Indische Stud. i. 385).

[127] This is the fourth of the twenty-eight Ágamas (see Foulkes' Catechism).

[128] *Aṇu?* "The soul, when clothed with these primary things (desire, knowledge, action, &c.), is an exceedingly small body" (Foulkes). Anaṇu is used as an epithet of Brahman in Bṛihad Ar. Up. iii. 8. 8.

[129] See Ind. Studien, i. 301.

[130] The mind or internal sense perceives soul (see Bháshá Parichchheda, śloka 49).

[131] Delete the *iti* in p. 84, line 5, *infra*.

[132] Cf. the Nakulíśa Páśupatas, p. 76, 4 (*supra*, p. 103).

[133] For these three classes see J. A. O. S. iv. pp. 87, 137. They are there described as being respectively under the influence of *áṇavam malam* only, or this with *kanmam malam*, or these with *mayei malam*. The *áṇavam* is described as original sin, or that source of evil which was always attached to the soul; *kanmam*is that fate which inheres in the soul's organism and metes out its deserts; *mayei* is matter in its obscuring or entangling power, the source of the senses. Mádhava uses "*kalá*," &c., for *máyá*. The reason is to be found in J. A. O. S. p. 70, where it is said that the five *vidyátattvas* (*kalá*, *vidyá*, *rága*, *niyati*,

and *kalá*) and the twenty-four *átmatattvas* (*sc.* the gross and subtile elements, and organs of sense and action, with the intellectual faculties *manas*, *buddhi*, *ahaṃkára*, and *chitta*), are all developed from *máyá*. This exactly agrees with the quotation from Soma Śambhu, *infra*. We may compare with it what Mádhava says, p. 77, in his account of the Nakulíśa Páśupatas, where he describes *kalá* as unintelligent, and composed of the five elements, the five*tanmátras*, and the ten organs, with *buddhi*, *ahaṃkára* and*manas*.

[134] See J. A. O. S. iv. p. 137. I read *anugrahakaraṇát* in p. 86, line 3.

[135] I omit the quotation, as it only repeats the preceding. It, however, names the three classes as *vijñána-kevala*, *pralaya-kevala*, and *sakala*.

[136] *I.e.*, thus including five of the *vidyátattvas* and all the twenty-four *átmatattvas*.

[137] This term seems to be derived from *purí*, "body" (cf.*puriśaya* for *purusha*, Bṛihad Ár. Up. ii. 5, 18), and *ashṭaka*(cf. also the Sánkhya Pravachana Bháshya, p. 135).

[138] Or rather thirty-one?

[139] *Manas*, *buddhi*, *ahaṃkára*, *chitta*.

[140] These are the seven *viḍyá-tattvas*, *kalá*, *kála*,*niyati* (fate), *vidyá*, *rága*, *prakṛiti*, and *guṇa*. Hoisington, however, puts *purushan* "the principle of life," instead of *guṇa*, which seems better, as the three *guṇas* are included in *prakṛiti*. He translates *kalá* by "continency," and describes it as "the power by which the senses are subdued and the carnal self brought into subjection."

[141] This "instrument" (*karaṇa*) seems to mean what Hoisington calls *purushan* or "the principle of life which establishes or supports the whole system in its operation;" he makes it one of the seven *vidyátattvas*. According to Mádhava, it should be what he calls *guṇa*.

[142] The thirty-one *tattvas* are as follow:—Twenty-four*átmatattvas*, five elements, five *tanmátras*, ten organs of sense and action, four organs of the *antaḥkaraṇa*, and seven *vidyátattvas*as enumerated above. (See J. A. O. S. iv. pp. 16-17.)

[143] I take *aṇu* in this verse as the soul, but it may mean the second kind of *mala* mentioned by Hoisington. The first kind of*mala* is the *máyá-mala*, the second *áṇava mala*, the third*kanma-mala* (*karman*).

[144] "The soul, when clothed with these primary things (desire, knowledge, action, the *kaládipanchaka*, &c.), is an exceedingly small body"

(Foulkes). One of the three *malas* is called *áṇava*, and is described as the source of sin and suffering to souls.

[145] The first three are the three kinds of *mala* in the J. A. O. S., viz., *áṇavam*, *kanmam*, and *máyei*, the last is the "obscuring" power of Máyesuran (cf. vol. iv. pp. 13, 14). The Śaivas hold that Páśa, like the Sánkhya Prakṛiti, is in itself eternal, although its connection with any particular soul is temporary (see J. A. O. S. iv. p. 228).

[146] These are the five, *vindu*, *mala*, *karman*, *máyá*, and *rodhaśakti*. *Vindu* is described in Foulkes' translation of theŚiva-prakáśa-patalai: "A sound proceeds out of the mystical syllable*om*;... and in that sound a rudimentary atom of matter is developed. From this atom are developed the four sounds, the fifty-one Sanskrit letters, the Vedas, Mantras, &c., the bodily, intellectual, and external enjoyments of the soul that have not attained to spiritual knowledge at the end of each period of the world's existence, and have been swept away by the waters of the world-destroying deluge; after these the three stages of heavenly happiness are developed, to be enjoyed by the souls that have a favourable balance of meritorious deeds, or have devoted themselves to the service of God or the abstract contemplation of the Deity, viz., (1.) the enjoyment of the abode of Śiva; (2.) that of near approach to him; (3.) that of union with him." *Vindu* is similarly described, J. A. O. S. iv. pp. 152, 153 (cf. also Weber, *Rámatápanyía Up*. pp. 312-315).

[147] See the same illustrations in J. A. O. S. iv. p. 150.

[148] Some forced derivation seems here intended as of *páśa*from *paśchát*.

[149] In p. 90, line 2, read *sá káryeṇa.*

[150] Read *bháván* for *bhávát*.

[151] Cf. *supra*, p. 113. Mádhava here condenses Abhinava Gupta's commentary. Abhinava Gupta lived in the beginning of the eleventh century (see Bühler's Tour in Cashmere, pp. 66, 80).

[152] I have seen in Calcutta a short Comm. on the Śiva sútras by Utpala, the son of Udayákara (cf. pp. 130, 131).—E. B. C.

[153] Cf. Marco Polo's account of the Indian yogís in Colonel Yule's edit. vol. ii. p. 300. *Párada-pána* is one of the practices of the Siddhopásakas in the Śaṅkara-digvijaya, § 49, to obviate*apamṛityu*, *akálamṛityu*, &c.

[154] The Vaiśeshikas are called Aulúkyáḥ in Hemachandra's*Abhidhána-chintámaṇi*; in the Váyu-puráṇa (quoted in Aufrecht's*Catal*. p. 53 b, l. 23), Akshapáda, Kaṇáda, Ulúka, and Vatsa are called the sons of Śiva.

[155] He is here called by his synonym Kaṇabhaksha.

[156] It is singular that this is inaccurate. The ninth book treats of that perception which arises from supersensible contact,& c., and inference. The tenth treats of the mutual difference of the qualities of the soul, and the three causes.

[157] For this extract from the old *bháshya* of Vátsyáyana, see Colebrooke's *Essays* (new edition), vol. i. p. 285.

[158] Cf. *Bháshá-parichchheda*, śloka 14.

[159] "Particularity" (*viśesha*) resides by "intimate relation" in the eternal atoms, &c.

[160] This clause is added, as otherwise the definition would apply to "duality" and "conjunction."

[161] This is added, as otherwise the definition would apply to "existence" (*sattá*), which is the *summum genus*, to which substance, quality, and action are immediately subordinate.

[162] Existence (*sattá*) is the genus of *dravya*, *guṇa*, and *kriyâ*. *Dravya* alone can be the intimate cause of anything; and all actions are the mediate (or non-intimate) cause of conjunction and disjunction. *Some* qualities (as *saṃyoga*, *rúpa*, &c.) may be mediate causes, but this is accidental and does not belong to the essence of *guṇa*, as many gunas can never be mediate causes.

[163] As all karmas are transitory, *karmatva* is only found in the *anitya*. I correct in p. 105, line 20, *nityá-samavetatva*; this is the reading of the MS. in the Calcutta Sanskrit College Library.

[164] *I.e.*, it can never be destroyed. Indestructibility, however, is found in time, space, &c.; to exclude these, therefore, the former clause of the definition is added.

[165] "Particularity" (whence the name Vaiśeshika) is not "individuality, as of this particular flash of lightning,"—but it is the individuality either of those eternal substances which, being single, have no genus, as ether, time, and space; or of the different atomic minds; or of the atoms of the four remaining substances, earth, water, fire, and air, these atoms being supposed to be the *ne plus ultra*, and as they have no parts, they are what they are by their own indivisible nature. Ballantyne translated *viśesha* as "ultimate difference." I am not sure whether the individual soul has *viśesha*.

[166] Mutual non-existence (*anyonyábháva*) exists between two notions which have no property in common, as a "pot is not cloth;" but the genus is the same in two pots, both alike being pots.

[167] "*Samaváyasambandábhávát samaváyo na játiḥ*," Siddh. Mukt. (*Saṃyoga* being a *guṇa* has *guṇatva* existing in it with intimate relation).

[168] The feel or touch of earth is said to be "neither hot nor cold, and its colour, taste, smell, and touch are changed by union with fire" (Bháshá-parichchheda, *sl.* 103, 104).

[169] The organ of touch is an aërial integument.—*Colebrooke.*

[170] Sound is twofold,—"produced from contact," as the *first* sound, and "produced from sound," as the *second. Janya* is added to exclude God's knowledge, while *saṃyogájanya* excludes the soul's, which is produced by contact, as of the soul and mind, mind and the senses, &c.

[171] The mediate cause itself is the conjunction of time with some body, &c., existing in time,—this latter is the intimate cause, while the knowledge of the revolutions of the sun is the instrumental cause. In p. 106, line 12, read *adhikaraṇaṃ*.

[172] *Paratva* being of two kinds, *daiśika* and *kálika*.

[173] Time, space, and mind have no special qualities; the last, however, is not pervading but atomic.

[174] The three other *padárthas*, beside soul, which are*amúrtta*,—time, ether, and space,—are not genera.

[175] All numbers, from duality upwards, are artificial,*i.e.*, they are made by our minds; unity alone exists in things themselves—each being *one*; and they only become two, &c., by our choosing to regard them so, and thus joining them in thought.

[176] *Saṃskára* is here the idea conceived by the mind—created, in fact, by its own energies out of the material previously supplied to it by the senses and the internal organ or mind. (Cf. the tables in p. 153.)

[177] Here and elsewhere I omit the metrical summary of the original, as it adds nothing new to the previous prose.

[178] Every cause must be either *jñápaka* or *janaka*;*apekshábuddhi*, not being the former, must be the latter.

[179] *Apekshábuddhi* apprehends "this is one," "this is one," &c.; but duality, for instance, does not reside in either of these, but in *both* together.

[180] The Vaiśeshikas held that the jívátman and space are each an all-pervading substance, but the individual portions of each have different special qualities; hence one man knows what another is ignorant of, and one portion of ether has sound when another portion has not. Dr.

Röer, in his version of the Bháshá-Parichchheda, has mistranslated an important Sútra which bears on this point. It is said in Sútra 26—

—*athákáśaśarírinạm, avyápyavṛittiḥ kshaṇiko viśesha-guṇa ishyate,*

which does not mean "the special qualities of ether and soul are limitation to space and momentary duration," but "the special qualities of ether and soul (*i.e.*, sound, knowledge, &c.) are limited to different portions and of momentary duration."

[181] The author here mentions two other causes of the destruction of *dvitva* besides that already given in p. 152, l. 14 (*apekshábuddhi-náśa*), viz., *áśrayanáśa*, and the united action of *both*:—

Column 1:
Ekatva-jñána
Apekshábuddhi
Dvitvotpatti and akatva-jñána-náśa
Dvitvatvajñána
Dvitvaguṇa-buddhi and apekshábuddhi-náśa
Dvitva-náśa and dravya-buddhi

Column 2:
Avayava-kriyá.
Avayava-vibhága
Avayava-saṃyoga-náśa
Dvitvádhárasya (i.e., avayavinaḥ) náśaḥ
Dvitva-náśa (i.e., of avayavin).
Avayava-kriyá
....

Column 3:
....
Avayava-vibhága.
Avayava-saṃyoga-náśa.
Ádhára-náśa (of avayavin).
Dvitva-náśa.

The second and third columns represent what takes place when, in the course of the six steps of *ekatvajñána*, &c., one of the two parts is itself divided either at the *first* or the *second* moment. In the first case, the *dvitva* of the whole is destroyed in the fifth moment, and therefore its only cause is its immediately preceding*dvitvádhára-náśa*, or, as Mádhava calls it, *áśrayanivṛitti*. In the second case, the *náśa* arrives at the same moment simultaneously by both columns (1) and (3), and hence it may be ascribed to the united action of two causes, *apekshábuddhi-náśa* and *ádhára-náśa*. Any*kriyá* which arose in one of the parts after the second moment would be unimportant, as the *náśa* of the *dvitva* of the whole would take place by the original sequence in column (1) in the sixth moment; and in this way it would be too late to affect that result.

[182] *I.e.*, from the destruction of *apekshábuddhi* follows the destruction of *dvitva*; but the other destructions previously described were followed by some production,—thus the knowledge of*dvitvatva* arose from the destruction of *ekatvajñána*, &c. (cf. Siddh. Mukt., p. 107). I may remind the reader that in Hindu logic the counter-entity to the non-existence of a thing is the thing itself.

[183] From the conjunction of fire is produced an action in the atoms of the jar; thence a separation of one atom from another; thence a destruction of the conjunction of atoms which made the black (or unbaked) jar; thence the destruction of the compound of two atoms.

[184] *I.e.*, a kind of initiative tendency.

[185] These are explained at full length in the Siddhánta Muktávalí, pp. 104, 105. In the first series we have—1. the destruction of the *dvyaṇuka* and simultaneously a disjunction from the old place produced by the disjunction (of the parts); 2. the destruction of the black colour in the *dvyaṇuka*, and the simultaneous destruction of the conjunction of the *dvyaṇuka* with that place; 3. the production of the red colour in the atoms, and the simultaneous conjunction with another place; 4. the cessation of the action in the atom produced by the original conjunction of fire. The remaining 5-10 agree with the 4-9 above.

[186] The Vaiśeshikas hold that when a jar is baked, the old black jar is *destroyed*, its several compounds of two atoms, &c., being destroyed; the action of the fire then produces the red colour in the separate atoms, and, joining these into new compounds, eventually produces a new red jar. The exceeding rapidity of the steps prevents the eye's detecting the change of the jars. The followers of the Nyáya maintain that the fire penetrates into the different compounds of two or more atoms, and, without any destruction of the old jar, produces its effects on these compounds, and thereby changes not the jar but its colour, &c.,—it is still the same jar, only it is red, not black.

[187] In p. 109, line 14, I read *gagaṇavibhágakartṛitvasya*.

[188] The Siddhánta Muktávalí, p. 112, describes the series of steps:—1. An action, as of breaking, in one of the halves; 2. the disjunction of the two halves; 3. the destruction of the conjunction which originally produced the pot; 4. the destruction of the pot; 5. by the disjunction of the two halves is produced a disjunction of the severed half from the old place; 6. the destruction of the conjunction with that old place; 7. the conjunction with the new place; 8. the cessation of the original

impulse of fracture. Here the second disjunction (viz., of the half of the pot and the place) is produced by the previous disjunction of the halves, the intimate causes of the pot.

[189] The original has a plural *vibhágán*, *i.e.*, disjunctions from the several points.

[190] *I.e.*, the disjunction of the hand and the points of space.

[191] The author of a commentary on the Bhagavad Gítá.

[192] For *dravyádi* read *pṛithivyádi.*

[193] I am not sure that it would not be better to read *viddhavevidhayá*, rewounding the wounded, instead of *vṛiddhavívadhayá.*

[194] Unless you *see* the rope you cannot mistake it for a serpent.

[195] In p. 110, last line, read *'bháve.*

[196] Read in p. 110, last line, *anavadhánádishu.Vidhipratyaya* properly means an imperative or potential affix implying "command;" but the pandit takes *vidhi* here as *bhávabodhaka-kriyá.* It has that meaning in Kávya-prakáśa, V. (p. 114, l. 1).

[197] The mind perceives *áloka-jñána*, therefore it would perceive its absence, *i.e.*, darkness, but this last is perceived by the *eye.*

[198] *I.e.*, light possesses colour, and we cannot see a jar's absence in the dark.

[199] Sound resides in the imperceptible ether, and cessation is the *dhvaṃsábháva*, or "emergent non-existence."

[200] The reading *pratyayavedyatvena* seems supported by p. 110, last line, but it is difficult to trace the argument; I have, therefore, ventured hesitatingly to read *pratyakshavedyatvena*, and would refer to the commentary (Vaiś. Sút. p. 250), "*yadi hi níla-rúpavan nílaṃ rúpam eva vá tamaḥ syát, váhyálokapragraham antareṇa chakshushá na gṛihyeta.*"

[201] Intimate relation has also no intimate relation.

[202] "Relative non-existence" (*saṃsargábháva*) is the negation of a relation; thus "the jar is not in the house" is "absolute non-existence," "it was not in the house" is "antecedent," and "it will not be in the house" is "emergent," non-existence.

[203] *I.e.*, the absolute absence of the jar is found in the jar, as, of course, the jar does not reside in the jar, but in the spot of ground,—it is the *játi ghaṭatva* which resides in the jar.

[204] The opposite is "there *is* colour in the air."

[205] Cf. Nyáya Sútras, i. 29.

[206] In p. 112, line 16, of the Calcutta edition, I read*doshanimitta-tattva* for *doshanimittakatva* (compare Nyáya Sút. iv. 68).

[207] Without this last clause the definition might include the objects (*vishaya*), as these are, of course, connected with right knowledge.

[208] Íśvara is a cause of right knowledge (*pramáṇa*) according to the definition, because he is *pramáyá áśrayaḥ*.

[209] On this compare Siddhánta-Muktávali, p. 115.

[210] On these compare my note to Colebrooke's Essays, vol. i. p. 315.

[211] "Our coming to the conclusion that there can be no smoke in the hill if there be no fire, while we *see* the smoke, is the confutation of there being no fire in the hill" (*Ballantyne*). Or, in other words, "the mountain must have the absence-of-smoke (*vyápaka*) if it has the absence-of-fire (the false *vyápya*")".

[212] Action (*pravṛitti*) follows after the ascertainment of the truth by *nyáya*.

[213] Cp. Vátsyáyana's Comment., p. 6. The Calcutta edition reads *prakírtitá* for *paríkshitá*.

[214] The printed text omits the third fault, "a stupid indifference, *moha*," which is however referred to presently.

[215] In p. 116, line 3, I would read *tannirvartakam* for*tannivartakam*.

[216] This refers to the couplet so often quoted in Hindu authors, "Logic, the three Vedas, trade and agriculture, and the eternal doctrine of polity,—these four sciences are the causes of the stability of the world" (cf. Manu, vii. 43). It occurs in Kámandaki's*Nítisára*, ii. 2, and seems to be referred to in Vátsyáyana's Com. p. 3, from which Mádhava is here borrowing.

[217] Compare the English proverb, "As soon as the cat can lick her ear."

[218] Literally the "bell-road," *i.e.*, "the chief road through a village, or that by which elephants, &c., decorated with tinkling ornaments, proceed."—*Wilson's Dict.*

[219] The cognition is produced in the first moment, remains during the second, and ceases in the third.

[220] See Nyáya Sút. i. 2.

[221] As otherwise why should we require liberation at all? Or rather the author probably assumes that other Naiyáyikas have sufficiently established this point against its opponents, cf. p. 167, line 11.

[222] See *supra*, pp. 24-32.

[223] All is momentary, all is pain, all is *sui generis*, all is unreal.

[224] In the form of the various *kleśas* or "afflictions."

[225] *Ávaraṇa*, cf. pp. 55, 58.

[226] But the Nyáya holds that the attributes of the soul, as happiness, desire, aversion, &c., are perceived by the internal sense, mind (Bháshá P. § 83).

[227] The reading *múrtapratibandhát* is difficult, but I believe that *pratibandha* means here *vyápti*, as it does in Sánkhya Sútras, i. 100.

[228] The true *summum bonum* must be *niratiśaya*,—incapable of being added to.

[229] *Yogyánupalabdhi* is when an object is not seen, and yet all the usual concurrent causes of vision are present, as the eye, light, &c.

[230] Alluding to the Vedic phrase, "*grávánaḥ plavanti*," see Uttara Naishadha, xvii. 37. The phrase *aśmánaḥ plavanti* occurs in Shaḍv. Br. 5, 12.

[231] Or perhaps "capable of being surpassed."

[232] Since the Supreme Being is a single instance.

[233] Since the Veda, if non-eternal, must [to be authoritative] have been created by God, and yet it is brought forward to reveal the existence of God.

[234] The Nyáya holds presumption to be included under inference, and comparison is declared to be the ascertaining the relation of a name to the thing named.

[235] Since ether is connected by contact with the parts of everything, as *e.g.*, a jar.

[236] The whole (as the jar) resides by intimate relation in its parts (as the jar's two halves). But the eternal substances, ether, time, the soul, mind, and the atoms of earth, water, fire, and air, do not thus reside in anything, although, of course, the category*viśesha* does reside in them by intimate relation. The word "substances" excludes *tantutva*, and "existing in intimate relation" excludes ether, &c.

[237] Intermediate between infinite and infinitesimal, all eternal substances being the one or the other.

[238] The *viruddha-hetu* is that which is never found where the major term is.

[239] This and much more of the whole discussion is taken from the Kusumáñjali, v. 2, and I extract my note on the passage there. "The older Naiyáyikas maintained that the argument 'the mountain has fire because it has blue smoke,' involved the fallacy of vyápyatvásiddhi, because the alleged middle term was unnecessarily restricted (see Siddhánta Muktáv. p. 77). The moderns, however, more wisely consider it as a harmless error, and they would rather meet the objection by asserting that there is no proof to establish the validity of the assumed middle term."

[240] For the *upádhi* cf. pp. 7, 8.

[241] As in the former case it would be clear that it is a subject for separate discussion; and in the latter you would be liable to the fault of *áśrayásiddhi*, a "baseless inference," since your subject (or minor term), being itself non-existent, cannot be the locus or subject of a negation (cf. Kusumáñjali, iii. 2). "Just as that subject from which a given attribute is excluded cannot be unreal, so neither can an unreal thing be the subject of a negation."

[242] If God is known, then His existence must be granted; if He is not known, how can we argue about Him? I read lines 15, 16, in p. 120 of the Calcutta edition, *vikalpaparáhatatvát*, and then begin the next clause with *syád etat*. The printed text, *vikalpaparáhataḥsyát tad etat*, seems unintelligible.

[243] The aggregate of the various subtile bodies constitutes Hiraṇyagarbha, or the supreme soul viewed in His relation to the world as creator, while the aggregate of the gross bodies similarly constitutes his gross body (viráj).

[244] The usual reading is *tasthur* for *tasthe*.

[245] For these divisions of the *anyonyáśraya* fallacy, see*Nyáyasútra vṛitti*, i. 39 (p. 33).

[246] For *tívra* cf. *Yoga sútras*, i. 21, 22.

[247] Mádhava here calls it the *práchí Mímáṃsá*.

[248] Cf. *J. Nyáyamálávist*, pp. 5-9.

[249] Thus it is said that he who desires to be a family priest should offer a black-necked animal to Agni, a parti-coloured one to Soma, and a black-necked one to Agni. Should this be a case for*tantra* or not? By *tantra* one offering to Agni would do for both; but as the offering to Soma comes between, they cannot be united, and thus it must be a case of *ávápa, i.e.*, offering the two separately (*J. Nyáyamálá*, xi. 1, 13).

[250] In p. 123, line 4, I read *vilakshaṇa-dṛishṭaphala*.

[251] In the former case it would be a *vidhi*, in the latter a *niyama*. Cf. the lines *vidhir atyantam aprápto niyamaḥ pákshike sati, tatra chányatra cha práptau parisaṃkhyá vidhíyate.*

[252] The Mímáṃsá holds that the potential and similar affixes, which constitute a *vidhi*, have a twofold power; by the one they express an active volition of the agent, corresponding to the root-meaning (*artha-bhávaná*); by the other an enforcing power in the word (*śabda-bhávaná*). Thus in *svargakámo yajeta*, the *eta* implies "let him produce heaven by means of certain acts which together make up a sacrifice possessing a certain mystic influence;" next it implies an enforcing power residing in itself (as it is the word of the self-existent Veda and not of God) which sets the hearer upon this course of action.

[253] These four "fruits of action" are obscure, and I do not remember to have seen them alluded to elsewhere. I was told in India that they were a thing's coming into being, growing, declining, and perishing. If so, they are the second, third, fifth, and sixth of the six *vikáras* mentioned in Śaṅkara's Vajrasúchi, 2, *i.e., asti,jáyate, vardhate, vipariṇamate, apakshíyate, naśyati.* I do not see how there could be any reference to the four kinds of*apúrva*, sc. *phala, samudáya, utpatti*, and *aṅga*, described in Nyáya M. V. ii. 1, 2.

[254] The *nigamas* are the Vedic quotations in Yáska's*nirukta*.

[255] See Nyáya-málá-vistara, i. 4, 19.

[256] The exact number is 915.

[257] This is to explain the last of the five members, the*saṃgati*.

[258] Cf. Aśvaláyana's Gṛihya Sútras, i. 19, 1.

[259] The *anuváda*, of course, implies a previous *vidhi*, which it thus repeats and supplements, and so carries with it an equal authority. The *anuváda* in the present case is the passage which mentions that the Veda is to be read, as it enforces the previous*vidhi* as to teaching.

[260] I read in p. 127, line 12, *anava-gamyamánasya*, and so the recension given in the Nyáya M. V. p. 14, *na budhyamánasya*.

[261] In the next two or three pages I have frequently borrowed from Dr. Muir's translation in his *Sanskrit Texts*, vol. iii. p. 88.

[262] The soul may be traced back through successive transmigrations, but you never get back to its beginning.

[263] Mádhava means that the author of this stanza, though unknown to many people, was not necessarily unknown to all, as his contemporaries, no doubt, knew who wrote it, and his descendants might perhaps still be aware of the fact. In this case, therefore, we have an instance of a composition of which some persons did not know the origin, but which, nevertheless, had a human author. The stanza in question is quoted in full in Böhtlingk's Indische Sprüche, No. 5598, from the MS. anthology called the *Subháshitárṇava*. For *muktaka*, see *Sáh. Darp.*, § 558.

[264] The eternity of the Veda depends on this tenet of the Mímáṃsá that sound is eternal.

[265] Eternal things (as the atoms of earth, fire, water, and air, minds, time, space, ether, and soul) have *viśesha*, not *sámánya* or genus, and they are all imperceptible to the senses. Genera are themselves eternal (though the individuals in which they reside are not), but they have not themselves genus. Both these arguments belong rather to the Nyáya-vaiśeshika school than to the Nyáya.

[266] The Mímáṃsaka allows that the *uchcháraṇa* or utterance is non-eternal.

[267] The inference will be as follows: "The Vedas were arranged after being acquired by other modes of proof, with a view to their manifestation, from the very fact of their having the nature of sentences, just like the compositions of Manu, &c."

[268] The argument will now run, "The Vedas were arranged after being acquired by other modes of proof, because, while they possess authority, they still have the nature of sentences, like the composition of Manu, &c."

[269] In assuming a material body, he would be subject to material limitations.

[270] The Jainas allow thirty-four such superhuman developments (*atiśayáḥ*) in their saints.

[271] Jaimini maintains that the vibrations of the air "manifest" the always existing sound.

[272] "What is meant by 'noise' (*náda*) is these 'conjunctions' and 'disjunctions,' occasioned by the vibrations of the air."—*Ballantyne, Mímáṃsá Aphorisms*, i. 17.

[273] The Nyáya holds that colour and sound are respectively special qualities of the elements light and ether; and as the organs of seeing and hearing are composed of light and ether, each will, of course, have its corresponding special quality.

[274] In p. 131, line 7, I read *pratyaksliásiddheḥ*.

[275] Cf. my note pp. 7, 8, (on the Chárváka-darśana) for the*upádhi*. The *upádhi* or "condition" limits a too general middle term; it is defined as "that which always accompanies the major term, but does not always accompany the middle." Thus if the condition "produced from wet fuel" is added to "fire," the argument "the mountain has smoke because it has fire" is no longer a false one. Here, in answer to the Nyáya argument in the text, our author objects that its middle term ("from the fact of its being a special quality belonging to an organ of sense") is too wide, *i.e.*, it is sometimes found where the major term "non-eternal" is not found, as, *e.g.*, in*sound* itself, according to the Mímáṃsá doctrine. To obviate this he proposes to add the "condition," "not causing audition," as he will readily concede that all those things are non-eternal which, *while not causing audition*, are special qualities belonging to an organ of sense, as, *e.g.*, colour. But I need scarcely add that this addition would make the whole argument nugatory. In fact, the Púrva Mímáṃsá and the Nyáya can never argue together on this question of the eternity of sound, as their points of view are so totally different.

[276] In the former case we have the *dhwaṃsa* of sound, in the latter its *prágabháva*.

[277] In p. 131, line 12, I read *samapauhi* for *samápohi,i.e.*, the passive aorist of *sam* + *apa* + *úh*.

[278] I do not know this legend. Tála and Betála are the two demons who carry Vikramáditya on their shoulders in the Siṃhásan-battísí. It appears to be referred to here as illustrating how one answer can suffice for two opponents.

[279] This is probably a work by Bhásarvajña (see Dr. Hall's*Bibl. Index*, p. 26).

[280] *Dhvani*, or our "articulate noise," produces the vibrations of air which render manifest the ever-existing sound. There is always an eternal but inaudible hum going on, which we modify into a definite speech by our various articulations. I take *saṃskṛita*here as equivalent to *abhivyakta*.

[281] I read in p. 131, line 15, *saṃskárakasaṃskáryabhávábhávánumánam*.

[282] It would be a case of *vyabhichára*. The Naiyáyika argument would seem to be something as follows:—Sound is not thus manifested by noise, since both are simultaneously perceived by the senses, just as we see in the parallel case of the individual and its species; these are both perceived together, but the individual is not manifested by the species. But the Mímáṃsá rejoins that this would equally apply to the soul and knowledge; as the internal sense perceives both simultaneously, and therefore knowledge ought not to be manifested by the soul, which is contrary to experience. But I am not sure that I rightly understand the argument.

[283] Here begins a long *púrva-paksha*, from p. 131, line 18, down to p. 133, line 9; see p. 198 *infra*.

[284] This is Prabhákara's view (see Siddh. Muktáv., p. 118). The first knowledge is in the form "This is a jar;" the second knowledge is the cognition of this perception in the form "I perceive the jar;" and this latter produces authoritativeness (*prámáṇya*), which resides in it as its characteristic.

[285] Substances are "intimate causes" to their qualities, and only substances have qualities; now if authoritativeness, which is a characteristic of right knowledge, were caused by it, it would be a quality of it, that is, right knowledge would be its intimate cause and therefore a substance.

[286] The eye, &c., would be its instrumental causes.

[287] The first three categories "substance," "quality," and "action," are called *játis* or species; the last four, "genus," "*viśesha*," "intimate relation," and "non-existence," are called *upádhis* or "general characteristics."

[288] The Púrva Mímáṃsá denies that recollection is right knowledge.

[289] Wrong knowledge is produced by the same instrumental causes (as the eye, &c.) which produced right knowledge, but by these*together with a "defect,"* as biliousness, distance &c.

[290] *Scil.* if there be *doshábháva* there is *pramá*; if not, not. In p. 132, line 20, I read *doshábhávatvena* for*doshábhávasahakṛitatvena.*

[291] *Anyathásiddhatvam* means *niyatapúrvavartitve sati anávaśyakatvam.*

[292] *Scil.* or the absence of "defect," *doshábháva.*

[293] Wrong knowledge has *doshábháva* or the presence of a "defect" as its cause, in addition to the common causes.

[294] Wrongness of knowledge (*apramátva*) can only reside in knowledge as a characteristic or quality thereof; it cannot reside in a jar. The jar is, of course, produced by other instrumental causes than those of knowledge (as, *e.g.*, the potter's stick, &c.), but it is not produced by these other causes *in combination* with being also produced by the instrumental causes of knowledge (with which it has nothing directly to do); and so by a quibble, which is less obvious in Sanskrit than in English, this wretched sophism is allowed to pass muster. The jar is not produced-by-any-other-instrumental-causes-than-those-of-knowledge,-while-at-the-same-time-it-is-produced-by-these.

[295] I suppose this is the argument given at the close of the previous long púrva-paksha.

[296] These words "and is other than defect" (*dosha-vyatirikta*) are, of course, meaningless as far as right knowledge is concerned; they are simply added to enable the author to bring in "wrong knowledge" as an example. Wrong knowledge is caused by the causes of knowledge *plus* "defect;" right knowledge by the former alone.

[297] The Nyáya holds that wrong knowledge is produced by a "defect," as jaundice, &c., in the eye, and right knowledge by a *guṇa* or "virtue" (as the direct contact of the healthy organ with a true object), or by the absence of a "defect."

[298] The *guṇa* (or βελτίστη ἕξις of an organ is not properly a cause of *pramá* but rather *doshábháva-bodhaka.*

[299] *Scil.* "doubtful" (*sandigdha*) and "ascertained non-authoritativeness" (*niśchitáprámáṇya*).

[300] *Utsarga* is a general conclusion which is not necessarily true in every particular case; but here it means the conclusion that "right knowledge has no special causes but the common causes of knowledge, the eye," &c.

[301] The first knowledge is "This is a jar," the second knowledge is the cognition of this perception in the form "I perceive the jar;" and simultaneously with it arises the cognition of the truth of the perception, *i.e.*, its authoritativeness or *prámáṇya.*

[302] This seems to be a quotation of Udayana's own words, and no doubt is taken from his very rare prose commentary on the Kusumáñjali, a specimen of which I printed in the preface to my edition. This passage must come from the fifth book (v. 6?).

[303] I read *tat-práchuryam* for *tatpráchurye* in p. 134, line 7.

[304] This stanza affirms that according to the Mímáṃsá school, while authoritativeness is self-proved, non-authoritativeness is proved from something else (as inference, &c.)

[305] I take *vyutpatti* here as used for *śakti*; *siddhe*means *ghaṭádau.*

[306] These are the two great Mímáṃsá schools. The former, called*abhihitánvaya-vádinaḥ*, hold (like the Naiyáyika school) that words by themselves can express their separate meaning by the function *abhidhá* or "denotation;" these are subsequently combined into a sentence expressing one connected idea. The latter, called *anvitábhidhána-vádinaḥ*, hold that words only express a meaning as parts of a sentence and grammatically connected with each other; they only mean an action or something connected with an action. In *gám ánaya*, *gám* does not properly mean *gotva*, but*ánayanánvita-gotva*, *i.e.*, the bovine genus as connected with "bringing." We cannot have a case of a noun without some governing verb, and *vice versâ*. Cf. Waitz, as quoted by Professor Sayce (*Comparative Philology*, page 136): "We do not think in words but in sentences; hence we may assert that a living language consists of sentences, not of words. But a sentence is formed not of single independent words, but of words which refer to one another in a particular manner, like the corresponding thought, which does not consist of single independent ideas, but of such as, connected, form a whole, and determine one another mutually."

[307] Mádhava uses this peculiar term because the grammarians adopted and fully developed the idea of the Púrva-Mímáṃsá school that sound is eternal. He therefore treats of *sphoṭa* here, and not in his Jaimini chapter.

[308] Rig-Veda, x. 9, 4.

[309] *Śabdánuśásana*, if judged by the apparent sense of Páṇini, ii. 2, 14, would be a wrong compound; but it is not so, because ii. 2, 14 must be interpreted in the sense of ii. 3, 66, whence it follows that the compound would only be wrong if there were an agent expressed *as well as* an object, *i.e.*, if such a word as*ácháryeṇa* followed. In the example given, we cannot say *áścharyo godoho śikshitena gopálena* (as it would violate ii. 2, 14), neither can we say *áścharyo gaváṃ doho' śikshitasya gopálasya* (as it would violate ii. 3, 66).

[310] That is, the *ubhayaprápti* of ii. 3, 66, is a*bahuvríhi* agreeing with *kṛiti* in ii. 3, 65. These points are all discussed at some length in the Commentaries on Páṇini.

[311] These actually occur in the Commentaries to Páṇini, ii. 2, 8; iii. 3, 117, &c.

[312] This takes in all cases of relation, *sambandha*(*i.e.*, *shashṭhí-sambandha*).

[313] As in such rules as vi. 2, 139.

[314] These compounds occur in Páṇini's own sútras (i. 4, 30, and i. 4, 55), and would violate his own rule in ii. 2, 15, if we were to interpret the latter without some such saving modification as*shashṭhí śeshe*.

[315] The very word *śabda* in *śabdánuśásanam* implies the Veda, since this is pre-eminently *śabda*.

[316] Compare Max Müller, *Sansk. Liter.*, p. 113. It is quoted as from the Veda in the Mahábháshya.

[317] In the Calcutta text, p. 138, dele *daṇḍa* in line 3 after *bhavet*, and insert it in line 4 after *śabdánám*.

[318] As in the so-called *pada* text.

[319] See Ballantyne's *Mahábháshya*, pp. 12, 64.

[320] *Achíkramata* seems put here as a purposely false form of the frequentative of *kram* for *achaṅkramyata*.

[321] Or it may mean "the developed universe." Compare the lines of Bhartṛihari which immediately follow.

[322] One would naturally supply *śabdasya* after *sámyam*, but the Mahábháshya has *naḥ sámyam* (see Ballantyne's ed., p. 27).

[323] *I.e.*, prepositions used separately as governing cases of their own, and not (as usually in Sanskrit) in composition.

[324] The *karmapravachaníyas* imply a verb other than the one expressed, and they are said to determine the relation which is produced by this understood verb. Thus in the example, *Śákalyasaṃhitám anu právarshat*, "he rained after the Śákalya hymns," *anu* implies an understood verb *niśamya*, "having heard," and this verb shows that there is a relation of cause and effect between the hymns and the rain. This *anu* is said to determine this relation.

[325] See Ballantyne's ed., p. 10.

[326] This is not very clear, the *anu* in *anugraha* might mean *krameṇa*, and so imply the successive order of the letters.

[327] In the Calcutta edition, p. 142, line 11, I read *kalpam* for *kalpanam*.

[328] In p. 142, line 3, I add *viná* after *nimittam*.

[329] The ghaṭṭa is the place where dues and taxes are collected. Some one anxious to evade payment is going by a private way by night, but he arrives at the tax-collector's house just as day dawns and is thus caught. Hence the proverb means *uddeśyásiddhi*.

[330] In p. 143, line 13, I read *sphoṭakabhávam* for*sphoṭábhávam*.

[331] Cf. Ballantyne's Transl. of the Mahábháshya, pp. 9, 32.

[332] The Mímámṃsâ holds that a word means the genus (*játi*) and not the individual (*vyakti*); the Nyáya holds that a word means an individual as distinguished by such and such a genus (or species).

[333] Cf. Rig-Veda Prátiś. xii. 5.

[334] He here is trying to show that his view is confirmed by the commonly received definitions of some grammatical terms.

[335] Since Devadatta is only its transient owner.

[336] So by the words "horse," "cow," &c., Brahman is really meant, the one abiding existence.

[337] Cf. Ballantyne's Mahábháshya, pp. 44, 50.

[338] In p. 145, line 8, read *asatya* for *aśvattha*.

[339] We have here the well-known four grammatical categories, *játi*, *guna*, *dravya* or *sańjná*, and *kriyá*.

[340] But cf. Siddh. Muktáv., p. 6, line 12.

[341] Thus we read in the Siddhánta Muktávali, p. 82, that the Mímámṃsá holds that a word means the genus and not the individual, since otherwise there would be *vyabhichára* and *ánantya* (cf. also Maheśachandra Nyáyaratna's note, Kávya-prakáśa, p. 10). If a word is held to mean only *one* individual, there will be the first fault, as it will "wander away" and equally express others which it should not include; if it is held to mean *many* individuals, it will have an endless variety of meanings and be "indefinite."

[342] This seems the meaning of the text as printed *tasmát dvayaṃ satyam*, but I should prefer to read conjecturally *tasmád advayaṃ satyam*, "therefore non-duality is the truth."

[343] *Scil.* they can only be the absolute Brahman who alone exists.

[344] *Scil.* the individual soul (*jíva*) and Brahman.

[345] The *Saṃvṛiti* of the text seems to correspond to the*ávaraṇa* so frequent in Vedánta books.

[346] This passage is quoted in the Maitrí Upanishad, vi. 22.

[347] *Adhividyam* occurs in Taitt. Upanishad, i. 3, 1, where it is explained by [']Saṃkara as *vidyásv adhi yad dar[']sanaṃ tad adhividyam.*

[348] I borrow this term from Dr. Hall.

[349] Compare Kusumáñjali, i. 4.

[350] One great defect in the Sáṅkhya nomenclature is the ambiguity between the terms for intellect (*buddhí*) and those for mind (*manas*). Mádhava here applies to the former the term*antaḥkaraṇa* or "internal organ," the proper term for the latter. I have ventured to alter it in the translation.

[351] It is singular that this is Mádhava's principal Sáṅkhya authority, and not the Sáṅkhya Sútras.

[352] *Vaikṛita* is here a technical term meaning that goodness predominates over darkness and activity. On this Káriká, comp. Dr. Hall's preface to the Sáṅkhya-sára, pp. 30-35.

[353] As produced, like them, from modified egoism. The reading *saṃkalpavikalpátmakam* must be corrected by the Sáṅkhya Káriká.

[354] Cf. Colebrooke Essays, vol. i. p. 256. The *tanmátras*will reproduce themselves as the respective qualities of the gross elements.

[355] A name of the Buddhists.

[356] *I.e.*, the nature of a thing (*Svabháva*) cannot be altered—a man cannot be made a cow, nor a woman a man.

[357] I take *arthántaram* here as simply *bhinnam* (cf. Táránátha Tarkavá-chaspati's note, *Tattva Kaumudí*, p. 47).

[358] Colebrooke's translation.

[359] Or "passion," *rajas*.

[360] In other words—on the one hand the existing misery of beings induced God to create a world in order to relieve their misery, and on the other hand it was the existence of a created world which caused their misery at all.

[361] Bondage, &c., reside in the intellect, and are only*reflected* upon soul through its proximity (cf. *Sáṅkhyapravachanabháshya*, i. 58).

[362] This apologue is a widely spread piece of folk-lore. It is found in the Babylonian Talmud, *Sanhedrim*, fol. 91, *b*, and in the Gesta Romanorum.

[363] On this see Dr. Hall's Pref. to Sáṅkhya Pr. Bhásh., p. 20; S. Sára, p. 11.

[364] *I.e.*, he revealed the Veda, and also originated the meanings of words, as well as instructed the first fathers of mankind in the arts of life.

[365] I read *ye* for *te* with Dr. Hall's MS. *Tapya* means rather "susceptible of suffering."

[366] This is really Vyása's comm. on Sút., iv. 21.

[367] Cf. *Bháshá-parichchheda*, 15, *a*.

[368] Śatapatha Br., xiv. 7, 2, 28.

[369] I read in the second clause *tadbháve'pi*, understanding by *tad* the different conditions which *atha* is supposed to assume as being necessarily present.

[370] These are, i., the discrimination of the eternal from the phenomenal; ii., the rejection of the fruit of actions here or hereafter; iii., the possession of the six qualities, tranquillity,& c.; and, iv., the desire for liberation.

[371] It may be *sukha-janaka*, but it is not itself*sukha*.

[372] Granting that *atha* does not here mean "auspicious," why should not this be the implied meaning, as all allow that the particle *atha* does produce an auspicious influence?

[373] *i.e.*, a word's incapacity to convey a meaning without some other word to complete the construction.

[374] This is found with some variations in the Mahábháshya (p. 7, Kielhorn's ed.)

[375] The commentators hold that the word *vṛiddhiḥ* is placed at the beginning of the first sútra, while *guṇaḥ* in the second is placed at the end (*ad eṅ guṇaḥ*), in order to ensure an auspicious opening, *vṛiddhi* meaning "increase," "prosperity," as well as "the second strengthening of a vowel."

[376] In the old Bengali poem Chaṇḍí, we have an interesting list of these omens. The hero Chandraketu, starting on a journey, has the following good omens: On his right hand a cow, a deer, a Bráhman, a full-blown lotus; on his left, a jackal and a jar full of water. He hears on his right hand the sound of fire and a cowherdess calling "milk" to buyers. He

sees a cow with her calf, a woman calling "jaya,"*dúrvá* grass, rice, garlands of flowers, diamonds, sapphires, pearls, corals; and on the left twelve women. He hears drums and cymbals, and men dancing and singing "Hari." It is, however, all spoiled by seeing a guana (*godhiká*). The author adds, "This is a bad omen according to all śástras, and so is a tortoise, a rhinoceros, the tuberous root of the water-lily, and a hare." Elsewhere, a vulture, a kite, a lizard, and a woodman carrying wood are called bad omens.

[377] These are the names of two out of the four sacrifices lasting for one day, in which a thousand cows are given to the officiating Bráhmans.

[378] He is here called *phaṇipati*, "lord of snakes,"—Patañjali, the author of the Mahábháshya, being represented as a snake in mythology.

[379] Cf. Śaṅkara, Vedánta-Sút., iii. 3, 49.

[380] This is the Mímáṃsá rule for settling the relative value of the proofs that one thing is ancillary to another. 1. *Śruti*, "a definite text," as "let him offer with curds," where curds are clearly an ancillary part of the sacrifice. 2. *Liṅga*, "a sign," or "the sense of the words," as leading to an inference, as in the text "he divides by the ladle;" here we infer that the thing to be divided must be a liquid like ghee, since a ladle could not divide solid things like the baked flour cakes. 3. *Vákya*, "the being mentioned in one sentence," *i.e.*, the context, as in the text "'(I cut) thee for food,' thus saying, he cuts the branch;" here the words "(I cut) thee for food" are ancillary to the action of cutting; or in the text, "I offer the welcome (oblation) to Agni," the words "the welcome (oblation) to Agni," as they form one sentence with the words "I offer," are ancillary to the act of offering. 4. *Prakaraṇa*, "the subject-matter viewed as a whole, with an interdependence of its parts," as in the *darśa-púrṇamása* sacrifice, where the *prayája*ceremonies, which have no special fruit mentioned, produce, as parts, a mystic influence (*apúrva*) which helps forward that influence of the whole by which the worshippers obtain heaven. Here the *prakaraṇa*proves them to be ancillary. 5. *Sthána* (or *krama*), "relative position" or "order," as the recital of the hymn *Śundhadhvam*, &c., "Be ye purified for the divine work," in connection with the mention of the *sánnáyya* vessels, where this position proves that the hymn is ancillary to the action of sprinkling those vessels. 6. *Samákhyá*, "title;" thus the Yajur-veda is called the special book for the*adhvaryu* priests; hence in any rite mentioned in it they are *prima facie* to be considered as the priests employed. The order in the aphorism represents the relative weight to be attached to each; the first, *śruti*, being the most important; the last, *samákhyá*, the least. Cf. Jaimini's Sútras, iii. 3, 14; *Mímáṃsáparibháshá*, pp. 8, 9.

[381] *I.e.*, Yogi-Yájñavalkya, the author of the *Yájñavalkya-gítá*. See Hall, *Bibl. Index*, p. 14; Aufrecht, *Bodl. Catal.*, p. 87 *b*.

[382] *Karman* seems here used for *kriyâ*, which properly belongs only to the body, as the soul is *drashṭṛi*.

[383] *Scil. samádhi*, or the restraining the mind and senses to profound contemplation.

[384] *Scil.* "forbearance, religious observance, postures, suppression of the breath, restraint, attention, contemplation, and meditation (*samádhi*)."

[385] See Bhoja, Comm. iii. 3, *samyag ádhíyate mano yatra sa samádhiḥ*.

[386] Thus, *e.g.*, the antecedent non-existence and the destruction of the pot are found in the two halves in which the pot itself (the counter-entity to its own non-existence) resides by intimate relation (*samaváya-sambandha*).

[387] I read *niroddhavyánám* for *nirodhánám*.

[388] *Chit-śakti* and *chiti-śakti* = soul.

[389] The *sattva* of the *buddhi* or the internal organ.

[390] This second substance, "mind" or "understanding" (*buddhi*, *chitta*), is like a looking-glass, which reflects the image of the object on a second looking-glass (*sc.* soul).

[391] Váchaspati explains *lakshaṇa* as *kálabheda*.

[392] I take *ádi* as meaning *asphuṭatva*. The change of state takes place between the several moments of the *lakshaṇa-pariṇáma*. Cf. the Commentaries on iii. 13.

[393] These are generally called the five states of the thinking principle, *chittabhúmayas* or *avasthás*. Cf. Commentary, i. 2, 18.

[394] These three conditions respectively characterise men, demons, and gods.

[395] Much of this is taken from Bhoja's Commentary, and I have borrowed Ballantyne's translation.

[396] Can *chitta* mean "soul" here?

[397] *I.e.*, as, *e.g.*, whether the senses produce the elements or the elements the senses, &c.

[398] In p. 164, line 4 *infra*, read *sukhaprakáśamayasya*.

[399] In p. 164, line 2 *infra*, read *sattámátra* for*sattva-*. Bhoja well distinguishes *asmitá* from *ahaṃkára*.

[400] For these see *infra*, and cf. Yoga S., ii. 3, 12, 13.

[401] I have ventured to alter the examples, to suit the English translation.

[402] Where the negation is prominent it is called *prasajya-pratishedha*; but where it is not prominent, we have the *paryudása* negation. In the former the negative is connected with the verb; in the latter it is generally compounded with some other word, as, *e.g.*—

(a.) "Not a drum was heard, not a funeral note."

(b.) "Unwatched the garden bough shall sway."

The former corresponds to the logician's *atyantábháva*, the latter to *anyonyábháva* or *bheda*.

[403] Cf. the *várttika* in Siddhánta Kaum., i. 401.

[404] Thus *adhana* stands for *avidya-mánadhana*, with*vidyamána* omitted in the compound.

[405] As its subject would confessedly be *buddhi*.

[406] As it is *avidyá* after all.

[407] In p. 165, lines 16, 17, read (with my MS. of Váchaspati's Gloss), *sarvavṛittinirodhasampannáyá api tathátvaprasaṅgát*.

[408] I read *tanvavasthááścha* with the printed edition of Váchaspati's Gloss. If *tanudagdhááścha* is correct, it must mean *tanutvena dagdháh*.

[409] As in *rámalakshmaṇau*, Ráma and Lakshmaṇa.

[410] I read *pakshatraye* for *pakshadvaye*.

[411] In his Comm. on Sút., ii. 5.

[412] Thus *inimicus* is not a "friend," nor, on the other hand, a "non-friend," but something positive, an "enemy." So *agoshpada* is said to mean "a forest."

[413] Cf. Yoga Sút., i. 8.

[414] In p. 166, line 4 *infra*, read *káyádau* for*káryádau*.

[415] This couplet is quoted by Vyása in his Comm. on Yoga Sútras, ii. 5, and I have followed Váchaspati in his explanation of it; he calls it *vaiyásakí gáthá*.

[416] Since the continued enjoyment of an object only increases the desire for more, and its loss gives correspondent regret (cf. Bhag. G. xviii. 38).

[417] Literally, "it has four feet."

[418] Thus "sight," or the power of seeing, is a modification of the quality of *sattva* unobstructed by *rajas* and *tamas*.

[419] "Let the affix *ṇini* be used after a root in the sense of what is habitual, when the *upapada*, or subordinate word, is not a word meaning 'genus' and ends in a case."

[420] "Let *vṛiddhi* be the substitute of a base ending in a vowel, when that which has an indicatory *ñ* or *ṇ* follows;" *ṇini*has an indicatory *ṇ*.

[421] Sc. *anuśaya* + *ini* = *anuśayin*.

[422] *Ini* and *ṭhan*, which respectively leave *in* and*ika*; thus *daṇḍa* gives *daṇḍin* and *daṇḍika*. The line is quoted by Boehtlingk, vol. ii. p. 217, on Páṇ. v. 2, 115, and is explained in the *Káśiká*, *ad loc*. The different prohibitions are illustrated by the examples:—(1.) *svaván*, *khaván*; (2.) *kárakaván*; (3.)*vyághraván*, *siṃhaván*; (4.) *daṇḍavatí śálá* (*i.e.*, *daṇḍá asyáṃsanti*).

[423] By iii. 3, 56.

[424] It is curious to see the great grammarian's favourite study obtruding itself here on such a slender pretext.

[425] See the *Káśiká* on Páṇ. v. 2, 115. For *vivakshártha*(meaning "general currency"), compare Commentary on Páṇ. ii. 2, 27. The edition in the Benares *Pandit* reads *vishayaniyamártha*.

[426] *i.e.*, Thus *nirodha* is not *vṛitter abhávaḥ*, but*abhávasyáśryaḥ*.

[427] I read in p. 168, last line, *prakáśapravṛittiniyamarúpa*, from Bhoja's comment on i. 12.

[428] See Káśiká, ii. 3, 36.

[429] This passage probably occurs in the *Yájñavalkya-gítá*of Yogi-yájñavalkya. See Colebrooke's Essays (ed. 2), vol. i. p. 145, note.

[430] Mímáṃsá Sútras, ii. 1, 35-37.

[431] The tantras are not properly concerned with what is*nitya* or *naimittika*; they are *kámya*.

[432] The *víja* of air is the syllable *jaṃ*.

[433] The *víja* of water is the syllable *baṃ*.

[434] *Hríṃ*.

[435] *Śríṃ.*

[436] *Táṇḍava* is the frantic dance of the god. Śiva and his votaries.

[437] Literally "they take severally in order the gender of one of the two." Cf. "Thebæ ipsæ quod Bœotiæ caput est," *Livy*, xlii. 44; "Animal hoc providum, acutum, plenum rationis et consilii, quem vocamus hominem," *Cic.*, *Legg*, i. 7.

[438] I have borrowed these terms from Ballantyne's translation of the Sáhitya-darpaṇa.

[439] Qualified indication arises from likeness, as the man is like an ox from his stupidity; pure indication from any other relation, as cause and effect, &c., thus butter is the cause of longevity.

[440] *I.e.*, an hour, a *ghaṭiká* being twenty-four minutes.

[441] The *náḍís* or tubular vessels are generally reckoned to be 101, with ten principal ones; others make sixteen principal *náḍís*. They seem taken afterwards in pairs.

[442] Mádhava uses the same illustration in his commentary on the passage in the Aitareya Bráhmaṇa (iii. 29), where the relation of the vital airs, the seasons, and the mantras repeated with the offerings to the seasons, is discussed. "The seasons never stand still; following each other in order one by one, as spring, summer, the rains, autumn, the cold and the foggy seasons, each consisting of two months, and so constituting the year of twelve months, they continue revolving again and again like a waterwheel (*ghaṭíyantravat*); hence the seasons never pause in their course."

[443] This refers to a peculiar tenet of Hindu mysticism, that each involuntary inspiration and expiration constitutes a mantra, as their sound expresses the word *so'haṃ* (i.e., *haṃsaḥ*), "I am he." This mantra is repeated 21,600 times in every twenty-four hours; it is called the *ajapámantra*, *i.e.*, the mantra uttered without voluntary muttering.

[444] *I.e.*, that which conveys the inhaled and the exhaled breath.

[445] I cannot explain this. We might read *guruvarṇánám* for*guṇavarṇánáṃ*, as the time spent in uttering a *guruvarṇa* is a*vipala*, sixty of which make a *pala*, and two and a half *palas*make a minute; but this seems inconsistent with the other numerical details. The whole passage may be compared with the opening of the fifth act of the *Málatímádhava.*

[446] Sixty *palas* make a *ghaṭiká* (50 + 40 + 30 + 20 + 10 = 150, *i.e.*, the *palas* in two and a half *ghaṭikás* or one hour).

[447] Cf. Colebrooke's Essays, vol. i. p. 256.

[448] Literally "the being ever more."

[449] For these colours cf. *Chhándogya Up.*, viii. 6;*Maitri Up.*, vi. 30.

[450] This is an anonymous quotation in Vyása's Comm.

[451] This seems a variation of Śloka 7 of the *Amṛita-náda Up.* See Weber, *Indische Stud.*, ix. 26.

[452] This is defined in the Yoga Sút., iii. 4, as consisting of the united operation towards one object of contemplation, attention, and meditation.

[453] *I.e.*, the internal organ (*chitta*).

[454] This couplet is corrupt in the text. I follow the reading of the Bombay edition of the Puráṇa (only reading in line 3 *chalátmanám*).

[455] Vishṇu-pur., vi. 7, 45, with one or two variations. The "perfect asylum" is Brahman, formless or possessing form.

[456] The old name for the central part of Bengal.

[457] A country comprising Khandesh and part of Guzerat; it is the Λαρικῄ of Ptolemy.

[458] In p. 178, l. 2, *infra*, read *pravṛitta* for*pravṛitti*. Cf. Yoga S., iii. 52 in Bhoja's Comm. (50 in Vyása's Comm.)

[459] Read *vikaraṇabhávaḥ*; Váchaspati explains it as "*videhánám indriyáṇáṃ karaṇabhávaḥ.*"

[460] Vyása has *karaṇapañchakarúpajaya*; Váchaspati explains*rúpa* by *grahaṇádi* (cf. iii. 47).

[461] I read in p. 179, l. 11, *vyava-sáyavyavaseyátmakánám*, from Vyása's Comm.

[462] *I.e.*, as past, present, or future.

[463] *Viśoká.*

[464] This is explained by Váchaspati, "The latent impressions produced by the states of the internal organ called*vyutthána* (when it is chiefly characterised by 'activity,' or 'darkness,' iii. 9) and *nirodha* (when it is chiefly characterised by the quality of 'goodness'), are absorbed in the internal organ itself; this in 'egoism' (*asmitá*); 'egoism' in the 'merely once resolvable' (*i.e., buddhi*); and *buddhi* into the 'irresolvable' (*i.e.,prakṛiti*)." *Prakṛiti* consists of the three 'qualities' in equilibrium; and the entire creation, consisting of causes and effects, is

the development of these 'qualities' when one or another becomes predominant.

[465] This curious passage occurs in the Taittiríya-Áraṇyaka i. 11, 5. Mádhava in his Comment, there explains it of the soul, and quotes the Śvetáśv. Up., iii. 19. Mádhava here takes *avindat* as "he pierced the jewel," but I have followed his correct explanation in the Comm.

[466] This is taken from Váchaspati's Comm. on Yoga S. ii. 15. Cf. the "four truths" of Buddhism.

[467] This probably refers to the Pañchadaśí. A Calcutta Pandit told me that it referred to the Prameya-vivaraṇa-saṅgraha (cf. Dr. Burnell's preface to his edition of the Devatádhyáya-bráhmaṇa, p. x), but, if this is the same as the vivaraṇa-prameya-saṅgraha, it is by Bháratítírthavidyáraṇya (see Dr. Burnell's Cat of Tanjore MSS. p. 88).

[468] The *upádhi* is the "condition" which must be supplied to restrict a too general middle term. If the middle term, as thus restricted, is still found in the minor term, the argument is valid; if not, it fails. Thus, in "The mountain has smoke because it has fire" (which rests on the false premise that "all fire is accompanied by smoke"), we must add "wet fuel" as the condition of "fire;" and if the mountain *has* wet fuel as well as fire, of course it will have smoke. Similarly, the alleged argument that "B is dark because he is Mitrá's son" fails, if we can establish that the dark colour of her former offspring A depended not on his being her son, but on her happening to have fed on vegetables instead of ghee. If we can prove that she still keeps to her old diet, of course our amended middle term will still prove B to be dark, but not otherwise.

[469] The Hindus think that a child's dark colour comes from the mother's living on vegetables, while its fair colour comes from her living on ghee.

[470] By Bháshá-parich. śl. 25, the four elements, earth, water, air, and fire, are *sparśavat*, but by śl. 27 of these air is neither *pratyaksha* nor *rúpavat*.

[471] This condition would imply that we could only argue from this middle term "the being produced" in cases of positive existence, not non-existence.

[472] "Soul," of course, is not external; but our topic was not soul, but air.

[473] As, *e.g.*, the mountain and Mitrá's first son in the two false arguments, "The mountain has smoke because it has fire" (when the fire-possessing red-hot iron ball has no smoke), and "Mitrá's first son A is dark because he is Mitrá's offspring" (when her second son B is fair). These two subjects possess the respective*sádhyas* or major terms "smoke"

and "dark colour," and therefore are respectively the subjects where the conditions "wet fuel" and "the mother's feeding on vegetables" are to be respectively applied.

[474] As, *e.g.*, the red-hot ball of iron and Mitrá's second son; as these, though possessing the respective middle terms "fire" and "the being Mitrá's offspring" do not possess the respective conditions "wet fuel" or "the mother's feeding on vegetables," nor, consequently, the respective major terms (*sádhya*) "smoke" and "dark colour."

[475] This will exclude the objected case of "dark jars" in (*a*), as it falls under neither of these two alternatives; for, though they are the sites of the *sádhya* "dark colour," they do not admit the condition "the feeding on vegetables," nor the middle term "the being Mitrá's son."

[476] *I.e.*, wherever there is fire produced by wet fuel there is smoke. The condition and the major term are "equipollent" in their extension.

[477] Where the *hetu* is found and not the *sádhya* (as in the red-hot ball of iron), there the *upádhi* also is not applicable.

[478] *I.e.*, one which requires no determining fact or mark, such as the three objected arguments required in § 137.

[479] The disputant says, "Fire must be non-hot because it is artificial." "Well," you rejoin, "then it must only be an artificiality which is always found elsewhere than in fire,—*i.e.*, one which will not answer your purpose in trying to prove your point." Here the proposed *upádhi* "the being always found elsewhere than in fire" answers to the definition, as it does not always accompany the*hetu* "possessing artificiality," but it does always accompany the*sádhya* "non-hot," as fire is proved by sense-evidence to be hot.

[480] As in the argument, "The earth, &c., must have had a maker because they have the nature of effects," where the Theist disputes the Atheistic condition "the being produced by one possessing a body." See Kusumáñjali, v. 2.

[481] In fact, it would abolish all disputation at the outset, as each party would produce a condition which from his own point of view would reduce his opponent to silence. In other words, a true condition must be consistent with *either* party's opinions.

www.ingramcontent.com/pod-product-compliance
Lightning Source LLC
LaVergne TN
LVHW041614070426
835507LV00008B/224

* 9 7 8 1 4 3 4 4 4 1 8 9 8 *